Archaeological Situations

This book is an introduction to theory in archaeology – but with a difference. *Archaeological Situations* avoids talking about theory as if it was something you apply but rather as something embedded in archaeological practice from the start.

Rather than see theory as something worked from the outside in, this book explores theory from the inside out, which means it focuses on specific archaeological practices rather than specific theories. It starts from the kinds of situations that students find themselves in and learn about in other archaeology courses, avoiding the gap between practice and theory from the very beginning. It shows students the theoretical implications of almost everything they engage in as archaeologists, from fieldwork, recording, writing up and making and assessing an argument to exploring the very nature of archaeology and justifying its relevance. Essentially, it adopts a structure which attempts to pre-empt one of the most common complaints of students taking theory courses: how is this applicable?

Aimed primarily at undergraduates, this book is the ideal way to engage students with archaeological theory.

Gavin Lucas is professor of archaeology at the University of Iceland. His main research interests are in archaeological method and theory and the archaeology of the modern world. He has published several books on archaeological theory, most recently *Writing the Past* (2019) and *Making Time* (2021), both published with Routledge.

Archaeological Situations
Archaeological Theory from the Inside Out

Gavin Lucas

LONDON AND NEW YORK

Cover image: Cover image by Gavin Lucas

First published 2023
by Routledge
4 Park Square, Milton Park, Abingdon, Oxon OX14 4RN

and by Routledge
605 Third Avenue, New York, NY 10158

Routledge is an imprint of the Taylor & Francis Group, an informa business

© 2023 Gavin Lucas

The right of Gavin Lucas to be identified as author of this work has been asserted in accordance with sections 77 and 78 of the Copyright, Designs and Patents Act 1988.

All rights reserved. No part of this book may be reprinted or reproduced or utilised in any form or by any electronic, mechanical, or other means, now known or hereafter invented, including photocopying and recording, or in any information storage or retrieval system, without permission in writing from the publishers.

Trademark notice: Product or corporate names may be trademarks or registered trademarks, and are used only for identification and explanation without intent to infringe.

British Library Cataloguing-in-Publication Data
A catalogue record for this book is available from the British Library

Library of Congress Cataloging-in-Publication Data
A catalog record for this book has been requested

ISBN: 978-0-367-56545-9 (hbk)
ISBN: 978-0-367-56010-2 (pbk)
ISBN: 978-1-003-09829-4 (ebk)

DOI: 10.4324/9781003098294

Typeset in Times New Roman
by Apex CoVantage, LLC

 Printed in the United Kingdom by Henry Ling Limited

Contents

List of Figures vi
List of Boxes ix
Acknowledgements xi

   Read This First 1
1 Who's Afraid of Theory? 5
2 Doing Fieldwork 22
3 Making Records 53
4 Writing Up 84
5 Building a Case 115
6 Doing Research 141
7 Defining the Discipline 165
   Coda: Theorizing Without Theory 192

   Index 195

Figures

1.1	Some contemporary responses to the current state of theory	6
2.1	Section drawing showing the interpretive problems of an interface: is the top of deposit 1203 a surface or a cut – perhaps a horizontal continuation of the cut 1211?	26
2.2	A comparison of two context sheets (left: Cambridge Archaeology Unit; right: Ardnamurchan Transitions Project)	27
2.3	Excavating the edge: Tony Baker excavates a second- and third-century "corn dryer", finding the edge of the clay foundation from the flue's infill deposit	31
2.4	Students planning with traditional tapes and paper (left) and a total station (right) at the university fieldschool in Iceland	33
2.5	Recording sensory distances over which sound (human shout and conversation, wooden whistle and stone striking) can be heard and human body movements can be communicated	37
2.6	Different levels of community engagement	45
2.7	Andrew Dafnis, Homeless Heritage project, surveying Turbo Island, Bristol, in 2010	48
3.1	The DIKW or data pyramid	55
3.2	The data trail	57
3.3	Map of excavations at Longstanton and Oakington, 5 km northwest of Cambridge (Northstowe Phases 1 & 2 [2014–2019]). The excavated areas revealed Middle to Late Iron Age, Roman and fifth- to seventh-century CE settlements, alongside other sites based on comprehensive trenching, geophysics and airborne transcription program [2005–2007, 2020–2021]. What data can you draw out from this map?	59
3.4	Extract from the CIDOC CRM pertaining to the category of "thing"; what kind of ontology does this entail?	65
3.5	Vessel types used for liquid and semi-solid foods in the Potomac typological system (POTS) which attempted to connect emic and etic classifications by matching terms from documentary sources (mostly probate inventories) with excavated pottery forms	68

3.6	Conceptual oppositions structuring a medieval longhouse in Dartmoor, England. Although not explicitly presented as a structuralist archaeology, the influence of structuralism in this example is clear	69
3.7	Making a pot: island of Sifnos, Greece	72
3.8	The Holywell witch bottle	74
4.1	The fragmentation and synthesis of the archaeological process	90
4.2	The architecture of the Rigny excavation archive	94
4.3	In the Virtual World of Second Life, Ruth Galileo stands on top of Okapi Island, aka the East Mound of Çatalhöyük, Turkey, surveying her team's construction in 2007–2008 of Neolithic houses (based on the South archaeological area) and, on the right, the shelter over the BACH archaeological area	97
4.4	Principal genres in archaeology and their relation to disciplinary knowledge	100
4.5	Principal modes of address in writing with hypothetical examples	106
5.1	Two views of archaeological knowledge. Left: jigsaw model, where the goal is to fill in the blanks by simply accumulating more pieces (induction). Right: crossword model, where the goal is to fill in the blanks by ensuring coherence between the pieces and correspondence with the clues	118
5.2	Diagram showing the structure of hypothesis testing in Lucero's example	120
5.3	Diagram showing the structure of IBE in Bogaard's example. Four hypotheses (H1-H4) are tested against three strands of evidence. Ticks indicate the presence of evidence showing only one hypothesis (H4) withstands all three tests	123
5.4	Diagram showing the structure of arguments adapted from an example in Chapman and Wylie (2016). A claim of provenance is made on the basis of specific data linked by warrants; note the criticisms (rebuttals) which largely focus on the warrants as the weak link in the argument	126
5.5	The hermeneutic spiral	129
5.6	The evidential relations and Peircean semiotics of fingerprints	133
5.7	Three types of binary thinking based on the nature of the relation between two concepts	137
6.1	Working out the value of a plate using George Miller's CC indices	151
6.2	Formal analogy between prehistoric stone gorgets and contemporary potter's tools	155
6.3	Jemez tribal member Aaron Tosa collecting obsidian and ceramic samples at the ancestral Jemez pueblo of Kwastiyukwa	161
7.1	A pavement on Mill Road, Cambridge, England; like an archaeological site, it is mix of multiple past events whose material presence persists in the present	167

7.2	Drift matter in Eidsbukta on the Sværholt peninsula, Finnmark, Norway	172
7.3	A tree growing around a sign in a park in north London, 2014; for whom does this sign matter?	174
7.4	The swinging pendulum of archaeology between the sciences and humanities	177
7.5	Diagram showing the different degrees of integration between multi-, inter- and trans-disciplinary research	182
7.6	Different ways to align archaeology depending on which aspect is privileged	183
7.7	The artefact as metaphor for two ways of looking at the archaeological record: as loss or as transformation (objects not to the same scale)	185
8.1	A plot from Google Ngram viewer using the search term "archaeological theory". How well does this reflect the status of theory in archaeology and if it does, what does it mean?	194

Boxes

1.1	The Three-Paradigms of Archaeological Theory	6
1.2	Three Views on the Relation Between Facts and Theory in Archaeology	11
1.3	Levels of Archaeological Theory?	13
1.4	Strong and Weak Theory	15
2.1	Total Recovery?	23
2.2	The Context Sheet	27
2.3	Following the Cut	30
2.4	Paper Versus Pixels	31
2.5	Gendered Fieldwork	34
2.6	Phenomenology and Fieldwork	36
2.7	Sutton Hoo in the Summer of '39	39
2.8	Research-Driven and Development-Led Excavation in Europe	41
2.9	What Do You Mean by Collaboration?	44
2.10	Community Archaeology as Intervention	47
3.1	What Do Maps Do?	58
3.2	AI and Machine Learning	62
3.3	Open Archaeology and Conceptual Reference Models (CRMs)	64
3.4	Making a Pot	71
3.5	Artefacts or Belongings?	75
3.6	Digital Collections and Archaeological Prosthetics	78
4.1	Honouring Ambiguity and Dealing With Doubt	87
4.2	Rigny Excavation: An Online Excavation Report	93
4.3	Virtual Reality at Çatalhöyük	96
4.4	Storytelling on the Acropolis	107
5.1	Hypothesis Testing and Mayan Household Rituals	119
5.2	A Process of Elimination: Modelling Neolithic Farming Practice in Central Europe	122
5.3	Networks of Trade and Networks of Inference: the Case of the Copper Ingots	125
5.4	Hermeneutics at Haddenham: Evolving Interpretations of a Neolithic Causewayed Enclosure	128
5.5	Bodies of Evidence or Silent Witness?	131

5.6	Binary Thinking, Dualism and Dialectics	136
6.1	Research Agendas and Grand Challenges	142
6.2	The Caring Archaeologist	144
6.3	The Unrepeatable Experiment?	152
6.4	Analogy in Archaeology	154
6.5	Creativity and Collaborative Archaeology	160
7.1	When Did the Neolithic End?	168
7.2	Archaeological Drift	171
7.3	Archaeology and the Two (or Three?) Cultures	177
7.4	Disciplinary Crossings	181

Acknowledgements

Writing this book has been a new experience for me. All my previous books have been written with an audience of peers in mind, but this work has been composed for the student reader, for someone relatively new to archaeology and its rich history. Although I have been teaching such students for two decades now, it is a different matter writing for them. I don't know how well I have succeeded in this and certainly I am aware of occasions where I slipped into old habits and assumed I was writing for my colleagues. One of my colleagues who read over a draft of the manuscript asked me whether this was intended for the teachers of a theory course or the students, pointing out what I feared. I suspect the final result may still be something in between. All I can hope is that those teachers who use this book in their courses will help their students navigate the more difficult parts.

That said, I want to acknowledge a number of people who kindly took time to help bring this book into being by offering valuable feedback and comments. First, to all the students who took my theory course at the University of Iceland over the last 20 years; it has changed radically since I first started and it was through those classes that I came to rethink what theory is. You are too numerous to mention, but without you, this book would not exist. My thanks also go to Matt Gibbons at Routledge who was very enthusiastic and supportive of the project; I also want to thank several reviewers who read the book at concept stage, including Lynn Meskell, Hannah Cobb and one other reviewer, who were so encouraging of the initial idea. In writing a book of this nature, I felt a greater than usual sense of obligation to the reader to get things right, and so I asked several people to read over either the whole manuscript or individual chapters and sections. I was quite overwhelmed that everyone agreed and I cannot express my gratitude for this, as such requests are always a "big ask" and I owe all of you a huge debt. For reading over the whole book: Craig Cipolla, Hannah Cobb, Bjørnar Olsen and Chris Witmore. For reading over individual chapters: Anna Beck, Matthew Johnson, Jeremy Huggett, Julian Thomas and Ruth Tringham. For reading specific sections: Zoë Crossland, Matt Edgeworth and Þóra Pétursdóttir; and especial thanks to Zoë for helping me come to grips with the complexities of Peirce's semiotics. To all of you, my deepest thanks. I don't doubt the book still has its flaws, but without your input, it would have been immeasurably poorer.

Finally, I want to thank several people who kindly shared images with me and/or allowed me to reproduce them in this book. To Matt Brudenell and Oscar Aldred/ Cambridge Archaeological Unit (Figures 2.2, 2.3 and 3.3); Hannah Cobb, Oliver Harris and Phil Richardson (Figure 2.2); Sue Hamilton and Mike Seager Thomas (Figure 2.5); Rachael Kiddey and John Schofield (Figure 2.7); David Austin and Julian Thomas (Figure 3.6); Lambos Malafouris (Figure 3.7); Nigel Jeffries and Andy Chopping/Museum of London Archaeology (Figure 3.8); Ruth Tringham (Figure 4.3); Cambridge University Press (Figure 6.2); Matthew Liebmann (Figure 6.3); Laurent Olivier (Figure 7.1); and Þóra Pétursdóttir (Figure 7.2).

Read This First

I studied archaeology as an undergraduate in the 1980s, and at the time, theory courses were fairly new and – at my university at least – optional. Forty years on, theory courses are now a regular part of the curriculum in many institutions and often mandatory, as they are where I teach. This shift has probably also been accompanied by changes in how students perceive theory. Archaeologists of my generation seemed to adopt a "marmite mindset" to theory – you either loved it or hated it, or rather perhaps you either embraced it as an indispensable part of doing archaeology or were suspicious of it and sceptical that it really had any useful role that wasn't already served by common sense. Part of the suspicion related to the historical background of archaeology and its separation from antiquarianism and emergence as a scientific field in the late nineteenth century. At worst, "theory" meant wild speculation, interpretation ungrounded in evidence while at best, it was a bias leading you to ignore evidence that did not fit your interpretation. Part of the scepticism is related to the abstract ideas and language that theory used, which seemed to be very detached from specific archaeological problems and issues. What does Heidegger really have to do with archaeology? For archaeologists of my generation, teaching theory often meant also trying to justify or defend it, even if only tacitly so. Many of the discussions in the 1980s and 1990s were about showing how theory was not separate from evidence, how it was not separate from archaeological practice.

I only started teaching theory in the new millennium and for a long time, I assumed my students inhabited the same "marmite mindset" of loving or hating theory, of embracing it or being suspicious or sceptical about it. Perhaps some did, but slowly it dawned on me that many of them didn't. I would see puzzled looks where I had expected resistance or acceptance. In other words, students simply didn't really have an opinion on the matter. At a British TAG session from 2017 called *Why Do Undergraduates Hate Archaeological Theory*, several of the speakers noted that students don't really hate theory – rather they are indifferent to it. I think this sums up my experience too. In some ways though, indifference is worse than hatred; at least with hatred, there is a sense of passion, of engagement; the problem with indifference is one tends to be detached, uninterested. The problem is one of getting the student engaged and connected to theory. But indifference can still have different inflections; it can be ingrained, an indifference

DOI: 10.4324/9781003098294-1

bred from disappointment. Or it can be an initial uncertainty, an indifference that is waiting to make up its mind. My feeling is most students' first encounter with archaeological theory is the latter. At the same time, students will vary between institutions (and generations), and one has to be careful extrapolating from one's own limited perspective; for people who are already interested in issues of political and social equality, theory is an important way to engage with the discipline and indifference is certainly not a quality one could ascribe to them. What about you? What is your attitude to theory?

If we teach theory in a defensive mode, then the chances are that it will be self-perpetuating; students will learn to love or hate it, regardless of how they first felt about it. What I mean by a defensive mode is more than implicit assumptions about whether theory is important or not, it is also about how this attitude spills over into the design of a course content and structure. Another of the recurrent themes in the TAG session I mentioned earlier was the importance of pedagogy and engaging students in theory, getting them to see its connections to other courses on their programme and countering the detachment and disconnection that many students experience when exposed to archaeological theory. Of course, such pedagogics are an important part of all courses and teaching, but often they seem especially amplified with theory courses. I love archaeological theory, yet for a long time, it was the course I hated teaching the most. I found it really difficult to engage the students, and while part of this was down to poor pedagogy on my part, part of it, I slowly came to realize, was the very way the course was structured. It was set up to fail.

The problem was precisely because I loved theory. I started reading philosophy around the same time I started reading archaeology; even before I took my optional theory course as an undergraduate in the 1980s, I was already predisposed to like theory. There will always be some students who share this same passion, but most who go into archaeology don't. For me, teaching archaeological theory as a series of schools of thought or -isms, or even as a series of concepts or topics, was like a duck taking to water. This was the way I was taught theory, and this is the way I taught theory for nearly 15 years. Most if not all existing archaeological theory textbooks are set up in the same way, even if there is great variety in style and manner of exposition. But teaching theory this way is already to begin with one hand tied behind your back; you are starting at a position already removed from what most students who go into archaeology are interested in learning about: excavation, analysing artefacts or bones, radiocarbon dating and so on. The best theory books – and teachers – bridge this divide, making the connections between personhood and a prehistoric burial apparent to students so they can see how theory relates. But why start with this disadvantage? Why not integrate the theory into the very core of these other things, like excavation and artefact typologies from the start?

There are good arguments against this. Setting concepts and ideas in their intellectual and historical context is important. Discussing a movement like postprocessualism in the context of historical developments in (mostly) Anglo-American archaeology is important for a deep appreciation of the history of our discipline; framing current theory like new materialisms in the context of theories of the body, phenomenology and actor network theory is crucial for a proper grasp of how its ideas are articulated. There is no question that for a deeper understanding of theory in archaeology, these ways of presenting theory are valuable. But for students starting out, especially those with more of an interest in osteology than object ontology, such an approach is, I believe, unnecessarily alienating. As teachers of archaeological theory, we are making our job harder than it needs to be and it doesn't matter if you present this approach to theory as a murder mystery or through practical case studies, you are still starting from a position of distance. For me, the immediate answer to this turned out to also reveal a deeper problem with theory. If teaching students archaeology was about helping them to learn how to *do* archaeology, surely teaching theory involved the same; it made me pose the question, how do we *do* theory? It was in trying to answer this question that I realized I don't do theory; at best, you might say I do a theoretical archaeology, but even if this characterization is not quite right either, it opened up a different way to approach the topic. To teach theory *as* archaeology, not theory in archaeology.

This book is an attempt to introduce archaeological theory to undergraduates at a basic level, that is, as a first- or second-year course, but through a very different approach. It merges theory with method and tries to teach theory as part of the normal process of learning archaeology. Instead of seeing theory as something apart, as a distinct topic, it integrates theory into the archaeological process. Hence the title which situates theory within concrete, archaeological situations. It is almost a mantra repeated by theoretical archaeologists that theory is everywhere, it underlies everything we do; taking this to the extreme though, it might suggest we shouldn't even be talking about theory anymore. If this book integrates theory with method, in what way is it an introduction to theory as opposed to an introduction to archaeology? I don't have a good answer to that question, but I would say that if you compare this book with a methods textbook, the difference should be obvious. At the same time, I am not sure I want there to be a distinction. In the end, any answer to this revolves around the question of what theory is; a question which I raise in the first chapter and return to briefly again at the end of the book. But however you might define theory, I hope at least, you will find some advantage to learning theory in the alternative mode offered in this textbook.

Let me end with a few final words about the contents of this book. I have tried to draw on the work of a diverse range of archaeologists and examples, but I know my own background shapes the topics covered within. As an English (and English-educated) archaeologist, I am inextricably part of the Anglo-American tradition, and this bias is difficult to shake off, especially in the field of theory. Certainly the centre of gravity of this book is North American and European, and this will likely be the main readership. To readers outside this sphere, I nonetheless hope you still find things of interest as the situations addressed are universal. The book is organized into seven chapters, each chapter addressing a specific domain of archaeological practice or concern. Each chapter begins with a short, fictional vignette which describes a situation that a student or junior scholar may find themselves in. The point of these vignettes is to foreground the situated nature of theory and to introduce it through an accessible and concrete example that the student can relate to as a way to set the scene for what the chapter addresses. The vignette is then returned to at the end of each chapter as a way of enfolding what has been covered, back into the original story.

Following the convention of many textbooks, there is no in-text citation in this book. Instead, I include a note on further reading at the end of each chapter, where I reference any works cited in the text as well as others the reader may find useful in connection to the topics discussed. A full list of references appends this. The references on each topic are by no means exhaustive; this is not a monograph but a textbook, so I have tried to select what I see as either key readings or readings with exemplary case studies. As this is meant as a textbook and teaching aid, I have also included a few exercises at the end of each chapter. These are small projects I have used in my classes and which the teacher can adapt and extend in their own way or the student can even try for themselves. As theory has traditionally been seen by many students as lacking a practical (or purposeful!) dimension, I consider such exercises an important part of this book, even if they take up little space. In my teaching, they take up half the time we spend in class. Finally, the reader will note that throughout the text, various words have been highlighted in **bold**, especially the first time it occurs. These words can also be found in the index at the back of the book. Sometimes, these terms are explained in the text but not always, and in many books, they might be connected to a glossary. Instead of providing a glossary, however, the terms in bold are an invitation to the student to make their own glossary as they work through the book or to serve as discussion points in class. In other words, this can serve as another exercise to engage students with archaeological theory in a more active way.

1 Who's Afraid of Theory?

> **Situation 1: In the Field**
>
> *This was my first year in the field with this particular team; it was a hot day and we were doing some heavy shovelling, removing backfill from the previous season, and so apart from having half an eye on the soil, this was fairly mindless digging. I was already known as an archaeologist with an interest in theory and I thought the person I was next to had an interest in Marxism, so I decided to throw out a question: "So what kind of theoretical perspective do you come from in your archaeology?" There was a short pause before they answered: "I guess I just come from a tradition of common sense archaeology". I am not sure he even stopped shovelling.*

Why Do We Need Theory?

You know how politicians almost never answer the questions they are posed – they deflect, ignore or best of all, tell you the question you *should* have asked and then proceed to answer that. Well, it's the same here. Why do we need theory? There are many ways of answering this question, but the cleverest is to argue that the question is all wrong; it is not even a choice. It is not about whether we need theory or not, as it is already inbuilt in everything we do. Rather the question is how we treat it; do we ignore it or bring it out into the open and cultivate it? The coded message here being: do we stick with our prejudices and bias, or do we expose them to scrutiny, to critique and so allow ourselves to grow, intellectually? This is an argument made nearly a century ago by American anthropologist Clyde Kluckhohn in 1939 and has remained a constant refrain ever since. One of the most popular theory textbooks today by Matthew Johnson makes the same point; although Johnson offers some justifications for why we need theory, he ends by affirming the point that all archaeologists are already theoretical whether they know it or not; what many people call **common sense** is just a cloak for a whole series of assumptions and perspectives which guide our thinking. They

6 *Who's Afraid of Theory?*

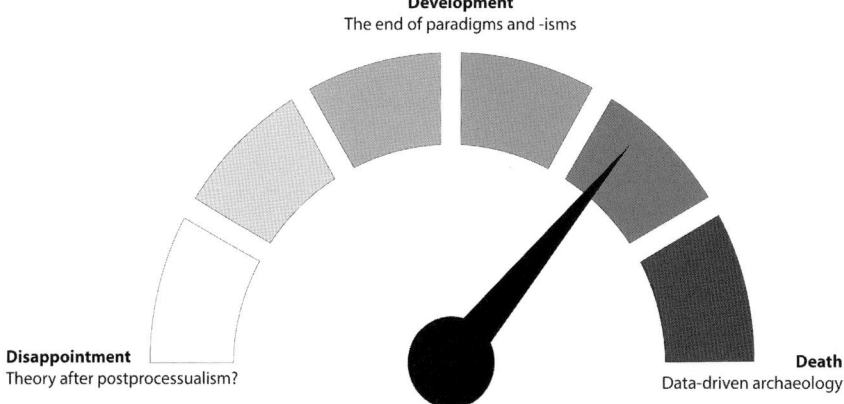

Figure 1.1 Some contemporary responses to the current state of theory.

may be sound, but maybe not; very likely they are shaped by specific cultural and historical contexts and one person's common sense might be another's nonsense. We will encounter some examples of this later in the book, especially in relation to what counts as archaeology.

The question then, is not "why do we need theory", but whether we should think about it or not, and given the implicit connotation that *not* thinking about theory is akin to being prejudiced, biased, uncritical – all the things that academic scholarship stands against, well then, who really would choose that? One conception of being theoretical therefore – and we will explore others later in this chapter – simply means bringing these assumptions out into the open so they can be challenged, developed or rejected. And yet in the last decade, there has been what you might call a backlash against theory which suggests not everyone agrees with this argument. The backlash has taken many forms, which I will rank from soft to harsh (Figure 1.1).

The first and softest has been a sense of disappointment in the wake of the last half century of theoretical debate. Other theory textbooks will give you this backstory; it is the typical three-part narrative where archaeology went through three phases of theory or what people usually call **paradigms**: culture history (1920s–1960s), processualism (1960s–1980s) and postprocessualism (1980s–2000; see Box 1.1).

Box 1.1. The Three-Paradigms of Archaeological Theory

1920s–1960s: Culture History – this is where the theory story traditionally begins, mainly because it was what the "real" theoretical revolution of the 1960s was reacting against. Sometimes portrayed as a-theoretical, culture history nonetheless represented a way of doing archaeology that focused on mapping material traits to specific cultures in time and space and understanding how these cultures changed over time through interaction and diffusion. Gordon Childe is often counted as the paragon of culture historical archaeology, yet both Marxism and nineteenth-century cultural evolution suffuse his writings. Go figure!

1960s–1980s: New Archaeology and Processualism – the 1960s was a period of social "revolutions" in the Western world, and archaeology was no exception. The New Archaeology was a movement that emerged around Lewis Binford in the US which sought to make archaeology both more scientific and more like anthropology. Critical of what they saw as the "stamp-collecting" mentality of culture history, they wanted to make the past come alive by offering images of living societies, not just catalogues of artefacts. They also wanted archaeologists to adopt a more rigorous methodology, one that aligned their discipline closer to the natural sciences and away from the humanities, and so their approach to studying past societies was framed by a search for generalizations and cross-cultural comparison.

1980s–2000: Postprocessualism – the conclusion to the story happens on the other side of the Atlantic with a largely English counteraction to processualism centred around Ian Hodder. Postprocessualism reacted to the heavy "sciencification" of archaeology under processualism, and although it shared its vision of making the past come alive, it had very different ideas about how to do this. In seeking to resurrect an interest in historical particulars but wedded to a more up-to-date social theory from within the humanities, postprocessualism acted as an umbrella term for a diverse set of interests from feminism to phenomenology.

The better narratives will qualify this story by saying each phase didn't replace the last, but they overlapped, and in fact aspects of culture historical and processual archaeology are still with us today. The better narratives will also remind you that this is largely an Anglo-American story though it spilled out into other parts of Europe and the globe. A typical clue to this Anglophone bias is if you hear some country or archaeologist being described as still being stuck in the "culture historical" phase; if this sounds familiar it is no surprise – it is also how North America and Europe often describe other parts of the world in terms of economic and social development. "Country X is now how England was in the 1800s". But the problem is, we are still teaching this narrative in the 2020s, two decades after the "end" of postprocessualism. It begs the question: what -ism are we in now? Julian Thomas has argued that theory has become a victim of its own historiography; by narrating the development of archaeological theory as one of paradigm shifts or revolutions, we are conditioned into expecting the next big thing. The fact that there has been no new obvious contender to replace postprocessualism – we have been waiting now for 20 years! – surely suggests an epic stalling of theory. Or does it? There are different ways to see this and it all depends on where you are situated. Arguably, given the predominantly Anglo-American nature of this three-part history of theory, it is only archaeologists bound to this tradition who see any crisis in the first place; for many other archaeologists outside this narrative, theoretical archaeology has never been more vibrant and creative and in some cases, is arguing for a redefinition of what archaeology is. From within the traditional Anglophone world of theoretical archaeology, however, it is another matter, and perceptions of the state of theory vary.

Thus there are some who have even proclaimed the death of theory in archaeology. Such a proclamation was somewhat hyperbolic though; its main proponents, John Bintliff and Mark Pearce, were chiefly referring to the demise of grand theory, of the big systems or schools, not theoretical reflection *per se*. Instead of theory referring to grand paradigms or systems – all those -isms and -ologies that form the stock in trade of basic theory courses – theory instead became about concepts and ideas. Concepts such as gender, agency or materiality gradually started to take centre stage over Marxism and Structuralism, or processualism and postprocessualism. Anthropologist Henrietta Moore characterized this as the shift from grand theory to concept-metaphors while archaeologist John Robb has described it as the difference between High Church and Low Church theory (personal communication). Many good theory courses today try and compromise and offer both historical narratives of the big schools alongside coverage of more specific concepts and topics. But ultimately the reason why there is no next big thing is that theory has changed its colours; it has metamorphosized into something less grand, more dispersed; for some it has finally grown up and come of age, fulfilling a promise first proposed by David Clarke in 1973 when he defined theoretical archaeology as the loss of innocence.

Yet a more hard-line approach exists, which constitutes the third and most critical backlash against theory, and this seems common to both Anglo-American and other European traditions. This is an approach which has been linked to the rise of big data and the resurgence of science in archaeology linked to work in aDNA and isotope analysis among others (see chapter 3). It is also linked to claims for a data-driven archaeology which no longer needs theory. The more naïve positions proclaim that the data deluge means that no theory or model can possibly account for the complexity of available data; rather we need to draw on statistical algorithms generated by computers to look for patterns and correlations. Finally, the old antiquarian dream has been realized: the data or facts *can* speak for themselves. Such a view is often called **empiricism** (see Box 1.2) although this term also covers rather more complex and diverse positions. Some archaeologists have challenged the naïveté of this position; facts can never speak for themselves, they always need some kind of framework and are, anyway, always pre-coded in some way that reflects some "theory". There is no such thing as raw data (see Chapter 3 for further discussion of this). On the whole, discussion of big data and science in archaeology has tended not to be so naïve. Rather than advocating any end of theory, it suggests that the usual relationship between theory and data be reversed. Instead of questions and problems being framed by theory, and where data are used to test theories, data-driven science argues that the questions and problems emerge from the data themselves, with theory being brought in afterward.

These various forms of backlash against theory in archaeology, from the soft sense of paradigm disappointment to the harder advocacy of data-driven interpretation, are important not so much in their details as in their general nature. For I would suggest they are symptomatic of an underlying uncertainty in how the discipline feels towards theory today, the ground is changing underneath our feet and we don't really know how or why. Philosopher Rosi Braidotti has identified this as part of a wider trend in the humanities that she calls "theory fatigue" – though in her case, it manifests itself more as an increasing rejection of the abstract and esoteric language (and language games) of high theory. In archaeology, the jargon of theory has always had its critics, but there is a deeper set of shared consequences of such theory fatigue: the return of anti-intellectualism and privileging of common sense over theory, all of which feed a dangerous political populism.

We started this section with the question "do we need theory?" and came to the conclusion that we are always theoretical whether we acknowledge it or not. This does not mean we are always engaging in theoretical reflection – no archaeologist does this and how could they? All it means is that everything we do has theoretical implications. So the better question is not "why do we need theory" but rather "why think about theory?" and the answer is: because it makes you a better scholar, a better archaeologist. But if we look more closely at this, we see that it makes certain assumptions about what theory is in the first place. Theory is taken to be the assumptions, perspectives, frameworks within which you think; these can be implicit (as in common sense) or explicit (as in, say Marxism or Feminism). In deflecting the question of why we need theory, we have adopted a definition of theory without really talking about what theory is. Now being critical and reflexive is surely a good thing; whatever our opinion on what theory is, these intellectual virtues should still stand as central tenets of academia and scholarship. But connecting theory to common sense as part of a broad umbrella concept makes certain assumptions about theory that perhaps we should question. Indeed, reviewing the various backlashes against theory in the new millennium, it is quite clear that definitions of theory are precisely what is at stake. So perhaps it is time we address the elephant in the room: *what is theory?*

What Is Theory?

Defining theory is not something many archaeologists are comfortable doing, though some have bravely tried. Consider the following statements about theory – only some of which I should stress were offered as explicit definitions:

- *Theory is the eat-your-vegetables part of archaeology. Everyone says it's good for you, but actually getting it down isn't considered much fun* (Adrian Praetzellis 2015).
- *Theory grabs the assumptions you hold dearest and shakes them until they fall apart* (Oliver Harris & Craig Cipolla 2017).

- *Theory does not provide answers, but it suggests a wider range of interesting questions* (Kevin Greene 1995).
- *Theory as revelatory, as opening up new spaces, as challenging assumptions* (Meg Conkey 2007).
- *Theory is the order we put facts in* (Matthew Johnson 2019).
- *I have come to think of theory as a pair of glasses. When you need to see things close-up, you grab some bifocals, when the sun is too bright, you need to filter it out, you put on sunglasses, when you need to see far away, you put on your distance glasses or binoculars . . . . Theories and schools of thought are frameworks designed to support particular idea structures* (Laurie Wilkie 2016).
- *Scientific theories operate at multiple levels of generalization and abstraction . . . . High-order theories, like world views, are filters through which reality is perceived, described, and explained* (Patricia Urban & Edward Schortman 2012).

The first one on this list is just fun, but underneath of course Praetzellis has a serious message we have already come across: theory is necessary for good intellectual health. The trouble is, it is very broad and vague, and it doesn't really say much about theory except it is "a good thing". The second statement by Harris and Cipolla is rather more specific and draws on the association between being theoretical and being critical but perhaps goes too far and merges their roles; theory *as* critical thinking. One might agree that it has this function, but is that all? Why not just call it critical thinking then? The third description is also connected to the same idea of critical and reflexive thought, but whereas the Harris and Cipolla focus on negative critique and pulling apart our preconceptions, Greene's observation fixes on positive stimulation and expanding our horizons. Again, we can surely agree that theory can do this, but it also reduces theory to a kind of lateral reading around one's subject. Theory as reading philosophy, anthropology, psychology and so on, which again is somewhat true – but is that all it is? The fourth statement by Conkey in some ways combines the best of both the previous ones – it is both critical in challenging assumptions but productive in clearing a space for new ideas.

The remaining three descriptions all take a slightly different tack. Johnson's definition of theory as something that structures or orders our facts is about seeing theory as a set of assumptions, perspectives or framework for thinking. It is this idea which also underlies the argument in the last section that theory is everywhere – it cannot be avoided. Wilkie's take on theory is very similar to Johnson's but expressed in a more concrete and familiar metaphor while the last statement quoted here by Urban and Schortman says much the same though with an interesting twist. They suggest that theory actually comes in different levels or layers and while the uppermost layer is akin to a "perspective", the lower levels are more empirically grounded and relate to a specific set of material or phenomena. I will come back to this question of levels of theory in a moment (see Box 1.3) as it is quite an old idea in archaeology.

To be fair, most of these quotes are not offered explicitly as a definition and elaborated upon through argument. They are more like "one-liners" and it would be unfair to hold the authors to these definitions too tightly. At the same time, it does emphasize how shy archaeologists – even theoretical archaeologists – have been about defining theory. It is one of those dangerous concepts that if you tinker with it too closely, it may blow up in your face. But there is perhaps a difference between the first four and the last three; the first four are what you might call *prescriptive*; they implicitly or explicitly suggest how theory *ought* to perform, ideally. Yet it would not be hard to find examples of archaeological theory that are not very critical or imaginative or even good for you! Yet somehow, we might still be happy to call them theoretical. The latter three definitions on the other hand are rather more *descriptive*; they purport to demonstrate what theory *actually does*, not what it ought to do or we would like it to do. In this way, theory can be good or bad, like anything else, but it is always with us.

For simplicity, let us return to Johnson's definition of theory as the order in which you put your facts. It is important because straightaway it highlights something that many archaeologists intuitively understand; theory stands in some relation or tension with facts. For some archaeologists, theory stands in *opposition* to facts; this is an old antiquarian view of theory which linked theory to speculation, interpretation in the *absence* of data and is often linked to a position known as **empiricism** which we encountered in the last section (also see Box 1.2). For Johnson though and probably most archaeologists, the relation is not oppositional but mutual. Facts without theory are just dry dust, trivial statements like "there were 234 sherds of pottery in the deposit" or "this wall has two re-builds"; theory is needed to arrange these atoms into some meaningful order. Yet Johnson's definition as it stands is still suitably broad to allow different views on what that mutual relation is (see Box 1.2). Under one view known as positivism, facts or data are construed as independent and used to test theory, while under another – conveniently labelled post-positivism – data are considered "theory-laden" while theories were regarded as "under-determined" by the data, all of which simply means that the separation of theory and data is more blurred and interdependent than in the former view.

Box 1.2 Three Views on the Relation Between Facts and Theory in Archaeology

Using artefact types cross-dated with coins as well as several radiocarbon dates, a site has been dated to the first half of the tenth-century CE. How are facts and theory implicated in this simple example? Depending on the archaeologist, you might hear at least three different versions of an answer.

Empiricism – this is the view that all knowledge is ultimately based on experience, that what we securely know – even complex beliefs – can be traced back to direct observations through our senses. In archaeology, this position usually manifests itself by a strong adherence to the privileging of facts – that is, observations made typically during fieldwork or in the lab – and the mistrust of theory as speculation or at best a temporary "filler" to be used in the absence of facts. It has close associations with **induction** which is discussed further in Chapter 5. For an empiricist, the dating in the aforementioned example makes use of no theory at all; it is based purely on the collation of several pieces of observed data: artefact types which have demonstrably been associated with coins minted in the early tenth century from other sites and the calibration of C14 isotope ratios recorded from samples recovered from the site. The facts all link up without any leaps of logic or speculation.

Positivism – with positivism, the role of theory becomes much more important, central even as it recognizes that no matter how many facts you have, they will never self-assemble into more than trivial knowledge without the aid of a theory or hypothesis. More than just a surrogate "filler" in the absence of data, theory acts as the glue to hold facts together in a meaningful way. At the same time, the facts remain independent of theory and as such act as an essential way to test the validity of any theory. Hypothesis testing, which formed a key method under positivism, is discussed further in Chapter 5. For a positivist, there is therefore theory involved even in this dating example, albeit of a subtle kind; the fact that coins have been found with artefacts of the same type on other sites does not automatically mean the same date can be applied here. It is always an assumption or hypothesis and as such they might want to check how often this association has occurred or know what the sample size is. They might even suggest that the radiocarbon dates from this site act as a further test on this typological dating, helping to corroborate or strengthen it.

Post-positivism – this last view is more an umbrella term for a variety of positions that reacted against positivism, but generally all share the position that facts and theory are not independent but mutually implicated. This means there is no such thing as a fact which isn't coloured by some theory, which is why the term theory-laden is often used to describe facts. Early versions of post-positivism often seemed to make theory all-powerful, so that data almost seemed to be at its complete mercy; however, it was recognized that because theory is not unified but heterogeneous, data could still resist one theory by being tied to another. In our dating example, a post-positivist would go one further with the typological association and argue that it doesn't matter how many times coins are found with a certain artefact type, there are still theoretical assumptions implicit in what counts as an "association". Do we count coins found with artefact types from the same deposit, regardless of how long or under what conditions it took that deposit to form? How do we define contemporaneity when it comes to objects being associated with one another? In other words, at no point do data escape a theoretical frame. On the other hand, the theoretical frame which structures typological dating is very different to the theoretical framework structuring radioactive decay, so when the results of both agree, we can argue that such theoretical frames do not need to be seen as taking us down a rabbit hole of circular reasoning as empiricists and positivists have claimed.

What empiricism, positivism and post-positivism all share however is a conception of theory which is articulated in relation to facts or data. It is thus easy to see why Johnson's definition cited earlier works and why it seems to be easy for archaeologists of very different outlook to accept it. Moreover, if theory is defined as the order in which we arrange our facts, it can also incorporate some of the shifts we observed in the last section around the softer backlash against theory. Whether you use theory to refer to grand systems, schools or paradigms, or to more specific concepts and ideas, it still works with Johnson's definition. It is this close pairing with data that has also informed the many attempts to create a classification of theory in archaeology, where different types of theory are defined in terms of the distance or degree of detachment between theory and data (Box 1.3).

Box 1.3 Levels of Archaeological Theory?

For some archaeologists, the close relation between theory and data suggests a need to discriminate different levels of theory, depending on how close a theory is to a set of facts. Inspired by sociological discussions of **middle range theory**, archaeologists suggested the need for a similar, archaeological middle range theory which bridged the abstract realms of high theory (e.g. evolutionism) and the facts on the ground. Lewis Binford was the first to adopt this idea in print and tied it to his interest with formation processes, though he was subsequently criticized for conflating two very different types of theory. In general though, middle range theory can be seen as a type of theory that has a very close relationship to data and is thus often empirically specific as opposed to very general theories which tend to be far removed from specific facts. Smith calls this kind of theory "empirical theory" to distinguish it from high-level social theory while Urban and Schortman, who we met earlier in this chapter, discriminate between high-level, middle-level and low-level theory, the latter largely overlapping with our notion of a fact. In Box 1.2, where I discussed the relation of theory and facts through the dating example, the theory there might be characterized as middle- or low-level theory.

> **High level** *Abstract theories about general social and historical processes (e.g. Marxism)*
> **Middle level** *Empirically tied theories about observable patterns in the archaeological record (e.g. mortuary rites)*
> **Low level** *Facts or empirical observations, usually patterned or recurring (e.g. typology)*

Other archaeologists have viewed this issue of the relation between theory and data in terms of the archaeological process; instead of being a purely conceptual issue which separate grand theory from middle range or low theory, the differences can be mapped onto the different stages of archaeological research. So the lowest levels of theory, those closest to the data, are also those that belong to processes of data generation and extraction – how sites are formed, how sites are excavated, while the higher levels of theory are those closest to data interpretation. Both David Clarke and Michael Schiffer offered versions of this kind of approach to different types of theory.

On the whole, this concern with levels of theory has largely been conducted within North America and more particularly within processual archaeology. There are several reasons for this but one major one probably relates to the way archaeology fits into a broader conceptualization of disciplinary knowledge. Traditionally in North America, archaeology is part of a fourfield division of a broader subject called anthropology; archaeology thus comprises one of four key fields along with linguistics, biological anthropology and cultural anthropology. There is a sense of a disciplinary hierarchy, where at the bottom, each field has its own empirical domain but at the top, they are all joined by a common body of social theory. Such a scheme has resulted in an anxiety peculiar to Anglo-American archaeology, that of being somehow always beholden to other disciplines who build theory, while archaeology remains a borrower.

The idea of archaeology belonging to a wider academic endeavour concerned with humanity is not unique to North America – indeed the English archaeologist Pitt Rivers also proposed a fourfield structure in the late nineteenth century. But in Europe and other parts of the world, this relation is conceived of in a much looser and more fragmented fashion, and as a result, the idea of social theory as something that floats above more parochial, disciplinary theories is less obvious. Indeed for many archaeologists, these levels are somewhat disingenuous as they ultimately perpetuate the separation of theory and data by mapping it onto a disciplinary hierarchy which separates the empirical side of research from its interpretation, one where archaeology – *as archaeology* – is primarily about fieldwork and data collection, while anthropology – as an umbrella field, not ethnographic fieldwork – is the domain of social theory (see Chapters 6 and 7 for further discussion of these issues).

All of this foregoing discussion suggests that Johnson's definition of theory seems to capture fairly well what archaeological theory is. And yet there remains something troubling about it.

Rethinking Theory

Defining theory in relation to facts or data carries certain assumptions about the nature of knowledge, about the nature of archaeological thought and practice. Even accepting that theory and data are mutually dependent, even constitutive of each other, there remains an important sense in which they are still different things. Johnson's definition of theory as the order in which we put our facts implicitly carries certain connotations of theory as active and facts as passive. Facts on their own are not enough, they need theory to make them meaningful, sensible. In the last section, we saw how some archaeologists were arguing that facts or data need to be given a more active, leading role; a data-driven archaeology is one which does not eschew theory but reverses the domination of theory over data. A similar argument has been made by archaeologists from what many would call, a more deeply theoretical position. Þóra Pétursdóttir and Bjørnar Olsen have argued for what they call weak theory (Box 1.4); weak theory is theory which does not impose itself on the material, on things, but which gives things the space to open themselves out and reveal aspects that might normally be closed off. Strong theory on the other hand is theory which imposes order and constraint on archaeological remains and more importantly, all significance is supplied by theory, not things.

Box 1.4   Strong and Weak Theory

The idea of strong and weak theory was first suggested by literary scholar Eve Sedgwick who linked strong theory to what she called paranoid reading – that in reading a text, we are always trying to find concealed or hidden meanings and treat the text with suspicion. In short, we always want to dominate the text by showing how much cleverer we are than the text itself. In contrast, she argued for reparative reading, one which was open to the text and its creative and emancipatory potential. Sedgwick's ideas which focused on texts were developed by anthropologist Kathleen Stewart in relation to our general sensory experiences of the world and the way we interact or respond to the things we encounter. From there, the idea was taken up by Þóra Pétursdóttir and Bjørnar Olsen in the context of archaeology, where they argue for the importance of allowing things to confront our expectations and that we should resist the desire to impose order that is normally part of the archaeological impetus to explain what we encounter.

> A key idea driving Pétursdóttir and Olsen's approach was the reaction against a view which saw theory as some kind of grazing omnivore, that whatever it encountered, it chewed it up and converted it into something for its own purposes. The very quality of theory that Johnson highlights – its ability to bring order to facts – is for Pétursdóttir and Olsen, a sign of tyranny. Seeing theory as something that floats above the world (especially in the "levels of theory" typical of North American processualism; see Box 1.3), as something that we have to bring down to earth and apply or "operationalize" is precisely what is wrong with this view of theory. It is wrong because such a view of theory ends up making the archaeological remains conform to shapes and forms of its own making. The danger is, one application of say, postcolonial theory will start to look like another, even if one has been applied on a site in Australia and another in South Africa. Of course, the empirical details will vary, but the interpretation – the relevance of the two case studies – may be hard to tell apart. And if that happens, what have we really learnt? The danger is that theory starts to reproduce, make multiple copies of itself in different places, while specificities of the place become superficial and interchangeable.
>
> To some extent, this is not a new critique; it was a key point in postprocessual attacks on the **grand narrative** in the 1990s. Any study of capitalism in the seventeenth or eighteenth centuries should always stress the local articulations of this concept rather than see the local as simply a manifestation of a global process. But what is new is the rebounding implications this has for our view of theory. What Pétursdóttir and Olsen have argued is that to avoid this "grand narrative" affect, we need to cut theory adrift from its privileged position of being the one that brings order to an archaeological situation. Theory will certainly affect the things it comes into contact with, but the reverse is equally true. Those things will affect theory – or ought to, if theory remains open to them. In Pétursdóttir and Olsen's succinct phase, *it matters to theory what it matters for*. In this way, weak theory is one which embraces this quality of openness, while strong theory is the opposite; it resists the agency of the things it encounters and tries to enfold them into its own image.

Structurally, the arguments from weak theory and data-driven archaeology are very similar; both argue for a reversal of dominance or at least symmetry between theory and data or things. But in other ways, the positions are very different. Data-driven archaeology frames theory within the context of abstract knowledge production; it is what you might call a purely conceptual view of theory and in this sense, it shares the same assumptions as Johnson's definition of theory. Both theory and data are concepts, ideas which are inextricably caught up in systems of meaning. Weak theory on the other hand frames theory differently, not against facts or data but things, objects, real stuff. Part of weak theory's argument is that there is more to things than meaning and by reducing theory to a conceptual field is to ignore the fact that archaeology deals with things. In defining theory as the order you put facts in, one is also defining theory as a meaning-making process. But meaning does not capture everything that soils, potsherds and flint axes present to us as archaeologists. Weak theory is all about acknowledging this. In a sense, weak theory is not a conceptual view of theory but an embodied or performative one.

Suddenly, a crack now opens in this definition of theory as something which would seem to be inevitably paired with facts or data. Indeed, many scholars who have been studying how scientists work, abandoned long ago such a conceptual framework in favour of a more practice-based or performative approach. The problem with this standard view of theory is that it frequently seems to entail another opposition: not just between theory and data but also between theory and practice. Theory as something abstract and cerebral, removed from the concrete and embodied work of archaeology. Maybe the uncertainty and backlash around theory that came with the new millennium is actually about this. If so, it is not enough to simply argue that theory has shifted from being about grand systems, schools and -isms to more localized concepts and topics. No, there is something even more radical afoot. Theory is no longer about conceptual schemes of any sort, big or small, no longer about the imposition of order, meaning or sense to an array of otherwise mute facts through the application of ideas. Indeed, arguably this was always a very (Anglo-)American view of what theory is, something you apply to your data. In many ways, this alternative view of theory takes us back to the first four statements about theory I quoted earlier, where theory is more like an attitude; Meg Conkey in particular elaborated upon this at length from a feminist position where she long ago contested the notion of theory as something to be applied in favour of something which opens up or discloses a terrain for thinking about the stuff we encounter as archaeologists.

Yet the traditional notion of theory as something applied to facts still has a strong hold and for obvious reasons. There is definitely a sense of the pragmatic here, of theory as something useful, something which helps you along. Such a view of theory informs the very structure of how students write their dissertations, how researchers frame their project: you outline your theory/theoretical framework, you present the methodology which operationalizes that framework and provides the bridge between theory and data, and then you bring in the data and apply the theory and methods to it in order to obtain your results. It is a deeply entrenched structure and of course it works. At the same time, it locks theory into a very confined role and helps to perpetuate the view of theory as a purely conceptual operation, of theory in relation to facts. But if theory is or can be something different, well then, this is a game-changer. Arguments for weak theory such as those discussed previously suggest that theory is or can be something different. Indeed, it is precisely this recognition that has motivated this book and why in it you won't be presented with a historical narrative of paradigms in archaeology or with a toolkit of theories and concepts set within their intellectual context. You will still encounter such theories and concepts in the pages that follow, but they will be embedded in a series of archaeological situations, the kind of typical and everyday situation that you will find yourself in when doing archaeology. In this sense, I have retained something of the pragmatism of the old view of theory, but instead of putting it as an add-on to theory as a conceptual operation, I have tried to make it central. In this sense, theory is no longer a tool used to assist archaeology but is part of the very fabric of archaeology itself. It is pragmatic in a performative sense, not a utilitarian one. Perhaps this is something most theoretical archaeologists have claimed theory is all along, but I would argue that the language of theory, especially the way theory has been traditionally defined in relation to facts and data, has in fact mitigated against this claim.

In the vignette which opened this chapter, two archaeologists were shovelling side by side; we had a "theoretical archaeologist" and a "common sense archaeologist". What do you think of these two characters having read this chapter? On the one hand, "common sense" has come in for some criticism in these pages. It is not that it is necessarily bad – we all start here after all – it is just never enough. For the theoretical archaeologist, the biggest problem with common sense is that it assumes a universal rationality and thus will be blind to its own biases – cultural, sexual or whatever. For the common sense archaeologist, however, the theoretical archaeologist appears to be deliberately introducing their own bias to the situation. How can a self-proclaimed Marxist not be biased? They would respond in turn by arguing that avoidance of bias is not the issue, but rather it is about putting any bias out front so it can be subject to and part of the discussion. And yet if the theoretical archaeologist seems to have come out looking better, this was short-lived. As the chapter progressed, our theoretical archaeologist who seemed to be disappointed by their fellow-digger's lack of theoretical position betrays an equally problematic position. An assumption that theory is something you bring to your work, like the tools they are using to dig with. They implicitly viewed theory as something to apply, something to render brute data meaningful. In this perception, theory itself becomes the active ingredient in archaeology without which no real interpretation is possible, a view which runs the risk of turning all archaeology into a game of mirrors. Ultimately, I hope you feel that neither of these characters are quite right; both are, to an extent, caricatures, yet ones that the discipline still works with.

Classroom Exercises

1. Go through a paper or even the abstract for a paper and identify what theoretical assumptions it makes or position it adopts.
2. Define what *you* think theory is, especially in the context of archaeology; write down 3–5 words or phrases and then discuss the results in the class. You can even try repeating this exercise at the end of the course to see how your answers have changed.

Further Reading

Why Do We Need Theory?

Most other textbooks on archaeological theory will give you a more detailed survey of the development of theory, usually framed through the "three-paradigm model" of culture history, processualism and postprocessualism (e.g. see Johnson 2019). For a more complex history of archaeology, the standard volume by Trigger can also be consulted (Trigger 2006). However, for a wider perspective on the history of theory outside the Anglo-American sphere, various volumes can be consulted including Hodder (1991), Ucko (1995) and Gramsch and Sommer (2011). For a prescient critique of the Anglo-American dominance of theory, see Olsen (1991).

For contemporary theory, this is a fast-moving river, so my suggestions here may need to be updated by your teacher. The "death of paradigmatic theory" was first proclaimed by Bintliff and Pearce (2011), but earlier, Baines and Brophy (2006) had questioned such schools, and Henrietta Moore (2004) has characterized a similar shift in anthropology. Advocates of big data and a new scientism include Kristiansen (2014) while Johnson (2011) offers a useful reminder of the dangers of a naïve empiricism (though for an alternative view on empiricism, see Witmore 2015). On "theory fatigue", see Braidotti (2019). More general papers reflecting on the current state of theory include Thomas (2015a, 2015b), Barrett (2016), Pétursdóttir and Olsen (2018) and Lucas and Witmore (2022).

What Is Theory?

Johnson (2014; also 2006) provides one answer for what theory is for as well as offering his own definition. The quotes used in this chapter come mostly from textbooks including Praetzellis (2015), Harris and Cipolla (2017), Green (1995), Wilkie (2016), Urban and Schortman (2012) and of course Johnson (2019). The exception is Conkey (2007), which is a journal article. The discussion of different types or levels of theory in Box 1.3 draws from Binford (1977), Smith (2011), and Urban and Schortman (2012); but also see Clarke (1973) and Schiffer (1988). For a revealing example of how levels of theory are connected to disciplinary hierarchies (and anxieties) in North American archaeology, see Lyman (2007); for reflections on archaeology as part of a fourfield anthropology outside of North America, see Hicks (2013) and Hodder (2005).

Rethinking Theory

For a critical discussion on levels of theory, see Lucas (2015). For strong and weak theory, see Sedgwick (1997), Stewart (2008), Pétursdóttir and Olsen (2018) and Lucas and Witmore (2022). For a classic postprocessual critique of "grand narrative", see Johnson (1999).

References

Baines, A. & K. Brophy. 2006. Archaeology Without -Isms. *Archaeological Dialogues* 13(1): 69–91.

Barrett, J. 2016. Archaeology After Interpretation. Returning Humanity to Archaeological Theory. *Archaeological Dialogues* 23(2): 133–7.

Binford, L. 1977. Introduction. In L. Binford (ed.), *For Theory Building in Archaeology*. New York: Academic Press, pp. 1–10.

Bintliff, J.L. & M. Pearce (eds.). 2011. *The Death of Archaeological Theory?* Oxford: Oxbow.

Braidotti, R. 2019. *Posthuman Knowledge*. Cambridge: Polity.

Clarke, D.L. 1973. Archaeology: The Loss of Innocence. *Antiquity* 47: 6–18.

Conkey, M.W. 2007. Questioning Theory: Is There a Gender of Theory in Archaeology? *Journal of Archaeological Method and Theory* 14(3): 285–310.

Gramsch, A. & U. Sommer (eds.). 2011. *A History of Central European Archaeology. Theory, Methods, and Politics*. Budapest: Archaeolingua.

Greene, K. 1995. *Archaeology. An Introduction*. London: Routledge.

Harris, O. & C. Cipolla. 2017. *Archaeological Theory in the New Millennium*. London: Routledge.

Hicks, D. 2013. Four-Field Anthropology. Charter Myths and Time Warps from St. Louis to Oxford. *Current Anthropology* 54(6): 753–63.

Hodder, I. (ed.). 1991. *Archaeological Theory in Europe: The Last Three Decades*. London: Routledge.

Hodder, I. 2005. An Archaeology of the Four-Field Approach in Anthropology in the United States. In D.A. Segal & S.J. Yanagisako (eds.), *Unwrapping the Sacred Bundle: Reflections on the Disciplining of Anthropology*. Durham, NC: Duke University Press, pp. 126–40.

Johnson, M. 1999. Rethinking Historical Archaeology. In P.P. Funari, M. Hall & S. Jones (eds.), *Historical Archaeology. Back from the Edge*. London: Routledge, pp. 23–36.

Johnson, M. 2006. On the Nature of Theoretical Archaeology and Archaeological Theory. *Archaeological Dialogues* 13(2): 117–32.

Johnson, M. 2011. On the Nature of Empiricism in Archaeology. *Journal of the Royal Anthropological Institute* 17: 764–87.

Johnson, M. 2014. What Is Theory For? In A. Gardiner, M. Lake & U. Sommer (eds.), *Oxford Handbook of Archaeological Theory*. Oxford: Handbooks Online.

Johnson, M. 2019. *Archaeological Theory. An Introduction*. Chichester: Wiley-Blackwell.

Kristiansen, K. 2014. Towards a New Paradigm? The Third Science Revolution and Its Possible Consequences in Archaeology. *Current Swedish Archaeology* 22: 11–34.

Lucas, G. 2015. The Mobility of Theory. *Current Swedish Archaeology* 23: 13–82.

Lucas, G. & C. Witmore. 2022. Paradigm Lost: What Is a Commitment to Theory in Contemporary Archaeology? *Norwegian Archaeological Review*. https://doi.org/10.1080/00293652.2021.1986127.

Lyman, R.L. 2007. Archaeology's Quest for a Seat at the High Table of Anthropology. *Journal of Anthropological Archaeology* 26: 133–49.

Moore, H. 2004. Global Anxieties, Concept-Metaphors and Pre-Theoretical Commitments in Anthropology. *Anthropological Theory* 4(1): 71–88.

Olsen, B. 1991. Metropolises and Satellites in Archaeology: On Power and Asymmetry in Global Archaeological Discourse. In R.W. Preucel (ed.), *Processual and Postprocessual*

Archaeologies: Multiple Ways of Knowing the Past. Carbondale: Southern Illinois University, pp. 211–24.

Pétursdóttir, Þ. & B. Olsen. 2018. Theory Adrift: The Matter of Archaeological Thinking. *Journal of Social Archaeology* 18(1): 97–117.

Praetzellis, A. 2015. *Archaeological Theory in a Nutshell.* Walnut Creek: Left Coast Press.

Schiffer, M.B. 1988. The Structure of Archaeological Theory. *American Antiquity* 53: 461–85.

Sedgwick, E.K. 1997. Paranoid Reading and Reparative Reading: Or, You're So Paranoid, You Probably Think This Introduction Is About You. In E. Sedgwick (ed.), *Novel Gazing: Queer Readings in Fiction.* Durham: Duke University Press, pp. 1–40.

Smith, M.E. 2011. Empirical Urban Theory for Archaeologists. *Journal of Archaeological Method and Theory* 18(3): 167–92.

Stewart, K. 2008. Weak Theory in an Unfinished World. *Journal of Folklore Research* 45(1): 71–82.

Thomas, J. 2015a. The Future of Archaeological Theory. *Antiquity* 89(348): 1287–96.

Thomas, J. 2015b. Why Are Archaeologists Discussing 'the Death of Archaeological Theory'? In C. Hillerdal & J. Siapkas (eds.), *Debating Archaeological Empiricism. The Ambiguity of Material Evidence.* London: Routledge.

Trigger, B. 2006. *A History of Archaeological Thought.* Cambridge: Cambridge University Press.

Ucko, P. (ed.). 1995. *Theory in Archaeology. A World Perspective.* London: Routledge.

Urban, P. & E. Schortman. 2012. *Archaeological Theory in Practice.* London: Routledge.

Wilkie, L. 2016. *Strung Out on Archaeology. An Introduction to Archaeological Research.* London: Routledge.

Witmore, C. 2015. Archaeology and the Second Empiricism. In C. Hillerdal & J. Siapkis (eds.), *Debating Archaeological Empiricism.* London: Routledge, pp. 45–75.

2 Doing Fieldwork

> **Situation 2: In the Trench**
>
> *The first week of the fieldschool, students are down on their knees, trowelling away, the supervisor is wandering around the site doing who knows what. Imagine if all the thoughts of these people were flashed above them in little cloud-bubbles like those cartoons: when is the lunch break? . . . . I have no idea what I am doing . . . they are cute . . . why didn't the supervisor put me over there? . . . this soil looks different to before . . . . Then suddenly all these bubbles pop as a voice breaks the silence, calling for the supervisor. A gleaming object has caught the eye of a student. "Is this anything?" the student asks, handing it to the supervisor. The supervisor examines the object, a rounded white pebble. After a brief moment of reflection, the answer comes back: "Probably not. It is a natural pebble, and although sometimes pebbles like this may have been intentionally brought to site – what we call manuports – this is probably not the case here". The supervisor hands it back to the student, who is still a bit unsure. "So . . . shall I keep it or throw it?"*

Fieldwork and Facts

What Counts as Archaeology?

Keep it or not? That is the question faced by any archaeologist when excavating and encountering things in the ground. For novices, such questions may be more frequent, but no matter how experienced you are, this dilemma will always crop up now and again. The fear is, of course, you may be discarding something meaningful or keeping something pointless. But either way, think about what happens in that moment of decision. If you keep it, the object gets registered and given a number, it goes through the same process as all the other finds and becomes a small fact about the site, a little bit of data. If you throw it on the spoil, it has become nothing and sinks into oblivion. There you are, at the birth of a fact – you are the midwife and perhaps you never even realized it.

Such decisions actually pervade our work all the time and underline the selective nature of fieldwork; we are always dividing the stuff we encounter into two groups: stuff that matters and stuff that doesn't. Because it isn't just about what object you keep or discard; it is also about whether that pile of rocks on the surface is a ruin or a natural pile; should I take a GPS reading or not? Whether that linear anomaly on a geophysical plot is an archaeological feature or an artefact of the software. Although a lot of the examples in this chapter will focus on excavation, almost everything discussed applies to other types of fieldwork. Indeed, perhaps this is what defines fieldwork in general: the act of transforming a farmer's field, a mountain valley or the seabed into an archaeological site. Crucially, we will adopt in this chapter, a notion of **the field** as anywhere this process of transformation takes place – which in recent times has included an increasing diversity of places, from an archaeologist's van to outer space!

The stuff that matters become our facts and data; the stuff that doesn't is ignored and eventually forgotten. Not everything that matters is always kept; the soil we are trowelling may get saved or sampled, but most of it ends up on, indeed creates, the spoil heap. But still we record things about it like its colour, its texture, composition and so on. But even here, we make selections; we cannot record *everything* about it. Is that even possible? We write down its colour, but not how it tastes; we measure its thickness, but rarely do we weigh it. The selections are endless, and in most cases we don't even think about them. As a student, this is part of what you learn, usually by following guidelines and rules about how to record stuff in the ground. These selections are not entirely arbitrary of course; in part, they have been honed over years and years of experience, but they are also informed by certain assumptions about what we think is important based on the research questions and general disciplinary background knowledge which lies behind all projects. Most of the time, what goes into the meaningful group, worthy of keeping or recording and what doesn't, is not subject to any deep reflection but taken for granted. But you only have to look at the history of archaeology to see that these divisions have not always been the same as they are today (Box 2.1).

Box 2.1 Total Recovery?

Excavators, as a rule, record only those things which appear important to them at the time, but fresh problems in archaeology and anthropology are constantly arising, and it can hardly fail to have escaped the notice of anthropologists, especially those who, like myself, have been concerned with the morphology of art, that, on turning back to old accounts in search of evidence, the points which would have been most valuable have been passed over from being thought uninteresting at the time. Every detail should, therefore, be recorded in the manner most conducive to facility of reference, and it ought at all times to be

> *the chief object of an excavator to reduce his own personal equation to a minimum.*
>
> (Pitt Rivers 1887)

> *Archaeologists who systematically record the position of a coke bottle or tin foil from a cigarette wrapper and then carefully bag and curate it as part of the archaeology of the site just make themselves (and other archaeologists) look silly.*
>
> (Drewitt 1999)

The late nineteenth century was a period when archaeologists were increasingly exhorting each other on the importance of mundane things and to recover as much as possible, especially in areas where art historical approaches often framed recovery protocols, that is, saving only museum-worthy objects. It is easy to portray the development of scientific archaeology as one where this shift in mindset marks a decisive break between antiquarianism and true archaeology. Yet the goalposts for recovery have constantly been shifting and often depend upon the kind of site you happen to be working on. Pitt Rivers, who worked mostly on prehistoric sites in England at the end of the nineteenth century, argued for total recovery while Flinders Petrie, who worked in Egypt at the same time, faced with tons of pottery as opposed to the handfuls that Pitt Rivers was used to encountering, argued for a selective retention policy. Yet even Pitt Rivers' methods were somewhat contradictory to his philosophy; he seems to have rewarded his workmen for the recovery of "nicer" finds and didn't always collect all bones but only the more diagnostic parts (skulls and long bones). And it goes without saying he will not have used sieves or flotation to recover smaller items.

Indeed, this last point reveals how recovery protocols are affected by broader frameworks of research; the rise in recovery of environmental samples from the 1950s is closely linked to an emerging interest in the ecological dimension of human cultures and societies. The same can be said about the interest in later modern periods, such as the archaeology of nineteenth and twentieth centuries remains which were – and still are in some places – neglected as outside the domain of archaeology. At the same time, no excavation can recover everything; has there ever been a site without a spoil heap? Most of the soil and stones are not kept. But recovery it is not just about materials; it also about the relations between materials: the location of finds, the stratigraphic position and shape of deposits, all the kinds of things we, of course, cannot keep simply because the very act of excavation destroys them. In this case, total recovery takes on a new meaning, one which places great burden on the written or visual record to "preserve" these aspects of a site more sensitive to our excavation. This is why excavation is sometimes called "preservation by record". Yet such claims, even when put in quotes, raise all kinds of questions about the extent to which a record can act as a copy of the site – what is often called the archive objective. This is a topic we will cover in more detail in Chapter 3.

What all this comes down to is quite simple really. We can argue and theorize all we like about what archaeology is, but every day, on every site, the boundary between what counts as archaeology and what doesn't is being made in the hundreds and thousands of small decisions about what to keep, what to record. Archaeological facts are not out there waiting to be discovered; they are made in these everyday events. But let's be clear here. When we say made, we don't mean made up; soils, stones, walls, pits and potsherds are all real things and they too play a role in these decisions. But when we describe something as "a natural pebble", that is not the same thing as the cold, smooth, rounded object you hold in your hand. Facts are always abstractions, representations of real things which begs the question: what is the relationship between the physical object and the fact?

Well, one thing we already know from the previous discussion is that facts are selective, they involve processes of sorting between what is deemed relevant and what isn't. Nobody can collect or record everything; we always make decisions based either on prior assumptions usually defined by the discipline or on-the-spot calls. When creating a fact about a layer, we regard colour as an important attribute but not usually how it tastes. When deciding if something is worth keeping as a find, we make judgements about whether it was made or at least used by humans and may therefore have cultural significance. But even if we accept that facts are selective, that they only give us partial representations of the things they refer to, that still leaves the question of how we understand the nature of that representation. Surely facts are, by definition, true? However selective or partial they may be, they still purport to be truthful statements about things. This layer was dark brown, it was not blue or pink; it was 12 cm thick, not 200 cm thick. Surely then, in making facts, one of the most important things we need to do is be truthful or faithful to the thing which we are representing? Archaeologists often refer to this fidelity as **objectivity** – but this is a difficult term, so let us put it to one side for now and explore this problem through a more familiar set of terms: description and interpretation.

Interpretation and Description

Archaeologists are a cautious bunch on the whole. Fieldwork is, like any good science, guided by protocols and rules which attempt to obtain truthfulness in the construction of facts. One of the most important traditions in fieldwork has been the importance of separating **description** from **interpretation**. A description is often depicted as factual, while an interpretation goes beyond the facts to speculate or infer something not immediately evident. I remember a conversation with a colleague once where he showed me two drawings; one was a plan of a site, to scale, using standard conventions drawn in the field. The other was a simplified drawing showing the same site but in a different style, one that tried to show what the features represented. He held up the first and said this was fact, the other interpretation. It is one thing to describe a layer as dark brown and 12 cm thick, quite another to identify it as a floor. Its colour and thickness we can see and measure, it is right in front of us. The notion that it might be a floor is surely more speculative; it refers to how that deposit was used in the past, a thing we cannot ever observe. So in calling this layer a floor, we have to accept that this is an interpretation because we are making inferences beyond what is observable.

To some extent, this seems like an intuitively correct way to separate description from interpretation; a description shows us what was there, while an interpretation goes beyond that, it makes inferences (Box 2.2). But how separate are they really? Let's go back to that deposit we are calling a floor and consider its interface with the deposit above it. The interface is that line on a section or profile drawing that marks the separation of two layers (Figure 2.1). Is that interface the surface of the deposit or could it actually be a horizontal levelling cut? Maybe the original upper surface of that deposit has been scraped away prior to the upper layer being laid down. How do we decide which of these two it is? Of course we use various clues to help, but this just underlines the point that this is an interpretive decision. Such examples can be multiplied; you only have to think about how difficult it can be sometimes to define the edges of a deposit at all; where does it stop and start? Often deposits blend or merge into one another and sites don't always conform to the neat, discrete layering shown in textbooks. Very often when you draw a section or profile of a trench or feature, you are faced with decisions about where to draw lines demarcating layers; even though we may use conventions to indicate where divisions are more (or less) distinct, such decisions can still be open to negotiation.

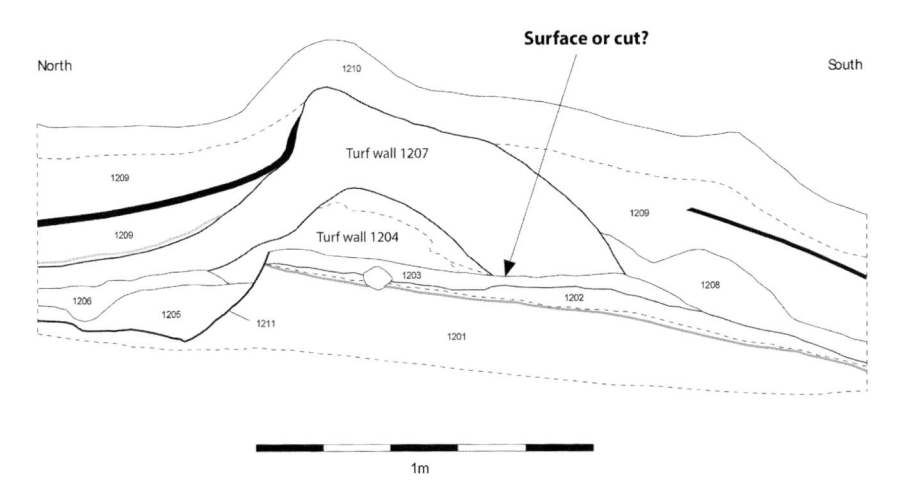

Figure 2.1 Section drawing showing the interpretive problems of an interface: is the top of deposit 1203 a surface or a cut – perhaps a horizontal continuation of the cut 1211?

Box 2.2 The Context Sheet

One of the common targets of criticism in field recording was the way description was separated from interpretation on *pro forma* record sheets for excavation units, known as context sheets in the UK. Moreover, description tended to take up the larger part of space on such sheets with the interpretation relegated to a small box at the bottom. The philosophy implicit in such traditional sheets is that subjective input should be both kept to a minimum and clearly separated from objective description. In the 1990s and early 2000s, many archaeologists argued against such divisions and tried to develop sheets which embodied a more reflexive and self-aware process of documentation where the relationship between description and interpretation is more fluid and recursive. Compare the two context sheets in Figure 2.2 and look at how they differ in respect to these issues.

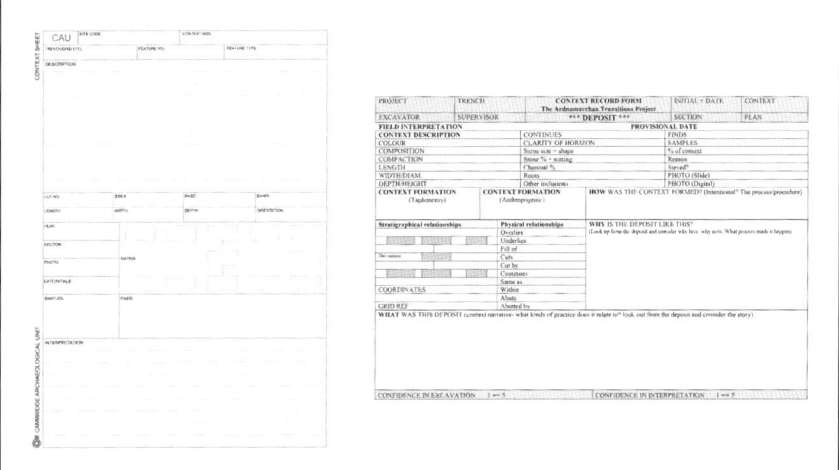

Figure 2.2 A comparison of two context sheets (left: Cambridge Archaeology Unit; right: Ardnamurchan Transitions Project).

All of this suggests that the distinction between description and interpretation is not as rigid as we might have thought; deciding whether the upper face of a deposit is an intact surface or has been truncated/cut away will start to affect our descriptions; not only do we have to decide if the deposit is complete or not, it will also affect whether we have one or two unit sheets to fill out: a single deposit with a surface or a deposit with a truncated surface on the one hand and a cut on the other. And if we open the door to this, then maybe we need to open it further.

You might think whether we call a deposit a floor or a midden won't change the description of it. It is still dark brown and 12 cm thick. Yes, but maybe we will start to pay closer attention to other aspects of the deposit we hadn't given much thought to before. If we see it as a floor, we might expect it to be more compact than other adjacent deposits, maybe we would go back and check our description, compare it and possibly modify it in light of this. On the other hand, if it clearly is not compact but rather soft and loose, maybe our interpretation of it as a floor needs to be questioned or explained why it is not more compact.

What this example suggests is that the relation between description and interpretation is recursive, that is, each informs how we construct the other. This does not mean they are completely circular though and can be collapsed. There does remain some autonomy between the two. Overall descriptions tend to follow more explicit protocols; we might have a checklist of attributes to go through, whereas an interpretation is more open and flexible. At one level, descriptions are always interpretive in the sense that they are selective and guided by some set of assumptions; protocols we use to describe a layer are based on theories of soil science and deposit formation which guide us in choosing what things to record and how. But the crucial thing here is that these general theoretical frameworks are independent from the specific interpretations you might make of features on a particular site. In this sense, the difference between description and interpretation still has some validity, though maybe the terms are not the most appropriate. In most cases what we mean by interpretation is some inference as to the past use or formation process of a deposit or feature. In the cases discussed here, whether we are dealing with the interpretation of an interface as a surface or cut, or of a deposit as a floor, the inference is how the deposit was formed or functioned in the past. These formational or functional attributions are different to the physical attributes of description because they are inferential. It is fair to say, both description and inference are interpretive, but in different ways which does not invalidate the distinction between them.

However, there is another dimension here we still need to consider. It is not just that description and inference are recursive, each helping to constitute the other. This recursiveness also extends out to how we interact and even excavate a deposit. If, for example, we decide that this deposit is a floor and not a midden, then it might also affect the way we excavate it. We might want to separate finds from the surface as finds contemporary with the use of the room with which the floor is associated and finds from the lower part of the deposit as mixed/re-deposited material brought in as part of the floor construction. In doing this though, it also reveals to us something even more important about the construction of facts in the field; it isn't just a purely mental or conceptual exercise. It is a deeply embodied and performative one. Everyone knows fieldwork is an intensely physical activity; you are outside, using your hands, arms and legs, and at the end of the day, your muscles can ache, especially at the beginning of the field season. This physical aspect of our discipline is not just one of the perks (or put-offs) of doing archaeology; it is also deeply implicated in the production of facts and production of archaeological knowledge. More importantly, as we shall see, it also shifts the balance of agency in terms of how facts are made: as joint endeavours constructed not only by the archaeologist but also by their tools and, of course, the ground itself.

Fieldwork as Lived Practice

Observation and Intervention

In the previous discussion about description and interpretation, I presented these ideas as if they were purely cognitive acts; I look at the layer and see it is dark brown, I notice the layer sits within four lines of stones I take to be walls and infer my layer must be a floor. It is as if we can make all these decisions at a distance, simply by gazing at the ground. It reminds me of that stereotypical image about how archaeologists used to excavate 150 years ago: sitting in an armchair under a parasol while directing the labourers, occasionally getting up to inspect the area, making notes. Doubtless this stereotype has some truth to it, which we will see later on in this chapter. But in terms of the previous discussion, such detachment seriously misrepresents the process of how facts are made. Quite possibly I can record the colour of a deposit at a distance, but if it is a hot day, it may help to moisten the layer to enhance its colour or at the very least, remove the top, dry crust to get a fresher exposure. In most cases, making facts requires not just detached observation but physical intervention. Certainly, there will be times when you do need to stand back; one of the reasons the supervisor seems to spend a lot of time wandering around the site doing nothing is that she is thinking about what is going on: how this layer relates to that, what that section of wall is doing there, why are these two features at different levels? But to answer these questions, usually also then requires some action: clear away that spoil, clean up that edge, remove this layer so we can better see what is going on.... Observation and intervention – like description and inference – are inextricably bound together.

But this relation is more complex than simply a recursive process of reflecting and acting. Into this mix, we also have to include recording. We often think of recording as something we do when the process of intervention has reached completion; when we have finally resolved the edges of a deposit, then we are ready to record it; when the section or profile has been cleaned and the stratification makes sense, we can start to draw it. But in some ways, recording actually *precedes* the intervention; one of the reasons we clean the top of a deposit to ascertain its edges is so we can draw it, measure it and so on. One of the reasons your supervisor tells you to keep the trench edges straight and vertical is that they want it to materially prefigure the drawing you might later make. We are sculpting and shaping the site to look like the record we will subsequently make of it. Why? Because the whole point of a record is to be a faithful copy or representation of the physical thing it records. If a drawing of a deposit looks like the deposit, then it is partly because we have moulded the deposit to look like the drawing, even before we have made it. This is the reason why sometimes, plans of different sites or parts of sites can look eerily familiar, why descriptions of soils can become very repetitive, especially when recording and archiving systems become highly standardized across projects.

Once again though, we must be careful not to over-state this. You cannot sculpt a site into any shape you like; as archaeologists, you are trying to learn to "read" the soil, to spot when there are changes or differences. The ground itself has its own properties, its own characteristics which will resist as well as conform to your actions. The point here is that recording on site is never a passive process of simply transferring what is there, on to paper or tablet; the record is always an active co-production between the archaeologists and the site (see Box 2.3).

Box 2.3 Following the Cut

The phrase "follow the cut" refers to the injunction given to archaeologists when excavating features like pits, postholes or ditches (Figure 2.3). These cut-down features filled with sediment require the excavator to find the edges between the "fill" and the surrounding (often "natural") soil. How should we characterize this action? Are we simply revealing what is there? And if so, how does the skill of an excavator seem to make such a difference in enabling this cut to emerge? Matt Edgeworth offers a very lucid discussion of this and argues that we are neither simply uncovering what is "really there" nor are we making it up.

The problem here is that, on the one hand, we traditionally see this cut as something which pre-exists the archaeologist, while on the other, the feature only becomes visible through the act of excavation. The problem exists because we have already assumed a separation of the cut (in the past) and archaeologist (in the present) at the start, whereas Edgeworth argues that the cut is never a static object. It was made in the past, presumably by humans like us but with very different tools; but it didn't then just freeze. It continued existing, interacting with the soil and other living organisms around it, its shape subtly being modified as the sides weathered and this process of "what the cut is" simply carries on when the archaeologist comes along and starts to excavate. The "cut" therefore is an extended co-production of many different agencies and materials from compact subsoil and long-dead humans and antler shovels to wind and rain to archaeologists and their trowels. At any one point in time, it is always an emergent thing, an object which is a conjunction of past and present forces and materials. Viewed in this way, the original problem and separation of a "pre-existing cut" and an "excavating archaeologist" no longer has any meaning or relevance. When the archaeologist is following the cut, it is as much about how the cut guides the archaeologist's hands as it is about the dexterity of those hands.

Figure 2.3 Excavating the edge: Tony Baker excavates a second- and third-century "corn dryer", finding the edge of the clay foundation from the flue's infill deposit (photo: Cambridge Archaeological Unit/Dave Webb).

But there is yet one final thing still to add. Even accepting that any record we make is dependent on this recursive process of observation and intervention with the ground, neither intervention nor observation can usually happen without the use of instruments. To observe the colour of the soil as dark brown, I need a spray bottle to moisten the soil or a trowel to turn over a fresh surface. To record the colour, I may even decide to use a Munsell chart book. To make a vertical face, I need a spade with a sharp edge, a flat-bladed trowel to clean up and maybe even a plumb line if I want to be extra precise. We can use our spit to moisten soil, our hands to dig holes – and often we do! But no excavation would be possible without the army of shovels, picks, trowels, buckets, total stations, paper, pens, manuals, string and so on, which accompany us onto the site. These are our microscopes, our particle accelerators – the instruments we need to gather our facts. And just like the microscope and the accelerator, they are not just passive tools used to record what is there; they play an active role in shaping and constituting those facts (Box 2.4).

Box 2.4 Paper Versus Pixels

Which is the better way to plan layers on a site: using a state-of-the-art 3D scanner or measuring tapes, pencil and paper (Figure 2.4)? If you believe planning is all about accuracy and precision, then you are likely to go for the modern technology. There is no doubt it will measure the edges and even topography of the layer or feature to a level of accuracy in a way that traditional tapes and levels could never compete with. Indeed, if you can scan in 3D, it far surpasses 2D drawings which have to rely on hachures or combine elevations and plans to capture a site in three dimensions. It will also be quicker. So surely the answer is obvious. But is it? Let's look at some of the counter arguments.

Colleen Morgan and Holly Wright have argued that important cognitive work is lost in the shift from hand drawing to digital recording. Given what we discussed earlier in the chapter about the problems with separating description from interpretation, planning a layer or feature is not only about accurately rendering the shape or size of a deposit, it is equally about understanding why it takes this form and how it relates to other layers on site. It is argued that drawing engages the archaeologist in an understanding of the site in ways that are lost with digital recording because it is a much more interactive and recursive process, especially so when more than one person is involved in making the drawing. In a follow-up study, they found moreover that this was especially acute with novice archaeologists and students because the impact of the technology is much greater on the inexperienced whose mental map of what it is they are recording is generally much more undeveloped. Indeed, when comparing people's descriptions of objects before and after drawing, it was commonly the case that the drawing greatly enhanced attention to details and aspects not noticed before.

Related to this is also a question of speed. It certainly can be beneficial to record a site faster, especially in the competitive world of commercial archaeology. But taking your time brings its own benefits; embracing the slower pace of low-tech tapes and pencils means you have time to think and once again engage with the site in a way that fast, automated technologies make harder. This is the impetus behind calls for a **slow archaeology** by archaeologists like William Caraher who has questioned our inbuilt assumptions that advances in field technology are always better. Indeed, there is a wider issue here which relates to the way highly refined methodologies – whether of fieldwork or scientific analysis – streamline the archaeological operation too much. Marko Marila has argued that this methodological streamlining which is especially associated with archaeological science encourages a "fast archaeology", which may produce speedy results but at the expense of narrowing the breadth of our knowledge. When excavation, for example, is too formalized and bound to protocols, how will we innovate?

At the end of day though, as Morgan and Wright conclude, it isn't a question of either/or but rather acknowledging that different technologies each have their own strengths and weaknesses but more importantly, construct knowledge in different ways, that the medium matters.

Figure 2.4 Students planning with traditional tapes and paper (left) and a total station (right) at the university fieldschool in Iceland (photos: the author).

But it isn't just our instruments that help to give form to our facts and records; we do too in terms of our subjectivities. If there is a difference between making a plan with pencil, paper and tapes versus making one with a total station or GPS (see Box 2.4), there is also a difference between the plans made by different people, though often subtly so (see Box 2.5). We are all different; some of us are better at drawing than others, some are colour blind, some dyslexic; all of our individual qualities can affect the record. Yet at the same time, one of the fundamental points about going on a fieldschool and learning field methods is to dampen or limit the effect of these personal traits. We train our bodies to use tools in a certain way, we train minds to think in certain ways, our senses to perceive certain things. Archaeological sites and facts are not just made by archaeologists; they make us. Our engagement with sites and with the instruments and tools we use, also shapes us, shapes our subjectivities; not to the same depth and extent that our parents or homes shaped us, but nonetheless, we are being moulded to perform in certain ways so that whenever we find ourselves on an archaeological site, this moulding, this training, kicks in. And it will also leak out into other situations; maybe a walk in the countryside might trigger your archaeological self or a stroll down a high street. You might notice things and think about things you wouldn't ordinarily have, if you hadn't been trained as an archaeologist.

Objectivity and Subjectivity

Such training can be seen as both shaping your subjectivity but also stripping it – making you more objective. We came across this term **objectivity** earlier; it usually has a sense of being impartial, free of bias, but one of the best ways to understand it is as the opposite of **subjective**. When archaeologists or other scientists talk about being objective, they mean not letting their subjectivity taint any description or creation of a record. We don't want any bias or prejudice to be skewing the production of facts.

> **Box 2.5 Gendered Fieldwork**
>
> We all know how gender is implicated in behaviour in everyday life, how cultural norms around the traditional binary of male and female gender roles leads to certain expectations, no matter how critical or reflexive we try to be. Archaeological fieldwork is no more exempt from these patterns than any other sphere of life as Joan Gero once demonstrated in a paper on gendered fieldwork. In particular, she found some quite startling differences in the way her male and female students dug and recorded. When the students were excavating around finds to leave them on pedestals of soil for later plotting, she noticed that the pedestals of male students tended to be larger than those of the female students who only left enough soil to support the find. Gero saw this as indicative of an (unconscious) masculine practice of drawing attention to their own finds as the eye is automatically drawn to these finds "framed" by larger pillars of soil. When it came to drawing, she also observed that the female students were much more open to ambiguity in what they were recording, using dotted lines in the plans and acknowledging uncertainty. In contrast, the male students were much more likely to use solid lines and produce a record that left little space for uncertainty.
>
> Such subtle, gendered differences in how male and female students engaged with the site is connected to broader philosophies of knowledge production where authority and certainty is valued over ambiguity, an issue Gero went on to write about in another paper (see Box 4.1). Indeed, the larger point here is not whether male and female archaeologists differ in how they excavate or record but rather whether a masculinist "logic" of how to do science has dominated archaeological practice throughout most of the history of our discipline. This is not about essentializing male and female ways of thinking but acknowledging that cultural norms of gendered behaviour impact science as much as any other cultural practice.

But what does removing subjectivity really mean? How can anyone get rid of their subjectivity? Isn't that what it means to be human? Does being objective mean becoming dehumanized? This is one way of looking at it, although in a moment we will see this is not quite right either. Let's think of it this way. Which do you think produces a more accurate plan: a total station using lasers, prisms and a computer chip, or a pair of archaeologists with tapes and pegs? The answer – as we saw in Box 2.4 – is of course the first and the reasons are manifold: it is a lot harder for humans to take account of sloping ground, humans are more prone to make errors transcribing numbers from tapes to paper or round numbers up and down, the wind and weather may also impact performance and so on. In short, compared to a machine, humans frequently don't measure up when it comes to certain operations. Using a total station is not just more accurate, it's more objective because the degree of human-induced error has been reduced; all we have to do is to point and press a button. It is quite literally, dehumanized recording. Still, there are other sources of inaccuracy with the older method using paper and tapes; the tapes may stretch and bend, gridded paper may shrink or expand. Nobody is arguing that instruments don't also have their problems, but the issue is rather which has the least. So let's wind this back one stage. Which is better for measuring the dimensions of a deposit: a measuring tape or the human body? I can certainly pace out the length of a layer or use my arms or hands as guides, but a measuring tape is certainly more useful, however much it may stretch or break; human paces and body parts are of variable length, whereas a tape measure is standardized. Once again, a tape measure is a more objective means of evaluating the dimensions of a feature than any human body on its own. Objectivity as it is being used here therefore means a situation where an act of recording has been delegated to an object.

So one way of characterizing what we mean when we talk about objectivity is really about minimizing subjectivity; we can never remove human involvement and subjectivity all together, but we can minimize the dependence on human eyes and hands to dehumanize the recording process as much as possible by delegating as much of this task to non-human instruments and tools as possible. This is what our recording tools do, whether they are cheap fibre glass tapes or expensive robotic total stations, cameras or soil pH meters. This is also what Munsell colour books and *pro forma* context sheets also do; by creating standardized protocols, they essentially turn the human mind and body into a supplement of these recording protocols. Ultimately, all the training you receive in learning how to do fieldwork and how to record could be seen as about learning to subordinate your agency to a variety of instruments and tools so that as objective a record as possible is made.

Yet describing this process of creating objectivity through delegation to non-human instruments as dehumanizing is misleading. One of the major theoretical developments in the last few decades has been an acknowledgement that objects like tools are what *makes us human in the first place*. In using cameras and total stations to record a site, we are not dehumanizing the process but actually reproducing what it is to be human, more specifically, to be an archaeologist as a special kind of human. Rather than see Munsell books and GPS as ways of minimizing subjectivity, we could argue that in fact they are ways of enhancing subjectivity or more precisely, archaeological subjectivity. This in fact has been a key argument of many archaeologists who talked about the role of material culture in the past, especially its role in human development and evolution. Whenever humans use other things, it often extends their abilities or powers in super-human ways; it is in this sense that some have claimed we have always been cyborgs. When humans domesticated horses, they increased their speed of movement umpteen fold; when they developed projectiles, they created a new ability to kill or maim other life at a distance. Tool use, whether of a palaeolithic hunter or an archaeologist in a trench, gives people capacities to act in new and sometimes very powerful ways. Just as a bow and arrow enhance the subjectivity of a human-as-hunter, so a trowel enhances the subjectivity of a human-as-archaeologist.

Arguably in discussing our instruments on site as tools for minimizing subjectivity, for dehumanizing the recording process, we have it the wrong way around. Rather we should claim such objects *develop* our subjectivity or humanity rather than strip it away – but develop it in very specific ways. Maybe all we really mean by objectivity is enhanced scientific subjectivity, and as such, objectivity is not opposed to subjectivity but simply a specialized facet of it. And we should stress that it is just *one* facet; archaeological subjectivity has in fact multiple facets, even in the field. Certainly when it comes to recording a deposit, we might value the use of measuring tools to obtain an accurate representation of its shape and dimensions; we might value the use of *pro forma* sheets to create some consistency between our descriptions. But on other occasions, we might actually wish to eschew such technology or develop alternative tools; sometimes, our bodies and senses are the best tools for the job (Box 2.6). Consider, for example, the case of human footprints in Peche Merle Cave, southern France, dating to more than 10,000 years ago; since their discovery in 1949, they had been subject to repeated archaeological investigation using morpho-metric techniques (i.e. counting, measuring and classification), but usually these only resulted in broad identification of the number of people and their age. Yet when archaeologists recently invited three indigenous trackers from the Ju/'hoan San people in Namibia to study the prints, whole mini-narratives emerged around the prints which often extended the number of people but importantly told them about how they were walking – a woman slipping, a middle-aged man walking slower than his companions and so on. Suddenly, the whole scene comes much more alive. Ultimately, the strength of our understanding comes from combining different approaches and being open to different ways of experiencing the archaeology.

Box 2.6 Phenomenology and Fieldwork

Our bodies are our most important tools for recording; even when we use cameras, digital surveying equipment and tablets or pencils and paper, we use our eyes and hands to operate these things, just as we use our whole bodies when fieldwalking or excavating. The problem is, most conventional recording technologies tend to privilege just one sense: vision. Colour, size, composition and spatial position all largely rely on our sense of sight, and moreover, on one that has been channelled in very specific ways. Why are sites typically presented as aerial, birds-eye views in our plans and maps? We almost never see them or experience them like this and nor did people in the past.

Many archaeologists, drawing on a philosophical movement called phenomenology, argued for broadening the experiential repertoire of how we engage with and record sites. Phenomenology in the philosophical tradition comprises a much richer set of ideas than implied here and archaeologists have drawn on it in other ways than described here (see Chapter 3). However, this approach, which is primarily associated with British postprocessualists studying the landscape, is perhaps the most well-known within the Anglophone world. Chris Tilley, who is the most famous exponent of this method, made it central to his fieldwork, especially of landscape survey, but the same approach has been used in excavation and artefact analysis. During fieldwork on site at Neolithic enclosures in Italy, Sue Hamilton and Ruth Whitehouse used various sounds such as human shouting and banging stones or wood together to try and map the soundscapes of these spaces by recording the relationship between audibility and distance and what role this might have played in social organization. Chris Tilley and Wayne Bennett used portable doorframes during the excavation of Bronze Age huts in southwestern England to gain a sense of viewshed from within the houses.

Figure 2.5 Recording sensory distances over which sound (human shout and conversation, wooden whistle and stone striking) can be heard and human body movements can be communicated (photo: M. Seager Thomas).

> Gavin McGregor decided to record a variety of affective properties of late Neolithic and early Bronze Age ornately carved stone balls from Scotland to see if they could help us better understand their meaning. What happens when you spin one of these balls, what visual effects does it create? In all these cases, the archaeologists were trying to interact with the archaeological remains in a way that made them come alive, made them active, rather than passive objects to be simply studied at a distance.
>
> Such approaches are not about trying to re-live past experiences but rather to foreground the fact that people in the past interacted with things and the environment in an embodied way that was not mediated through tapes and surveying instruments but other everyday objects like cowbells or doorframes – or simply their bodies. Again, it is not about the historical veracity of these alternate "props" that necessarily matters but an openness to experimentation and exploration of sensory qualities of the archaeological remains as these may open up new avenues of interpretation and thinking about the past.

However, developing archaeological subjectivity in the field is even broader than simply experimenting with new approaches or new tools. Archaeologists' engagement with a site is not just through or alongside their tools and equipment; it is also an engagement alongside other people including, as well as other archaeologists, developers, planning control officers, local and descendant communities, digger drivers, landowners and so on, all of whom will have a greater or lesser interest in the site and what you are doing with it. This is important as the conditions under which fieldwork takes place can be quite different – especially between research-led and development-led projects, which impacts knowledge creation.

Who Is an Archaeologist?

As a student studying archaeology, you may find yourself on a training excavation which may also be your first ever time on a dig. Hopefully it is exciting and probably, you imagine you are there to learn how to excavate. Are you an archaeologist? Maybe that's an unfair question; does it have to be either/or? One is learning to become an archaeologist for sure, but when do you know you have *become* an archaeologist? When you have your degree in hand? When you have become a member of a recognized society of archaeologists? When you get your first *paid* job on an archaeological project or with an archaeological organization? Your teacher might tell you, you never stop learning, you never stop becoming an archaeologist, which is true of course but also an easy answer from someone standing on the other side of the lecture theatre drawing a regular salary! Because while your teacher may have a point, if you look again at what goes on in real-life archaeological situations, there is a constant and often subtle and unspoken set of divisions that suggest something otherwise. Let's look at some of them.

Profiling the Profession

Who dug the tomb of Tutankhamen? Howard Carter you might think and of course he was there on site, but the bulk of excavation was carried on by hundreds of labourers whose names almost nobody knows today. In former colonial contexts like Egypt during the 1920s, the majority of the fieldwork was conducted by local men, women and children: teams of diggers and spoil removers under the supervision of experienced foreman. Flinders Petrie had a permanent staff of six Egyptian foremen under a chief supervisor, who ran digging teams of hundreds from the 1880s. So what did Petrie or Carter do if they weren't digging? Usually they organized and boxed up finds and made the records – drafted plans, took fieldnotes, recorded finds, often with the assistance of other Europeans. And it wasn't just in Egypt and other former colonial settings this happened; back on European soil, local labourers also did most of the digging, while the "archaeologist" made the records, wrote up the site or presented the results to learned societies (Box 2.7). You may have heard of Flinders Petrie, but have you heard of Ali al-Suayfi, his chief excavator? You may have heard of Pitt Rivers, but have you heard of Herbert Toms, one of his best field assistants? Not to mention the countless, un-named and largely forgotten people who wielded the shovels and spades, moved baskets, buckets and wheel-barrows of soil off the site. Tell me, who are the archaeologists here?

Box 2.7   Sutton Hoo in the Summer of '39

Sutton Hoo is a site in eastern England, famous for its Anglo-Saxon burial mounds, including a ship burial. The earliest excavations here took place in the late 1930s, just before the beginning of the Second World War. The landowner of the site, Edith Pretty instigated the initial excavations and hired a local, self-taught archaeologist Basil Brown affiliated with a nearby museum to conduct the work, with help from workers on Pretty's estate. The second summer of work, they struck gold – literally. But what was really impressive about the second season was the discovery of a ship burial, as it was this that grabbed the attention of Charles Philips at Cambridge University. Discussions between the local and British Museum and other institutions resulted in Philips taking over the excavations from Brown with a team of archaeologists who were or became key figures in British archaeology during the early-mid twentieth century including W.F. Grimes, O.G.S. Crawford and Stuart Piggott. But during that summer of 1939, the events around the project also offer a glimpse of how power was distributed within an excavation and connected to issues of class and gender.

The original excavator Brown was a farmer, and archaeology was something he originally did in his spare time until the local museum and then

> Petty paid him. But whatever skills he had as an excavator were deemed unimportant compared to the status of a Cambridge scholar and his sidelining on the excavation after the arrival of the "professionals" anticipated the increasing divergence of amateur and professional in British archaeology over the mid-twentieth century. But Brown wasn't the only one sidelined. There were also women working on the site, both archaeologists such as Stuart Piggott's then wife, Margaret Guido, an exceptional excavator and finds specialist, and the photographers Mercie Lack and Barbara Wagstaff who took high quality images of the ship burial. The dynamics of these relationships, especially of Brown, was recently the subject of a Netflix film *The Dig* and although some of the "facts" have been played with, the basic storyline offers an incisive insight into the social politics of archaeology in England at this time.

Issues of class and race are obviously bound up here with these valuations which is why theories of Marxism and Postcolonialism can be helpful. Pitt Rivers was part of the English landed gentry with connections to nobility on his mother's side while Toms was the son of a gardener who married a maid in Pitt Rivers household. Flinders Petrie was a middle-class Englishman, while Ali al-Suayfi was Egyptian, better known as Ali Muhammad Swafi of al-Lahun who also worked as a site guard. Whatever the complexities of the real relationships between these men and the archaeology they did, at the end of the day they have been reduced to grossly simplistic positions which revolve around class and race which have determined who gets to be called or recognized as an archaeologist. Indeed, at this time the idea of an archaeologist as a professional was somewhat anachronistic; Pitt Rivers was, if anything, a soldier by profession. But it is not just race or class that is implicated here, gender is also a key factor. It should not have escaped your notice that Pitt Rivers, Petrie, Toms and al-Suayfi are all men. And yet just as we dig behind Pitt Rivers to discover Herbert Toms, so if we dig behind Toms, we will find his wife Christine Sophie Marie Huon, who worked alongside Toms on most of his earthwork surveys. Indeed, although there are some well-known female archaeologists from the late nineteenth and early twentieth centuries, there are many more who are invisible. Many of them did fieldwork, but a large number were also involved in processing the finds from excavations, and as the feminist archaeologist Joan Gero later put it, women frequently became associated with the "domestic, indoor" work of archaeology while their male colleagues dominated the excavation trench.

This is all history, you might say. This may have been how things were in the 1920s, but in the 2020s, we do things differently. Think again. For example, even if the gender ratio among your fellow students is roughly similar, studies have clearly shown that as you progress throughout your career, whether it is in academia or commercial archaeology, a gender imbalance will start to appear. Not only are there more men than women in the older age groups, men also tend to dominate in the more prestigious and better paid jobs. This is changing, but slowly and painfully. Given what we discussed in the last section about the formation of archaeological subjectivities, it should now be very obvious if it wasn't already, how broader social and cultural structures impact archaeology simply because it impacts who becomes or is counted as an archaeologist. Other aspects of fieldwork also carry over old and deeply rooted social hierarchies. In Germany, there is often still a traditional division between those who excavate – called *Techniker* – and the archaeologist whose job it is to analyse and interpret the finds and site. What is going on here is a manifestation of a deep cultural prejudice and assumption about how work is valued: intellectual labour is more important than manual labour and is linked to class distinctions in society. Brain over brawn.

Of course, the situation differs between countries and places. In the UK, the division between those who dig and those who think was to some extent undermined by the rise of rescue and development-led archaeology in Europe after the Second World War and an increase in trained archaeologists emerging through university programmes. Although a gradual process, fieldwork in such contexts became gradually democratized, to the extent that the use of local labourers gradually disappeared as the numbers of trained archaeologists increased. Fieldworkers now both dig and record. Yet ironically, as this happened, a split also emerged between those archaeologists working in development-led archaeology and those based in universities and research. As late as the 1980s, a lot of the fieldworkers came into archaeology through unemployment schemes, and it is only in the last decades that undergraduates with a degree in archaeology make up most field staff on commercial projects. In countries like the UK, a new division emerged between commercial and academic archaeology and even if this is now changing, it is still a slow process in part because the system underlying it helps to perpetuate it: those working in academia have time and are paid to write articles, do research, attend conferences, while those in commercial world are only paid to dig and write technical reports. I remember an occasion when, having newly finished my PhD, I went to work on a development-led excavation in London and even though I had been working in projects like these since I was 16, because I had just come out of my doctoral studies, most of the staff assumed I didn't even know how to hold a trowel. But this was 25 years ago.

Box 2.8 Research-Driven and Development-Led Excavation in Europe

Although your experience as a student of archaeology is largely framed by the academic environment, most archaeologists are not working in academia but in development-led or preventative archaeology. The chances are, if you look for a job in archaeology after graduating, or even in the summer, it will be in development-led archaeology. How this operates varies between countries; in some places like France and Denmark, such work is closely tied to museums and state institutions; in others like Britain and the Netherlands, independent companies carry out the work. Such a division has been characterized as a socialist versus capitalist model of heritage management. There has a been a lot of discussion about what kind of system works best, and each has their merits. One argument made by Kristian Kristiansen has been that the research dimension in countries which have gone down the capitalist route has suffered in development-led archaeology, because of the way financial considerations are privileged. In other words, in development-led archaeology, the work becomes almost mechanical, churning out lots of basic data on sites and finds, but none of it "interpreted" or incorporated into larger research questions. In the UK, Richard Bradley ran a project which attempted to sift through all the grey reports produced by development-led archaeology and integrate them into our knowledge of British prehistory, a fact which seems to lend support to this criticism.

However, the division between research-driven and development-led excavations involves a problem more complex than what social model a country adopts. This is exemplified, for example, in the case of Sweden. When Kristiansen wrote his review of this topic in 2009, he singled out Sweden – which he defined as a mixed model of socialist and capitalist, but one that privileged research over money – as a model of good practice. Yet voices from within the development-led community of archaeologists in Sweden became increasingly critical of how the situation there has stifled innovation. When Åsa Berggren tried to incorporate a reflexive methodology drawn from her experiences working at Çatalhöyük, onto development-led projects in Sweden, the result was not entirely successful. Indeed, responses from the archaeologists working on the project tended to fall into two contradictory categories: people either felt they were already being reflexive or reflexivity was seen as a luxury add-on, which few had time to properly implement.

What is going on here? The problem is that the divide between framing research questions and conducting fieldwork still exists in Sweden, but *within* development-led archaeology. In Sweden, the problem is that the major research questions and agenda are being set by people in heritage offices, while the people in the field are still largely just fulfilling a job set by someone higher up the chain of command. As Lise Börjesson's research has found, despite the heavy emphasis put on research within the larger domain of development-led archaeology in Sweden, when it comes to fieldwork it is still primarily about collecting and documentation. As a result, people conducting excavations often feel constrained when it comes to experimenting or making fieldwork more "theoretical", a problem which is only exacerbated by the way fieldwork practices have become highly codified and uniform. The problem here then is not a lack of theory or research-thinking in development-led archaeology but rather its separation from the process of excavation and documentation. In a sense, the fieldworkers job is to provide data for those higher up in this system to interpret. Sound familiar?

Outside of Europe, the people involved in fieldwork also continue with legacies from earlier times. In places like Egypt or Turkey, local labour is still used on excavations, even if archaeological students, professionals and researchers make up a large part of the team and now dig as well as record. Alison Mickel's work on local labour on archaeological projects in Turkey and Jordan, for example, has highlighted the issue of lucrative non-knowledge, where it pays for local labourers to feign ignorance or downplay their skills, otherwise they would not be hired. After all, they are being hired usually as labourers, not archaeologists. However, the legacy of colonialism is not just felt in how excavation teams are composed; it is also evident in which countries engage in fieldwork outside their own. How North American, British and German archaeologists, for example, don't see national boundaries as a constraint on where to do research and even have "research outposts" in these places such as the various British Institutes and Schools in Amman, Ankara, Athens, Rome and Nairobi. The appropriation of other pasts has long been acknowledged within archaeology, and it is not just about physical appropriation through excavation and – at least originally – export of finds back to Europe or North America, it also the conceptual appropriation, one of writing "others" history – and ironically, even monopolizing the postcolonial critique of this appropriation.

Collaborative Archaeology

If the inequalities within the profession affect who is counted as an archaeologist, the situation is no less complex when we consider the interaction between archaeologists and other interest groups, especially local communities. One of the most important developments of the last decades in archaeological projects has been the collaboration of archaeologists with local communities. In almost all places that archaeologists work, there are local communities already living there and who may have deep roots and ties to the place. For them, the past can be a living and personal thing. The archaeologists are only visitors, staying in the area for the duration of the project or seasonally. In most cases, the archaeologists cannot work without some degree of interaction with the local community – at a bare minimum, they may need landowner permission, local government permits and the hire of local services, whether it is someone to operate a JCB or provide accommodation. But is that as far as our engagement should go?

In many countries like the US and Australia where archaeology is often conducted among descendant communities of indigenous people, this is nowhere near enough. The archaeological remains are part of their heritage, their history and usually, not only is their endorsement needed but their participation and sometimes, their instigation. The terms collaborative and community archaeology actually cover quite a wide spectrum of relationships between archaeologists and local people (Box 2.9). At one end of the scale, archaeologists might simply seek approval for their project and keep the community informed of the results through meetings and presentations. In other cases, archaeologists will facilitate greater engagement, involving people in the excavation and finds processing, and perhaps even encouraging younger people to study and become archaeologists.

When I ran a small project in South Africa among a descendant slave community, we interviewed people, consulted with them about their own views on their heritage, explained our aims, gave a talk on site to a party of local school children and invited a couple of teenagers to help on the excavation. All very laudable, but of course, it wasn't enough. Looking back, it was clear that my own agenda was steering the project and the relationship was still deeply asymmetrical.

Why? Because the engagement was still largely on my terms, about letting the community into my archaeological project, not about co-creating the project with them. And this is where the big difference turns: the extent to which local communities are not passive consumers of archaeological research but active participants. As Sonia Atalay has put it, it is about archaeology with, by and for local communities. Which means more than having locals work on site. It means having them co-determine the direction of the research, shape the research questions, even to the extent that it might challenge or go against some of the deep philosophical assumptions you are working under, including what counts as knowledge, what counts as archaeology and what counts as ethically appropriate. This is ultimately about making archaeology open up fully to other perspectives and belief systems because archaeology is not a neutral science – it offers a view of human history and society which is grounded in a western, modernist perspective, yet most of the societies and histories it studies never shared this perspective. Which kind of archaeology is better: one which tries to forge a dialogue with these other perspectives or one that ignores them?

Box 2.9 What Do You Mean by Collaboration?

What does collaborative or community-based archaeology mean to you? Sonya Atalay is an Anishinaabe-Ojibwe indigenous archaeologist who has worked in both North America and Turkey on community-based participatory research (CBPR) projects. She has offered a really useful way to see collaborative and community archaeology as a spectrum or continuum, based on the extent of community participation and the degree of their involvement in decision-making. This is important as there are a number of terms which are used, often interchangeably, yet they can mean subtly different things: public archaeology, community archaeology and collaborative archaeology are among the more common. But what do they involve?

Atalay suggests that we see this along a continuum of five broad levels (Figure 2.6). At the bottom is legally mandated consultation which is the bare minimum and may involve nothing more than getting a permit to do research. Above that comes public archaeology and outreach, which typically means the archaeologist presenting their work to select members of the community. Next up the scale is the involvement of various stakeholders in the interpretation of the research and is typically described through

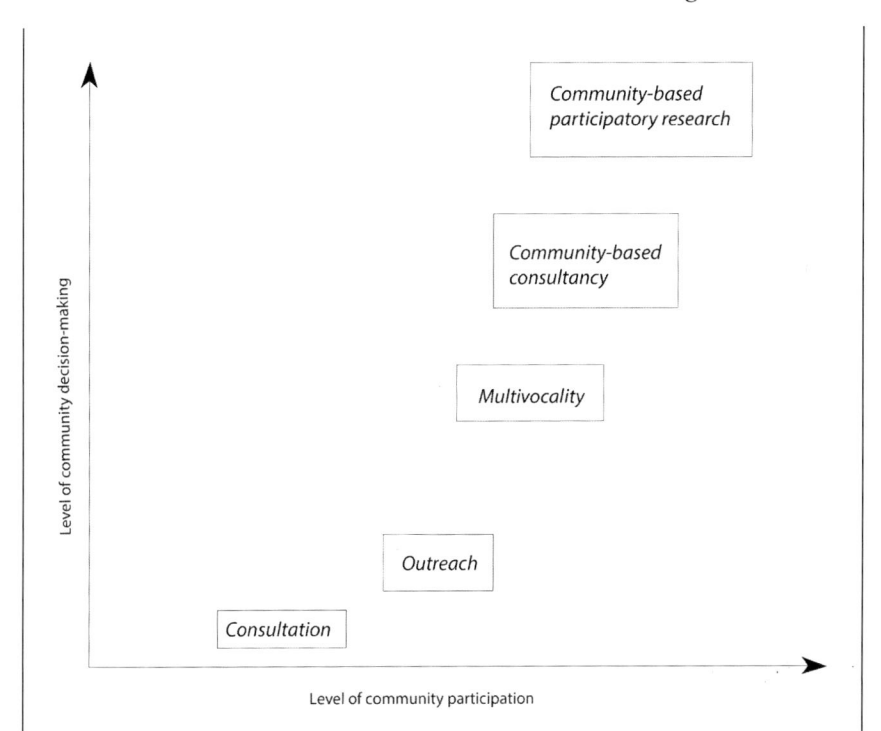

Figure 2.6 Different levels of community engagement (adapted from Atalay 2012).

terms such as multivocality. Then comes the community-based consultancy model where the archaeologist is hired by a local community to work for them on a project at their instigation, and finally, there is CBPR, where the whole process is community driven and fully participatory. The various definitions of public archaeology, community archaeology and collaborative archaeology can vary a lot depending on who is using them, but on the whole, public archaeology has tended to be closer to the more passive end of the scale while collaborative archaeology towards the active end, while community archaeology can cover almost the whole spectrum.

Ultimately, what matters here is what the extent and nature of collaboration is rather than the label – of which there are many more than I have listed here.

Indubitably the level of community interest in the archaeology of an area varies; most of my archaeological projects have not occurred in places like South Africa but Europe, mainly England and Iceland. Here, there are no indigenous or descendant communities in the sense normally understood, though this needs qualification. Contemporary groups like neo-pagans will claim spiritual connections to prehistoric sites, while there are many communities with longer traditions that have a material heritage that archaeologists will encounter: Jewish cemeteries, Roma camps, not to mention the more obvious cases such as the Saami in northern Scandinavia. But even in the absence of such "interest groups" or stakeholders, one should never assume one is working in a vacuum. When I was excavating on an urban plot surrounded by residential tower blocks in the east end of London in the late 1990s, there was never any sense of community connection to the prehistoric and Roman remains we were digging. This doesn't mean people weren't interested though. Excavating at an abandoned farm in rural Iceland, some folks are curious or fascinated by what you are doing, some have no real interest. But in some ways, the same issues apply in these places. One can just respond to local interest by giving talks or site tours and simply adjust one's level of community engagement according to their interest, or one can be more pro-active in seeking out local involvement. Various projects have tried to stimulate what is called participatory research or citizen science; in Scotland, local communities have been conscripted to help register sites, especially sites under threat from coastal erosion using everyday technology of the GPS on smartphones and designed apps. I have a PhD student who is engaging local diving clubs to help register underwater sites, a method which has been used in many other places with great success. Where would you place this on Atalay's scheme? (see Figure 2.6)

These kinds of projects are very different in one way to those working among indigenous communities. In Scotland or Iceland, the local communities usually share the same broad world view as the archaeologists and willingly adopt the protocols set up by archaeologists. Moreover, they are usually not contributing to the design or conception of archaeological projects but acting as data collectors through a crowdsourcing model. To some extent, the same approach underlies policies which encourage metal detectorists to bring their finds into museums for appraisal; in this case though, the metal detectorist also usually has their own, personal interest in the data and finds collected which may align with archaeologists, but not always. Indeed, what metal detectorists show us is that even when doing archaeology in Europe, there can remain difference of opinion and even conflict over archaeological remains. Normally, of course, archaeology as the state-backed steward of the past is considered to have the last word, but how do we balance such competing claims?

Let us end by simply asking ourselves the question again: who is the archaeologist? At the beginning of this section, we saw how labourers, skilled and experienced foremen, supervisors and other people were frequently marginalized or written out of history as archaeologists because they weren't white, middle/upper class European men. We also saw that even today, though there is more diversity, the iniquities of this former condition still effect and shape the profession today. But as diversity and inclusion has expanded under the banner of community and collaborative archaeology, how shall we draw the line today? In some ways, trying to define who is the archaeologist might seem like the wrong question; the fact that we have institutions which establish qualifications like a degree in archaeology and membership of professional societies suggests that being an archaeologist will always be bound up with these institutional contexts. A metal detectorist or a village elder are not archaeologists, no matter how closely they collaborate with the profession. On the other hand, if being an archaeologist means doing archaeology, then the answer is not so straightforward. The ultimate point here is really to understand that what really matters are not labels like "archaeologist" but actions. And if doing fieldwork is part of what it means to do archaeology, then it involves a lot more people than we might include under the label "archaeologist" and that archaeology is therefore always done by more people than "archaeologists".

Box 2.10   Community Archaeology as Intervention

In many ways, the closest parallels to working with indigenous communities in Europe are those projects which engage with a specific sub-population, especially a marginalized or subaltern group who, for whatever reasons, are not integrated into "mainstream" society. A wonderful example of this is John Schofield and Rachael Kiddey's work with homeless people in Bristol. As an example of contemporary archaeology, their work sought to not only understand the materiality of homelessness in a western, twenty-first-century urban environment but equally to work *with* homeless people in the project – not only as informants but as full participants who helped shape the direction of the research, work at the excavations and create exhibitions. Moreover, for Kiddey this project was a natural extension of her own personal activism and links back to the motivations all of us have for doing archaeology (see Chapter 6 for a discussion of this issue).

A somewhat different community project is Operation Nightingale which uses archaeology to promote the well-being of military personnel and veterans. Serving and ex-soldiers have participated in a variety of excavations as part of a rehabilitation process, supported by the Ministry of Defence, and some of the participants have gone on to study archaeology at university. Works by Paul Everill and colleagues on evaluating the impact of programmes like Operation Nightingale have shown that levels of depression and anxiety dropped substantially after participating in these projects while general well-being increased. What is especially interesting here though is that with community archaeology for groups like veterans, the focus is much more on the community – the archaeology itself might or need not have any direct relevance to the "community"; that is, the excavations do not necessarily focus on sites relating to the backgrounds of the veterans (although in one case at least, excavations at Hougoumont Farm in Belgium was selected because of its association with regimental history and the Battle of Waterloo).

Figure 2.7 Andrew Dafnis, Homeless Heritage project, surveying Turbo Island, Bristol, in 2010 (photo: John Schofield).

Who would have guessed fieldwork was so theoretical? For many, excavation is the part of archaeology that has its feet firmly on the ground, far removed from the abstract realm of theory. Yet as we have seen, at every turn issues have popped up to suggest otherwise. Indeed archaeological fieldwork is actually one of the best places to look for archaeological theory. Not because we can sit around the site hut talking about Heidegger but quite the opposite. Archaeological theory does not have to be about calling on some (usually dead) French or German philosopher, but actually using our engagement with archaeological stuff as the foundation for theoretical reflection and the contexts and structures within which this takes place. Certainly many of the ideas discussed in this chapter have origins in other contexts, but the point is how they have been adapted, shaped and altered by their encounter with an archaeological situation. The same can be said for the subsequent chapters in this book. For our student in the trench deciding what to keep and what to throw, it is really the same problem they face when encountering ideas – wherever they have come from.

Exercises for the Classroom

1. Find a place – like your classroom – and imagine it is the "field" or an archaeological site; how does it alter the way you inhabit and interact with that place?
2. Divide the class into two debate teams: for and against total recovery on site.

3. Make your own context sheet.
4. Record an everyday object as if it was an archaeological find; discuss what aspects you are choosing to record and whether other sensory qualities which are relevant to the use or understanding of the object might have been more useful.

Further Reading

Fieldwork and Facts

Discussion about total versus selective excavation can be found in Carver (1990) and Lucas (2012, pp. 42–51), while the debate around interpretation and description is addressed by Hodder (1997; also 1999), Andrews et al. (2000) and Chadwick (2003), who also discusses context sheets. For a more extended discussion of context sheets and textual records on site, see Pavel (2010). The quotes in Box 2.1 came from Pitt Rivers (1887) and Drewitt (1999), while discussion of Pitt Rivers' field methods can be found in Bradley (1983). A recent volume exploring the intersection of theory and fieldwork through a variety of papers is by Cobb et al. (2012), including the Ardnamurchan Transitions Project, while the impact of Hodder's reflexive methodology at Catalhöyük is explored in Hodder and Marciniak (2015).

Fieldwork as Lived Practice

One of the earliest works to explore the performative nature of archaeology is by Shanks and McGuire (1996); also see Pearson and Shanks (2001) where the notion of the cyborg was also explored. The performative nature of fieldwork is examined from a variety of perspectives, including phenomenology (Bender et al. 2007; Hamilton & Whitehouse 2006, 2020; MacGregor 1999; also see van Dyke 2014), ethnographies of archaeological fieldwork (Edgeworth 2006, 2012), feminist archaeology (Gero 1996, 2007) and science studies (Lucas 2001; Lucas 2012, pp. 215–257; Olsen et al. 2012, pp. 58–77). Edgeworth's discussion of "following the cut" can be found in Edgeworth (2012). Recent debates about the impact of digital recording on site include papers by Morgan and Wright (2018), Morgan et al. (2021), Hacigüzeller (2012, 2019) and Taylor et al. (2018), while slow archaeology is addressed by Caraher (2019) and Marila (2019). For the "craft" of drawing, see Wickstead (2008, 2013) and McFadyen (2016). The study on Peche Merle cave is from Pastoors et al. (2015).

Who Is the Archaeologist?

For studies on the role of role of local labour in archaeology in the Middle East, see Quirke (2010), Doyon (2015) and Mickel (2021) while Shepherd (2003) provides a good example from South Africa; for the valuation of different fieldworkers in

50 *Doing Fieldwork*

European archaeology, see Bradley (1989), G. Carver (2012), Everill (2012) and Cobb and Croucher (2020). On Sutton Hoo, see M. Carver (1998). For gender politics and the division of labour in archaeology, see the classic paper by Joan Gero (1985) and also the website trowelblazers.com. For general surveys of the profession, see Aitchison (2013, 2014). For the issues of research in development-led archaeology, see Kristiansen (2009) and Bradley (2006); the case of Sweden is explored in Berggren (2009) and Huvila and Börjesson (2019). On the impact of colonialism on archaeology, the literature is vast, but see Trigger (1984) for a seminal paper. For collaborative archaeology, especially in the context of indigenous communities, see Colwell-Chanthaphonh and Ferguson (2008) and Atalay (2012). On the use of citizen science, see Dawson et al. (2017), while Kiddey's work on homeless heritage can be found in Kiddey (2017) and for Operation Nightingale, see Everill et al. (2020), while for a more general statement on archaeology as activism, see Kiddey (2020).

References

Aitchison, K. 2013. Discovering the Archaeologists of Europe. In J.H. Jameson & J. Eogan (eds.), *Training and Practice for Modern Day Archaeologists*. New York: Springer, pp. 15–29.

Aitchison, K. 2014. Discovering the Archaeologists of the World. *Archaeologies* 10(3): 207–10.

Andrews, G., J. Barrett & J.S.C. Lewis. 2000. Interpretation Not Record: The Practice of Archaeology. *Antiquity* 74: 525–30.

Atalay, S. 2012. *Community-Based Archaeology. Research With, by, and for Indigenous and Local Communities*. Berkeley: University of California Press.

Bender, B., S. Hamilton & C. Tilley. 2007. *Stone Worlds. Narrative and Reflexivity in Landscape Archaeology*. Walnut Creek, CA: Left Coast Press.

Berggren, Å. 2009. Evaluation of a Reflexive Attempt. The Citytunnel Project in Retrospect. *Archaeological Review From Cambridge* 24(1): 23–37.

Bradley, R. 1983. Archaeology, Evolution and the Public Good: The Intellectual Development of General Pitt Rivers. *Archaeological Journal* 140: 1–9.

Bradley, R. 1989. Herbert Toms – A Pioneer of Analytical Field Survey. In M. Bowden, D. Mackay & P. Topping (eds.), *From Cornwall to Caithness: Some Aspects of British Field Archaeology. Papers Presented to Norman V Quinnell*, BAR Brit Ser, 209, pp. 29–47.

Bradley, R. 2006. Bridging the Two Cultures – Commercial Archaeology and the Study of Prehistoric Britain. *The Antiquaries Journal* 86: 1–13.

Caraher, W. 2019. Slow Archaeology, Punk Archaeology, and the 'Archaeology of Care'. *European Journal of Archaeology* 22(3): 372–85.

Carver, G. 2012. How to Archaeologize With a Hammer. In H. Cobb, O.J.T. Harris, C. Jones, P. Richardson (eds.), *Reconsidering Archaeological Fieldwork. Exploring On-Site Relationships Between Theory and Practice*. New York: Springer, pp. 15–30.

Carver, M. 1990. Digging for Data: Archaeological Approaches to Data Definition, Acquisition and Analysis. In R. Francovich & D. Manacorda (eds.), *Lo scavo archeologico: dalla diagnosi all'edizione*. Firenze: All'Insegna del Giglio SAS, pp. 45–120.

Carver, M. 1998. *Sutton Hoo: Burial Ground of Kings?* London: British Museum.

Chadwick, A. 2003. Post-Processualism, Professionalization and Archaeological Methodologies. Towards Reflective and Radical Practice. *Archaeological Dialogues* 10(1): 97–117.

Cobb, H. & K. Croucher. 2020. *Assembling Archaeology. Teaching, Practice, and Research*. Oxford: Oxford University Press.

Cobb, H., O.J.T. Harris, C. Jones, & P. Richardson (eds.). 2012. *Reconsidering Archaeological Fieldwork. Exploring On-Site Relationships Between Theory and Practice*. New York: Springer.

Colwell-Chanthaphonh, C. & T.J. Ferguson (eds.). 2008. *Collaboration in Archaeological Practice: Engaging Descendant Communities*. Lanham: AltaMira Press.

Dawson, T.C., C. Nimura, E. Lopez-Romero & M-Y. Daire (eds.). 2017. *Public Archaeology and Climate Change*. Oxford: Oxbow.

Doyon, W. 2015. On Archaeological Labour in Modern Egypt. In W. Carruthers (ed.), *Histories of Egyptology. Interdisciplinary Measures*. London: Routledge, pp. 141–56.

Drewitt, P. 1999. *Field Archaeology*. London: Routledge.

Edgeworth, M. (ed.). 2006. *Ethnographies of Archaeological Practice. Cultural Encounters, Material Transformations*. Lanham: AltaMira Press.

Edgeworth, M. 2012. Follow the Cut, Follow the Rhythm, Follow the Material. *Norwegian Archaeological Review* 45(1): 76–92.

Everill, P. 2012. *The Invisible Diggers. A Study of British Commercial Archaeology* (2nd edition). Oxford: Oxbow Books.

Everill, P., R. Bennett & K. Burnell. 2020. Dig in: An Evaluation of the Role of Archaeological Fieldwork for the Improved Wellbeing of Military Veterans. *Antiquity* 94(373): 212–27.

Gero, J. 1985. Socio-Politics and the Woman-at-Home Ideology. *American Antiquity* 50: 342–50.

Gero, J. 1996. Archaeological Practice and Gendered Encounters with Field Data. In R.P. Wright (ed.), *Gender and Archaeology*. Philadelphia: University of Pennsylvania Press, pp. 251–80.

Gero, J. 2007. Honoring Ambiguity/Problematizing Certitude. *Journal of Archaeological Method and Theory* 14: 311–27.

Hacigüzeller, P. 2012. GIS, Critique, Representation and Beyond. *Journal of Social Archaeology* 12(2): 245–63.

Hacigüzeller, P. 2019. Archaeology, Digital Cartography and the Question of Progress: The Case of Catalhöyük (Turkey). In M. Gillings, P. Hacigüzeller & G. Lock (eds.), *Re-Mapping Archaeology. Critical Perspectives, Alternative Mappings*. London: Routledge, pp. 267–80.

Hamilton, S. & R. Whitehouse. 2006. Phenomenology in Practice: Towards a Methodology for a 'Subjective' Approach. *European Journal of Archaeology* 9(1): 31–71.

Hamilton, S. & R. Whitehouse. 2020. *Neolithic Spaces: Social and Sensory Landscapes of the First Farmers of Italy* (Volume 1). London: Accordia Research Institute.

Hodder, I. 1997. "Always Momentary, Fluid and Flexible": Towards a Reflexive Excavation Methodology. *Antiquity* 71: 691–700.

Hodder, I. 1999. *The Archaeological Process*. Oxford: Blackwell.

Hodder, I. & A. Marciniak (eds.). 2015. *Assembling Catalhöyük*. London: Routledge.

Huvila, I. & L. Börjesson. 2019. Contract Archaeology. In L. Börjesson & I. Huvila (eds.), *Research Outside the Academy. Professional Knowledge-Making in the Digital Age*. Cham: Palgrave Macmillan, pp. 107–22.

Kiddey, R. 2017. *Homeless Heritage. Collaborative Social Archaeology as Therapeutic Practice*. Oxford: Oxford University Press.

Kiddey, R. 2020. I'll Tell You What I Want, What I Really, Really Want! Open Archaeology That Is Collaborative, Participatory, Public, and Feminist. *Norwegian Archaeological Review* 53(1): 23–40.

Kristiansen, K. 2009. Contract Archaeology in Europe: An Experiment in Diversity. *World Archaeology* 41(4): 641–8.

Lucas, G. 2001. Destruction and the Rhetoric of Excavation. *Norwegian Archaeological Review* 34(1): 35–46.

Lucas, G. 2012. *Understanding the Archaeological Record*. Cambridge: Cambridge University Press.

MacGregor, G. 1999. Making Sense of the Past in the Present: A Sensory Analysis of Carved Stone Balls. *World Archaeology* 31(2): 258–71.

Marila, M. 2019. Slow Science for Fast Archaeology. *Current Swedish Archaeology* 27: 93–114.

McFadyen, L. 2016. Practice Drawing Writing Object. In T. Ingold (ed.), *Redrawing Anthropology. Materials, Movements, Lines*. London: Routledge, pp. 33–44.

Mickel, A. 2021. *Why Those Who Shovel Are Silent. A History of Local Archaeological Knowledge and Labor*. Louisville. University Press of Colorado.

Morgan, C., H. Petrie, H. Wright & J.S. Taylor. 2021. Drawing and Knowledge Construction in Archaeology: The Aide Mémoire Project. *Journal of Field Archaeology* 46(8): 614–28.

Morgan, C. & H. Wright. 2018. Pencils and Pixels: Drawing and Digital Media in Archaeological Field Recording. *Journal of Field Archaeology* 43(2): 136–51.

Olsen, B., M. Shanks, T. Webmoor & C. Witmore. 2012. *Archaeology. The Discipline of Things*. Berkeley: University of California Press.

Pastoors, A., T. Lenssen-Erz, Tsamkxao Ciqae, Ui Kxunta, Thui Thao, R. Bégouën, M. Biesele & J. Clottes. 2015. Tracking in Caves: Experience Based Reading of Pleistocene Human Footprints in French Caves. *Cambridge Archaeological Journal* 25(3): 551–64.

Pavel, C. 2010. *Describing and Interpreting the Past: European and American Approaches to the Written Record of the Excavation*. Bucuresti: Editura Universitatii din Bucuresti.

Pearson, M. & M. Shanks. 2001. *Theatre/Archaeology*. London: Routledge.

Pitt Rivers, A.H.L.F. 1887. *Excavations in Cranbourne Chase*. Privately Printed.

Quirke, S. 2010. *Hidden Hands: Egyptian Workforces in Petrie's Excavation Archives, 1880–1924*. London: Duckworth.

Shanks, M. & R. McGuire. 1996. The Craft of Archaeology. *American Antiquity* 61(1): 75–88.

Shepherd, N. 2003. 'When the Hand that Holds the Trowel Is Black...': Disciplinary Practices of Self-Representation and the Issue of 'Native' Labour in Archaeology. *Journal of Social Archaeology* 3(3): 334–52.

Taylor, S., J. Issavi, Å. Berggren, D. Lukas, C. Mazzucato, B. Tung & N. Dell'Unto. 2018. 'The Rise of the Machine': The Impact of Digital Tablet Recording in the Field at Çatalhöyük. *Internet Archaeology* 47.

Trigger, B. 1984. Alternative Archaeologies: Nationalist, Colonialist, Imperialist. *Man* (NS) 19(3): 355–70.

Van Dyke, R.M. 2014. Phenomenology in Archaeology. In C. Smith (eds.), *Encyclopedia of Global Archaeology*. New York: Springer. https://doi.org/10.1007/978-1-4419-0465-2_295.

Wickstead, H. 2008. Drawing Archaeology. In L. Duff & P. Sawdon (eds.), *Drawing: The Purpose*. Bristol: Intellect Books, pp. 13–27.

Wickstead, H. 2013. Between the Lines: Drawing Archaeology. In P. Graves-Brown, R. Harrison & A. Piccini (eds.), *The Oxford Handbook of the Archaeology of the Contemporary World*. Oxford: Oxford University Press, pp. 549–64.

3 Making Records

Situation 3: In the Lab

It's a pottery class and the teacher is explaining how to tell the difference between eighteenth- and nineteenth-century porcelain and industrial whiteware pottery; although the clays are very similar, porcelain is fired at a higher temperature, which causes the clay to vitrify making it semi-translucent. When you tap porcelain, it sounds different, it has a little "ping" whereas the whiteware returns a dull "thunk". You can also hold it up to the light and if you can see your finger move behind it, it is porcelain whereas if you can't, it's whiteware. You have examples in front of you so you can actually try out these little "tests" and sure enough, they seem to work. Then another student asks: what about china? Is that whiteware or porcelain? The teacher answered, saying that although the word originated in relation to imported Chinese porcelain, it quickly became a term to cover any fancy table or tea ware in contrast to utilitarian and kitchen pottery. So the answer is: "china" can be both and is therefore a term one should generally avoid using. You reflect on this and something bothers you about it. While the teacher and the textbook is telling you that it is important to distinguish between porcelain and whiteware because they are the result of different production processes, the people who may have actually used these vessels didn't differentiate between them. But if my goal as an archaeologist is to try to understand the people who used these things, surely "china" is a useful category after all?

Recording Technologies

Facts, Data and Records

What you call things matters. In the last chapter, we looked at facts and you will remember that one of the important things about them is that a fact is not the physical thing but a representation of it; the fact that a layer is "dark brown" or "20 mm thick" is an abstraction of the tangible bit of soil that your trowel scrapes over. Facts are what we call things. However, we now need to get a bit more fussy and make a distinction between **facts** and **data**. Often, archaeologists will use these terms interchangeably, but they do have historically and etymologically different roots. The word "fact" derives from the Latin *factum*, a deed, action or occurrence with the implication that it is something that actually happened. Similarly, the word "data" is derived from the Latin *datum*, something which is given with the implication that we take it for granted, as incontestable. There is a strong overlap between facts and data as something we consider to be true, but there are also subtle differences; a fact as "deed" reflects the idea of an achievement, something attained, whereas data as "given" reflect the idea of something we have received.

Data as something "given" play off **empiricism** as a view of science based purely on observations, where observations are thought of as composed of "sense data" – things "given" to our senses, like a blue sky or a hard stone (see Box 1.2). By data, we usually mean simple values or attributes, small little nuggets or atoms of meaning like the thickness of a layer (e.g. "20 mm"), the colour of a deposit ("dark brown"), the material of an artefact ("iron"), the identity of an item ("femur") and so on. In contrast, a fact is generally a broader concept as it can refer to fairly simple observations such as "this layer is 20 mm thick", but it can also be used for more complex statements such as "this site dates to the late 4th century", which condenses a much larger number of inferences and variables relating to dating methods and understanding of formation processes. This distinction largely overlaps with that made by philosopher of science Sabina Leonelli between small and big facts. Small facts are similar to what we might think of as data: meaningless on their own but valuable as part of a wider set. For example, the length of a stone arrowhead is banal unless it forms part of a database of other arrowheads where its similarity or difference to other lengths can become potentially informative. Big facts on the other hand come with more embedded meaning; the fact "stone arrowheads of type X are usually 40–50 mm long" incorporates all kinds of generalizations about the form and size of arrowheads that conceals smaller facts about specific objects. The distinction between small and big facts is arguably one of a continuum rather than a discrete difference, and so the same might be said of the distinction between data and facts.

This difference between small and big facts or between data and facts can be aligned with a particular model of knowledge known as the data or knowledge pyramid, where at the bottom, there is the basic building blocks of all knowledge – data and facts – on which more successively complex understanding is constructed; in the most common version known as the DIKW pyramid, above data are information, followed by knowledge and at the apex, wisdom. As you climb the pyramid, so data become more processed and rendered meaningful (Figure 3.1). However, the problem with this model is that it often assumes that the stuff at the bottom – data and facts – are un-processed, whereas we saw in the last chapter, there is no such thing as "raw data". Let's take a really simple example. The fact that a layer is 20 mm thick might seem basic, but that single bit of data – 20 mm thick – always implies some action. Where along the layer was this measurement taken? Was the layer uniformly thick? Maybe the layer was 19 mm at one end and 21 mm at another, and by describing it as 20mm, we are

Making Records 55

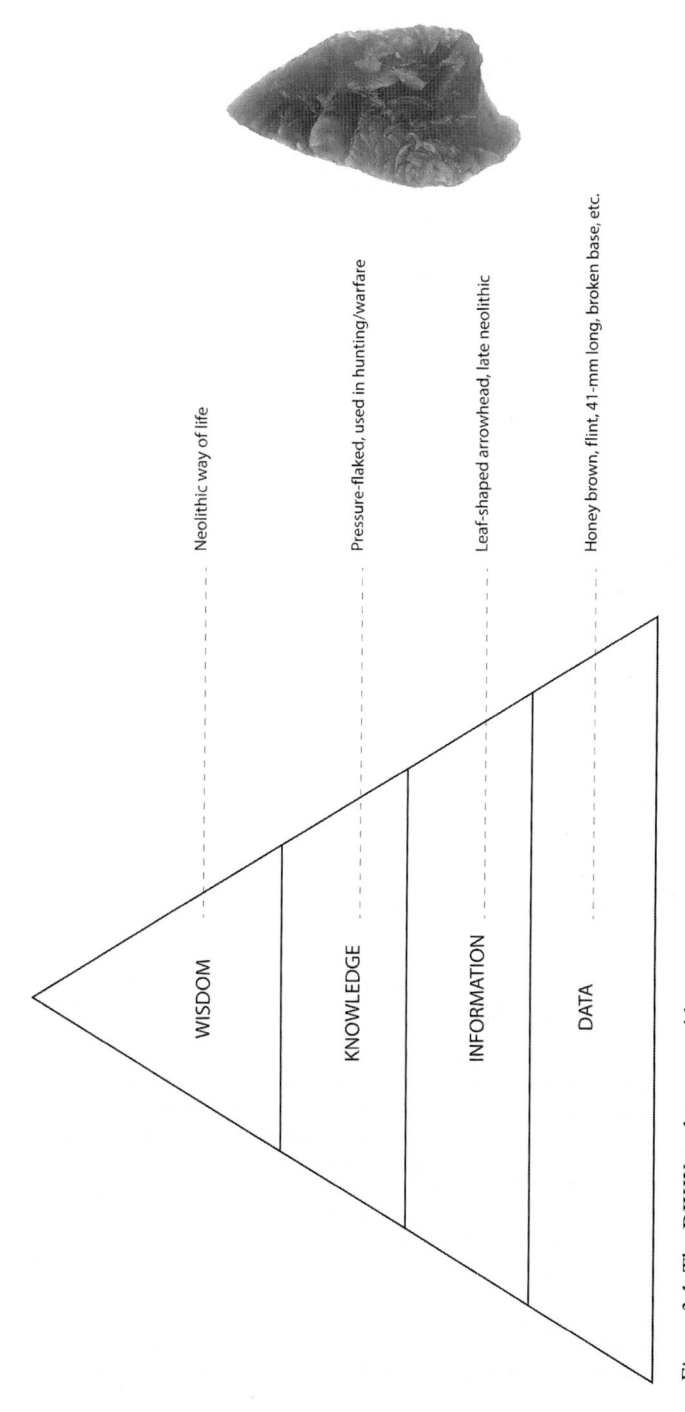

Figure 3.1 The DIKW or data pyramid.

WISDOM — Neolithic way of life
KNOWLEDGE — Pressure-flaked, used in hunting/warfare
INFORMATION — Leaf-shaped arrowhead, late neolithic
DATA — Honey brown, flint, 41-mm long, broken base, etc.

adopting an average or median measure. Recall the etymological distinction between data and fact above – facts as achievements, data as givens. Historically, this difference became blurred because over time data became something that was increasingly used to refer to the outcome of experiments or fieldwork which implies an entanglement with something more active, even if there remains a sense in which data are what is given in return for an action. For example, if you measure the depth of a posthole, the data returned is the depth in centimetres or whatever unit is used; if you use a pH meter to test the acidity of the soil, data is returned as a value, usually between 1 and 14.

What this suggests is that deciding on what constitutes facts and data may not be as important as the recognition that both are tied into specific actions. It is what you do to create them that matters. Remember in the last chapter we talked about the difference between observation and intervention in the context of fieldwork: that is, the difference between a view of knowledge which implies a detached mode of observation as opposed to an active, engaged or practical mode of learning. The "given" nature of data, such as the depth of a posthole, is never just "given", but rather returned as part of an action such as placing a hand tape into the hole and reading off the measurement. By foregrounding the practical nature of data, we can avoid hierarchical models like the data pyramid for just as it is important to understand the actions involved in data creation, so it is important to understand the actions that data themselves create. In short, to think of data and facts simply in terms of what they can do. Let's go back to that posthole; if you stick in a hand tape and read off the measurement, you have some data – its depth. What can you do with that bit of data? To do almost anything with it, you need to record it in some manner – as a number on a form or as a point on a drawing. These kinds of inscriptions are central to any science and some might argue that until you have it recorded, it doesn't even count as data. But what matters here is what data can do, and to answer this, it is important to pay attention to the form they take as inscriptions or records. Indeed, although we might talk about data collection when we are in the field or the lab, what we are usually doing when collecting such "data" is in fact making records – filling out a context sheet, making a site plan, keeping a log of readings and entering values in a database.

The important aspect about these records is that they are usually fairly structured; the context sheets typically stipulate the kind of data recorded (see last chapter, Box 2.2), a section drawing uses conventions of scale and line. Commonly, highly structured data tend to have a numerical or taxonomic base. Measurements and counts form a key part of visual and textual records but so do classifications such as those of colour (e.g. Munsell classification), material (e.g. flint), or artefact type (arrowhead). This kind of standardization or conventionalization serves a very practical purpose: comparability. If things are coded in the same way, then they also become easier to compare. If someone records a pot as large and another as 400 mm tall, how easy is it to compare these two pieces of data? How large is "large"? This is why data so often take numerical form; it does not have the monopoly on standardization or comparability, but it is almost the only universal data form that one sees across all the sciences, from sub-atomic physics to archaeology. As data, numbers have huge potential. In rendering an object as a number, it massively increases our ability to compare objects, often objects which might otherwise be very dissimilar. Pots and stone axes have almost nothing in common in terms of their material properties, yet both can be counted and weighed.

Records do vary in the degree of their organization of course; the traditional site diary often allows for free-form text, while a context sheet can be simply a series of check boxes. When it comes to what data can do though, structure is usually a good thing – especially if you want your data to be ampliative, that is to generate more data. Compare a sketch plan to a measured plan; the former can be certainly very informative and useful, but it will be hard to generate more data from it, whereas from a measured plan, new data are obtainable. For example, in plotting the outlines of a layer, I can calculate its area – data which were not recorded in the field. I can also compare its location relative to other layers that may not be currently visible as their records occupy a shared co-ordinate space. More productively, consider a database of animal bones recorded from an excavation; each record in the database will include a whole host of values and variables such as the species, skeletal element, degree of completeness and so on. All of this data are recorded individually from the bones, like the point co-ordinates on a map; but from this, new data emerge, such as the ratio of different species in the assemblage as represented by their individual skeletal elements (i.e. NISP) or age at death profiles based on variables like tooth eruption and bone fusion. These might even be visually displayed using graphs and charts which constitute another type of "record" of this emergent data (Figure 3.2).

To sum up: what matters is not how processed or "raw" data are (as with the pyramid model), but how generative or productive it is. Can your data go forth and multiply? Instead of a static, hierarchical model as with the DIKW pyramid, we have a fluid, horizontal model of data being mobilized and mutating as they are put to work – what we might call a data trail rather than a data pyramid. Having said that, it is important to recognize that records can be generative in other ways than simply producing more data. This is especially true of many visual records, for although measured drawings can generate new data, they can also do other things. For example, images like measured drawings and especially photographs do "presence" a thing in a way that numbers and words can never do, and that is because as records, they engage our senses – primarily of course our eyes – whereas numbers and words involve more abstract, conceptual thinking. Not that an image does not involve such abstract thought either – maps or even technical drawings require us to think, but they have this added visual quality

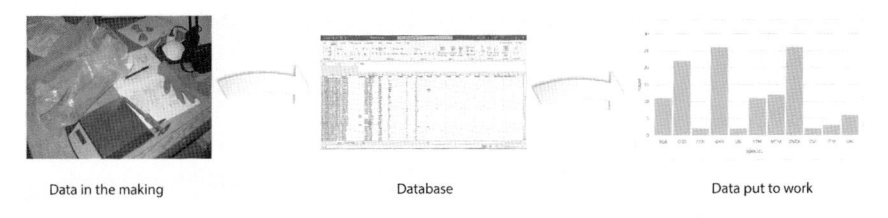

Data in the making   Database   Data put to work

Figure 3.2 The data trail.

which is usually backgrounded when reading a list of numbers or string of text. Images draw attention to themselves as things in their own right in a way that is less evident with words and numbers. How aware are you of the marks on the page or screen in front of you as your read this sentence? This sensory quality of an image is also the reason why debates about **realism** and "objectivity" seem to be so much sharper and more pertinent when dealing with images as opposed to numbers and words. No one expects numbers or words to be "realistic", because it is obvious they are conventionalized, abstract representations.

At the same time, we all know that images – whether drawings or photographs – are also conventionalized. Artefact drawings, sections, plans all use certain conventions and follow protocols in their production; site and artefact photographs are staged, with controls of framing, lighting, scale bars. The only reason we put a greater burden of "realism" on images is that they remain sensory, they engage our sense of sight; even if we use sight to read numbers and text, the sensory aspect is backgrounded. Similarly, even if images might elicit a verbal response, it is their visual quality that is foregrounded. It is this sensory quality to images that allows them to work in ways other than data tables or even textual descriptions. We will explore these roles of images in more detail in the next chapter, but this does bring us to the issue of how data fit into wider forms of knowledge construction.

Box 3.1   What Do Maps Do?

Maps are one of the most basic records archaeologists make – from individual feature plans to landscapes, the representation of space in two dimensions is a core product of archaeological fieldwork. Traditional surveying techniques and instruments remained relatively unchanged over most of the late nineteenth and twentieth centuries, but with the gradual advent of digital technology and "paperless plans" since the 1990s, map-making has been transformed. However, although 3D scanning is becoming increasingly more popular, the final product of most digital technologies is often very similar to that produced under older technology: a two-dimensional image. Indeed, often the same conventions are used which enable us to read or understand a map, even though it may depict a place or thing we have never personally seen. Universal conventions such as scales and north arrows, and legends to identify more specific symbols, are central to map-making which although ostensibly depicts a real thing are still never simply given but rather an achievement, a construction. The bird's eye view that a map affords suggests a certain element of "realism", although it can rarely hide its artifice.

Moreover, the basic way in which the image is built is not that different: the use of trigonometry. Using angles and distances to convert points in the field into a digital or paper space and then joining the points up with lines

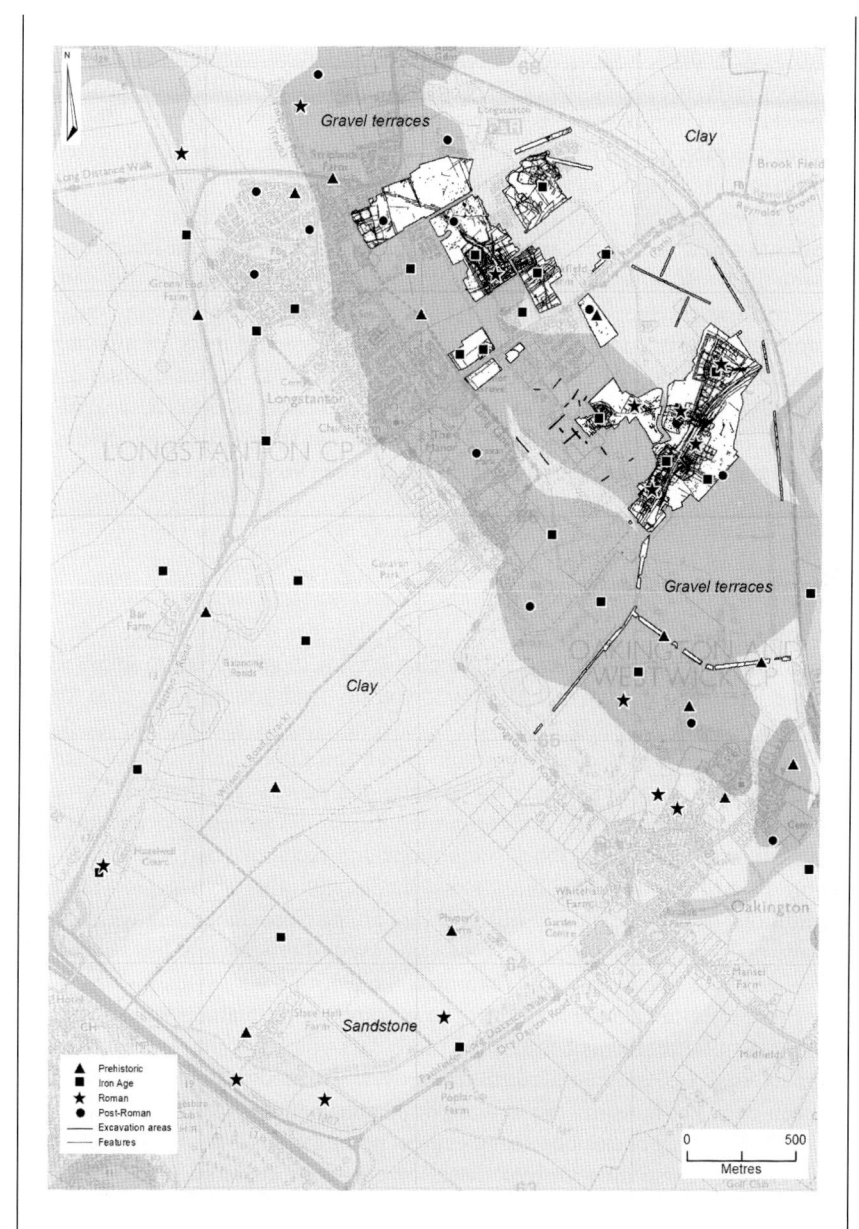

Figure 3.3 Map of excavations at Longstanton and Oakington, 5 km northwest of Cambridge (Northstowe Phases 1 & 2 [2014–2019]). The excavated areas revealed Middle to Late Iron Age, Roman and fifth- to seventh-century CE settlements, alongside other sites based on comprehensive trenching, geophysics and airborne transcription program [2005–2007, 2020–2021] (map credit: Cambridge Archaeological Unit/Oscar Aldred). What data can you draw out from this map?

to create shapes, a key part of map-making, involves recording numerical data which recede into the background and are largely invisible in the final product – even if they can be later extracted. But here is the amazing thing; once the map exists in its own digital or paper space, it can be interacted with, manipulated in a way that allows new information to emerge that was not necessarily recorded. Think of how you use a map to navigate your way around a new or unfamiliar place. But maps aren't just tools for interacting with the world; in archaeology especially, maps are tools for interacting with a virtual world, that on the paper or screen. Maps are not solely representations of features on a site or in a landscape; they are also tools for thinking about the spatial and temporal relations between these features. Although the use of GIS has expanded the instrumental nature of maps as analytical and exploratory tools, even the traditional, flat static maps embody this dynamic. Look at the map in Figure 3.3; what can you make it do?

Data, Big Data and Databases

You know how every time you go to a website like Amazon, it recommends purchases for you? Or how adverts on Facebook miraculously seem to know what you are interested in – or not! Of course you do. And you probably also know why and how they do this. There isn't someone doing a background check on you; instead someone wrote an algorithm which can automatically collate data on the sites visited, how long you spent on a site or a page, even where you paused, scrolling down the page. The algorithm continuously gathers and updates this information to tailor-make those suggestions and recommendations. This is the visible face of big data, and most social media and other apps exploit the fact the millions of people who use this software are also providing data which have commercial value. It is also exactly the same kind of process that lies behind the use of artificial intelligence (AI) and machine learning with finds identification (see Box 3.2). Big data are really "in" now; some people claim it will solve a lot of our scientific problems because the more data you have, the better and more complex analyses you can perform. Moreover, with today's computing power, you can even get the software to tease out patterns in the data by running endless data crunching operations, using endless permutations and combinations. We don't need to come up with hypotheses or questions anymore – the computer will just do that for you and spit out the best answers and by implication, the best questions.

Well, of course it is not that simple. There is no doubt there are some clever programs and algorithms out there, and there is no doubt that having the computer power to deal with complex operations on massive datasets is a wonderful thing. But the myth that the big data revolution will pre-empt the need for thinking, for coming up with interesting questions and the need to be sophisticated about interpreting and making inferences from data is just that: a myth. We touched on this in the last chapter; it is the myth of induction or empiricism, that the data will speak for themselves. Not only can they not do this, data itself are never just "given" despite what the Latin etymology implies. This is the second myth, that of raw data. All data are pre-packaged, pre-coded and to a degree, come pre-interpreted, set up in a certain way so that it prefigures the range of inferences that can be made of it, and similarly, forecloses others.

Let's take a closer look to see how this works. Imagine your teacher gives you a bag of pottery from an excavation and asks you to register it into a database. From your pottery class, you already know some of the basic things you are supposed to look out for: what kind of ware is it (e.g. porcelain or whiteware?), how is it decorated, what kind of vessel does it come from and so on. But now recall our discussion in the last chapter on what to keep or not, what to record or not. If I record the kind of vessel, I can do analyses on the proportions of different vessel types; but if I don't record the size of the vessel (using rim diameter as a proxy for example), then any patterns relating to size will be missed. This is the first and most obvious level at which coding determines the subsequent analysis. But it also works at another, more complex level. Let's say my pottery wares are based on the quality of their fabric – so I have finewares and coarsewares. Now, all analysis on wares will reflect this. But what if, instead of quality I had chosen colour, giving me redwares and greywares? Now the ware analysis will be different.

These are somewhat simplistic examples and in reality, a good ceramic database will try and capture multiple dimensions. But however good your database is, it will always be based on prior judgements and decisions about what to record in terms of how an object presents itself, and there will always – *always* – be another way to code and organize your data. Because the object, as well as affording certain observations, equally holds qualities back because of the way the archaeologist and object interact. This is why there is no such thing as raw data – but also why there is no such thing as judgements and decisions in a vacuum. These issues have taken on new relevance and importance in the wake of big data and the digital humanities. Digital humanities is a term coined early in the new millennium and refers to the impact computing is having on disciplines in the humanities, both in terms of digitizing archives but also how these archives can be examined in new ways and indeed, how digitization can facilitate new forms of publication. I will touch on some of these issues again in the next chapter, but in terms of database management and digital data, this is something that has a longer history as computers entered most academic disciplines from the late 1960s and 1970s, archaeology included. When I was an undergraduate in the early 1980s, computers were still relatively new and exotic things but by the time I was doing my PhD a decade later, I was using databases for my research on a Macintosh Classic II. What has changed since then of course is not only the computational power and memory of using digital databases, it is also the increasing user-friendliness of the software.

Box 3.2 AI and Machine Learning

In the last chapter, we discussed the problems of separating description from interpretation in the field and the same applies when recording finds. When a pottery specialist or zooarchaeologist records sherds or bones, the decisions of what to record, and how are based on both experience and wider disciplinary traditions. But can this process be automated and if so, what issues does it raise? The use of AI and machine learning in artefact recognition is one of the most exciting and cutting-edge developments in the discipline. The Italian-led ArchAIDE project (archaide.eu) uses shape and decoration on potsherds to produce automated identification of select Roman and post-medieval pottery sherds; based on data capture of thousands of examples, by using the camera on your smartphone the ArchAIDE app will ideally give you an identification. Just think of face recognition software as a comparable operation. Accuracy is currently not perfect, but this is due not to the capability of the algorithms but rather the amount of comparable data; for AI to work, it really needs *lots* of data (i.e. big data). Like most AI systems, the more people use the app, the more data it gathers and the better it gets at identification.

But is this use of AI simply a means of supplementing specialist knowledge or replacing it? If you are in the field and there is no pottery specialist on hand, it certainly can be useful to have such an app. If you are in commercial archaeology, maybe it is even cheaper than hiring a specialist – though identification is of course, only one part of any specialist work. Turning all those identifications into a meaningful analysis and interpretation is another matter – although even here, it has been claimed that AI can help. But even with identifications, it has been suggested that AI may actually improve on human performance. Another team working in the US on machine learning for identifying Ancestral Pueblo pottery suggested such programs will iron out problems in classifications that may incorporate inconsistencies or ambiguities or even suggest alternate classifications. They will, in effect, improve our typologies.

There is no doubt this is exciting and pioneering work and a lot still remains to be done to make such software widely functional in the "real world" of archaeology. But what is interesting about all such programs is that they combine what are traditionally two discrete steps in working with data: the generation of one kind of data (a classification) from the capture of another type of data (digital images). The operations are highly structured and it would be a grave mistake to see this as about the input of raw data and the output of a meaningful typology; rather it is simply about putting data to work. But is it the algorithms that are solely responsible for the resulting classifications?

Perhaps more than anything, the biggest change in digital technology has been the coming of the internet and ability for both sharing and accessing databases so multiple users can work on the same database at different locations and stations. In short, the issue here is connectivity. Even if I was using a digital database in the early 1990s, I just missed out on the internet revolution of the mid-1990s. What this changed was not simply the ability of archaeologists to share data but also to realize the great potential that lay in the development of larger databases. Instead of each scholar working on their own, isolated database, as I did for my PhD, what if these databases could be made to work with each other? This is where the notion of big data starts to take on meaning in archaeology; what if the ceramic database from my site can be joined to the one from yours – and the hundreds of others by scholars working on similar material. Imagine what analytical potential this could have. This is a great vision, but this is also where the problems start.

Because what if I coded my pottery differently to you? Even though archaeologists tend to try and follow conventional classifications so that we all know what we are talking about when we say "pearlware", there are always idiosyncrasies, differences which makes what is called inter-operability much harder. And this is precisely why issues of coding have surfaced in archaeology and why some scholars are working hard to create what are called cyberinfrastructures that are able to co-ordinate the different codings used by different archaeologists by using metadata. Metadata are data that provide information about other data; for example, the metadata of a digital photograph from an excavation might say what the photograph is of, while metadata about a digital report might give its title, author and keywords. Metadata come in different kinds. Process metadata or paradata, for example, deal with the processes behind data collection, such as excavation methods and competence of the excavator. Another type of metadata called reference metadata focus on concept definition and application and involves the creation of what Jeremy Huggett has called an e-ontology: the range of terms that a cyberinfrastructure uses, the objects it recognizes as valid entities. What an e-ontology attempts to do is create a master system which can incorporate and mediate between all the local and variable codings used by individual databases. However, all the issues around coding in an everyday database are simply magnified with concept metadata. This is very apparent, for example, in what has become the professional standard concept metadata model CIDOC, which works under a basic division of things into material and immaterial (see Box 3.3). Such issues lead us to a topic of major theoretical concern in archaeology today: **ontology**.

In the next section, we will define this term and explore what it means for archaeology in more detail. To a large extent, the predominant concern of this book so far has been with problems of knowledge – how we know what we know, how this knowledge is produced. This is at the core of any science-like archaeology. Matters of knowledge production are linked to the concept of **epistemology** and for a long time, epistemology was regarded as the "first philosophy" – that is, it was the most important topic which preceded all others. Think of Descartes and his famous "I think therefore I am" (*cogito ergo sum*); his whole approach started from the question "What can I know for certain?" Ontology however is concerned with matters of existence: what is the nature of existence and what exists. If you look at Descartes statement, his existence seems to be guaranteed by his ability to think. For him, ontology as an investigation into the nature of existence and what exists depended on sorting out what we can know first. But this relation was inverted in the last century by Heidegger among others who put questions of existence first. To understand knowledge, how I know things, I first need to know what kind of being I am. But what has all this got to do with archaeology? Well think of the facts and data we have been examining in this chapter so far; they incorporate both epistemological and ontological issues in one, tangled-up mess. To say something meaningful about the stuff we encounter, we need to classify it, codify it, count it; but all these operations presuppose something about the way reality is structured. But more than that, all acts of knowing are always situated, they exist as part of concrete situations like digging a posthole; they are not disembodied, so knowledge practices always implicate existential questions. The relation between epistemology and ontology – knowing and being – between I think and I am – is probably a chicken and egg situation, but either way, we cannot afford to ignore either. Since much of our attention so far has been devoted to archaeological epistemology, let us turn now to ontology.

Box 3.3   Open Archaeology and Conceptual Reference Models (CRMs)

Since the advent of the internet, archaeologists have realized its potential for making data more accessible and easier to share. Some pioneering projects like the Archaeological Data Service (ADS) set up by the University of York have now been running for two decades and provide an important platform for such accessibility (https://archaeologydataservice.ac.uk/). In the US, similar repositories include the Digital Archaeological Record (tDAR; tdar.org) and also Open Context (opencontext.org), both of which are intended to be international in scope.

At one level, these repositories can act simply as data stores, where scholars can upload and download data making it more accessible and shareable. So long as this is only about accessing one particular dataset, this is fine. But if you want to compare or *combine* multiple datasets in analytical ways, then a whole new problem has to be addressed: inter-operability. The European project ARIADNE (https://ariadne-infrastructure.eu/) was set up precisely to deal with this issue and is based on the CIDOC conceptual reference model or CRM which establishes a common platform where different data sources can be uniformly described and accessed. Because different archaeologists will often use different terminology or vocabulary to talk about the same entities, the platform provides a way to overcome this through a common infrastructure. The basic philosophy behind all digital

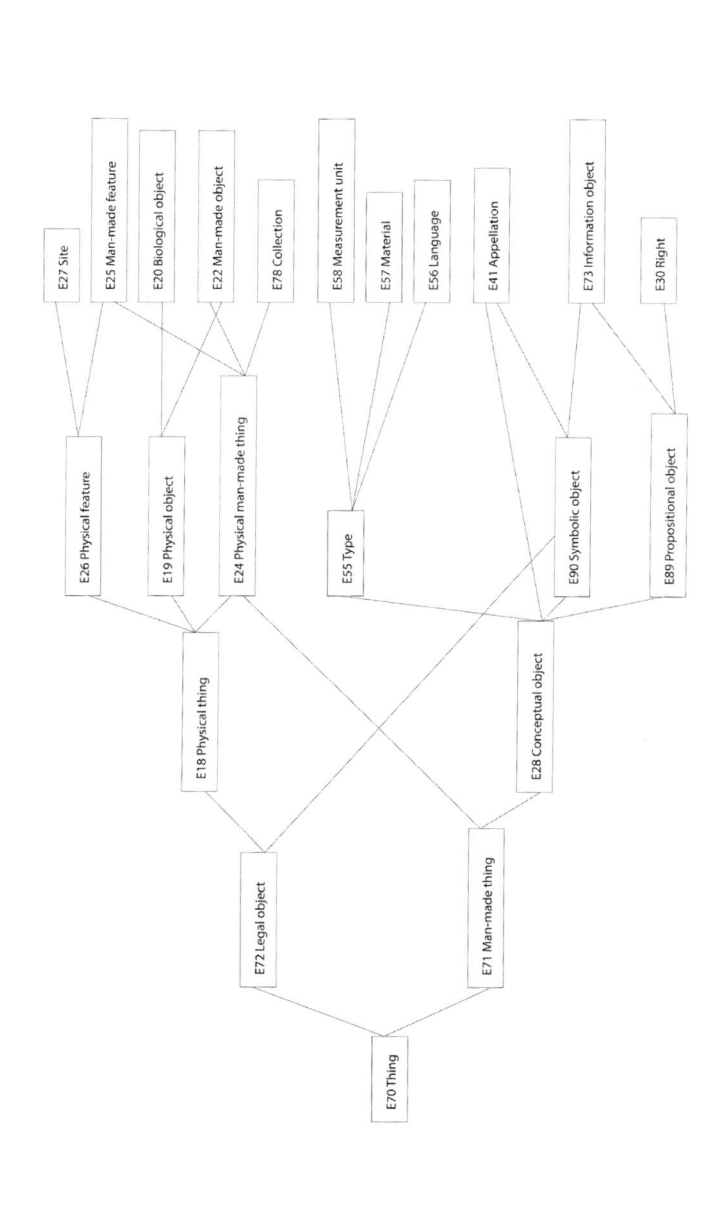

Figure 3.4 Extract from the CIDOC CRM pertaining to the category of "thing" (redrawn from https://cidoc-crm.org/); what kind of ontology does this entail?

66 *Making Records*

> archaeological data services today is summed up in the acronym FAIR: data should be findable, accessible, interoperable and reusable.
>
> But any data infrastructure and CRM – like any archaeological classification – will have some kind of metaphysical or ontological bias built in. That is, how it classifies data implies a certain view of reality. Look at how the CIDOC CRM classifies different kinds of entities grouped under the category of "things" (code E70 in the CRM) in Figure 3.4: what kind of ontology does this classification embody?

Sorting Out Stuff

Let's go back to the artefact class. Now you have a bag of mixed finds in front of you and you are asked to sort them out and then register them; how will you do it? The usual procedure is to start by separating objects by material: metal in this pile, ceramic in that, bone over here and so on. Even within a category, you might focus on material first; with metals you might sort them on the basis of metal types (iron, copper alloy, lead, etc.) or with pottery on the basis of fabric. Material commonly seems to be the first, default basis of any sorting process. To some extent, there are practical reasons for this in terms of conservation and storage; separating metals, organics, ceramic, etc. is important because different materials usually require very different conservation measures. But these classifications existed before conservation was a major concern and point to the fact that there is a deeper logic behind it. It is a logic that sees artefacts as cultural transformations of natural matter: how a tree is converted into a chair, clay into a pot, a rock into a hand axe. This is also why technologies of production are such a dominant feature of learning about them, from the "raw material", through its various stages of processing, to the finished object.

This basic division between nature and culture is closely related to the one between the material and immaterial that we met in the previous section. The very term **material culture** points to this; remove the first word "material" and what are you left with? There is an underlying sense that "material culture" is a bit of an aberration, an apologetic adjective to remind us that some aspects of culture have a material basis. This is not the place to rehearse the deep history of the term material and materiality in the humanities or its recent (re-)habilitation in contemporary theory; instead, let us just examine how deeply this opposition remains entrenched within archaeology. I remember once joining a new project and causing consternation when I registered all animal bones as part of a general finds catalogue. Finds were artefacts, bones were something else. Ecofacts is one word that has been used in archaeology, but on this site I think they called them samples, to indicate their affinity with soil samples from which plant remains were extracted. But you see to me, they were finds – because we found them. Nonetheless, the discipline commonly tends to preserve a broad division between artefacts (or material culture) and ecofacts or environmental data, which reproduces this split between nature and culture. Remember that white pebble found by the student at the start of the last chapter? The decision of whether to keep or throw was informed by which category we decide to place it in. Of course, many archaeologists have railed against this and most who work with these categories usually go on to think of them in more integrated and messy ways. But none of this changes the way they are originally sorted and registered on site.

So the ways in which we sort out stuff reflect our own culturally and historically-derived predilections about how the world is partitioned. Our categories and classifications not only embody a particular way of seeing things, they also help to realize and reinforce the reality of these divisions through our actions. By separating boxes of ceramics from boxes of bones, by training scholars to become expert in the analysis of these things, the reality of these things as "natural kinds" becomes more and more established. At the same time, archaeologists are not blind to this; we are fully aware that our own systems of classification are culturally situated and that other ways of ordering things are possible. We are also aware of the implications this has for the re-usability of our data. That if I systematically ignore the collection of white pebbles from my sites, my sites have little value for someone wishing to analyse the distribution of these pebbles in case they reveal some broader pattern. More to the point, as scholars whose job it is to study past cultures and customs, we are acutely aware that the people whose objects we are studying may have had a very different way of ordering the same stuff. Indeed, this has even encouraged archaeologists to think about how past ways of ordering the world might be discernible in things.

One of the first major discussions about this related quite specifically to artefact classifications. In the 1950s, there was a lot of discussion in the US about the extent to which archaeological classifications reflected past systems of categorization or were simply expedient and purely archaeological tools of analysis. This debate was tied in with the distinction between what are known as emic and etic classifications, where the former refers to past people's categorizations, also known as ethno-taxonomies, and the latter to the archaeological typologies (Figure 3.5). For some, etic systems (i.e. archaeological typologies) should try and capture the emic systems (i.e. native classifications) as closely as possible, while for others, this went against the whole point of archaeology as an objective science. What mattered is whether meaningful patterns emerged from using these classifications, not whether the people in the past used them. On the whole, the latter position became the one that most archaeologists adopted, seeing classifications as heuristic devices for analysing patterns in the archaeological record. This is not to say that such classifications are purely arbitrary; they are embedded in empirical criteria that objects present to the archaeologist and in that sense, they could also have been salient properties for the people who made and used them in the past. But the point is, such properties don't need to have been consciously recognized to have social or historical relevance.

Yet an interest in past ways of ordering the world did not disappear. In the 1970s, the influence of **structuralism** began to be felt in archaeology and so began another wave of discussion which was later amplified under postprocessualism as

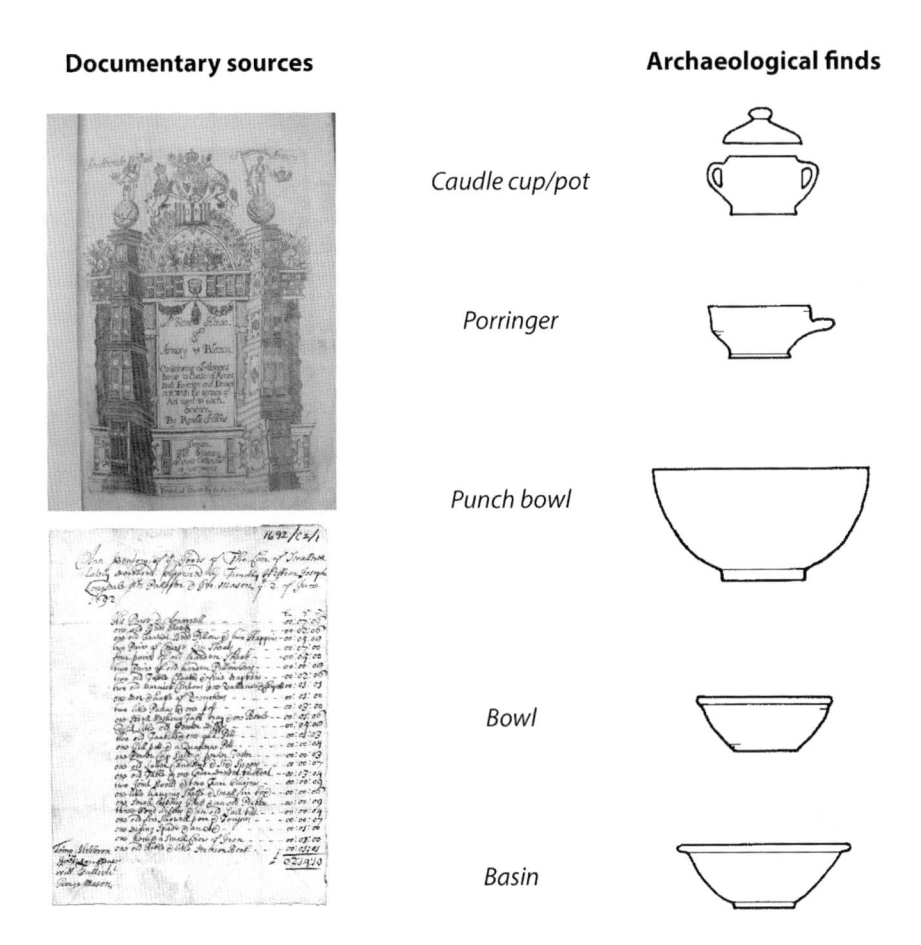

Figure 3.5 Vessel types used for liquid and semi-solid foods in the Potomac typological system (POTS) which attempted to connect emic and etic classifications by matching terms from documentary sources (mostly probate inventories) with excavated pottery forms (adapted from Beaudry et al. 1983; Beaudry 1988).

part of its interest in trying to "recover the mind" of past societies. This time, however, it did not revolve around narrow issues of artefact classification and typology as in the 1950s but rather was about understanding how the deeper conceptual logic of a culture or society is manifest through diverse contexts such as artefact decoration, spatial organization or contextual association (Figure 3.6). Structuralism was originally a theory developed by a Swiss linguist de Saussure to explain the underlying structure of language as a human phenomenon. From the 1960s, French scholars started to re-work these ideas in other fields such as Levi-Strauss in anthropology and Roland Barthes to modern French culture, both of whom looked at how things like myths, fashion, advertising and kinship systems embodied a specific cultural logic that operated on the same structuring principles

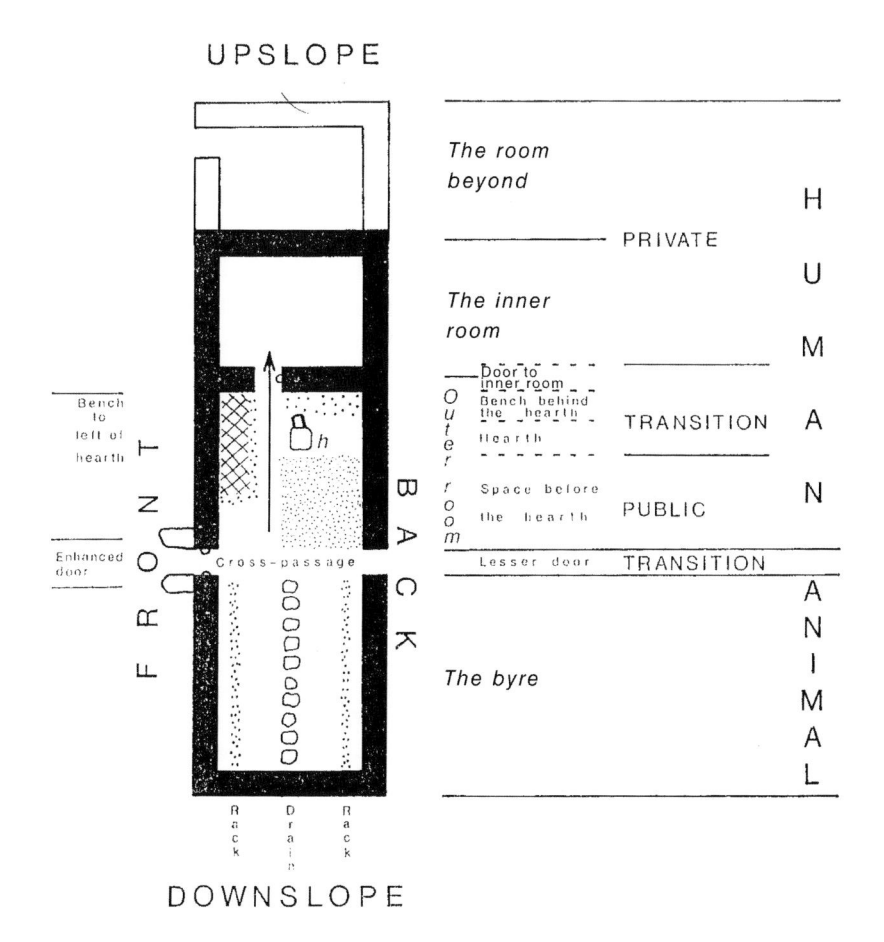

Figure 3.6 Conceptual oppositions structuring a medieval longhouse in Dartmoor, England (adapted from Austin & Thomas 1990). Although not explicitly presented as a structuralist archaeology, the influence of structuralism in this example is clear.

as Saussure had suggested for language. When archaeologists picked up on this in the 1970s and 1980s, they simply extended these approaches into material culture.

In the last decade, we might identify a third phase of discussion, one that revolves around the concept of **ontology**. Ontology, as we briefly mentioned previously, is a concept that in archaeology, generally addresses the question "what is a thing?" or "what kind of existence or being do things have?" The issue here is not really about specific things like potsherds and postholes but rather about the general range of entities and their nature. This ontological perspective digs deep into our cultural systems of classification because it suggests that we cannot treat classification as a purely methodological or epistemological issue; it carries ontological commitments about how we view the world in general. In archaeology, the question of ontology has tended to be addressed from two major directions. One is situated within the European philosophical tradition and is especially linked to phenomenology. Recall we met this in the last chapter in relation to fieldwork (see Box 2.6), but as we mentioned there, phenomenology comprises a much richer set of ideas. The other has been informed by indigenous perspectives on reality and has largely entered archaeology through social and cultural anthropology. Let us look a little further at each in turn.

Phenomenology and Relational Ontologies

A classic philosophical example of ontology is the debate over mind and matter or the mental and material, where reality is split into these two main kinds of things. This is a position usually linked to philosopher Descartes and called **Cartesian dualism**, and ever since he set it up like this, philosophers have debated whether mind can be reduced to matter (or vice versa) or whether the dichotomy is irresolvable. Our earlier discussion about the division between nature and culture relates to this as nature is often associated with the material and culture with the mental. This distinction is thus not just an issue of classification, it is also an issue of ontology as it frames the way we look at the world. For example, traditionally the job of archaeology was viewed as getting at people through their artefacts, that is trying to understand human culture, beliefs or behaviour *through* the things they left behind. Under this view, artefacts were merely proxies or ciphers for humans; on the one side you have the world of humans (the mental) and on the other, the world of things (material).

With phenomenology, however, this dualism was rejected in favour of a view which saw humans and the world as irreducibly entwined and so for philosopher Martin Heidegger, the important distinction was not between two basic kinds of stuff – mind and matter – but between different modes or states of being. That's why when we see any reference to Heidegger or his concepts (in English translation), they often use hyphens to underscore this entwining (e.g. being-in-the-world). In Heidegger's famous example of the hammer, when we use it as a tool to drive in a nail, its existence is of a very different kind to when the hammer head falls off the shaft and becomes a broken object. In the first case, it is so embedded in our action, to our being that we don't even notice it; it is part of us, this human-with-hammer exists as a joint being. In the latter case with a broken hammer, we now see it as a separate object because it is no longer part of something we are doing. As our relation to the hammer changes, so does the being of the object – and indeed us too. The point is, states of existence are *relational*, which was a key part of the philosophy of another phenomenologist Maurice Merleau-Ponty who explored the nature of human embodied existence.

Although early work in phenomenology defined relationality in terms of the human–thing relation, a thing's state of existence could also be defined by its relation to other things. So in a later example of Heidegger, the existence of a jug as a thing was defined by the way it gathered or enfolded other things around it: not just a human hand to grasp its handle but also wine to fill its inside, a table for it to stand on. This notion of a thing as something which "gathers" or "assembles" plays off the old Germanic word *thing*, which also refers to an assembly or gathering. This more "democratic" approach to the relational nature of what things are connects with more recent approaches which have had a big impact on archaeology such as **actor network theory** (ANT), most famously associated with philosopher Bruno Latour and **assemblage theory**, drawn from the work of philosophers Deleuze and Guattari. Here, what matters are not human actors but **agency**, not bodies but forces, that is, how actions are distributed across a network or assemblage composed of both humans and non-humans. That Heidegger's jug, for example, cannot be seen as the product of purely human creation since its form is dependent on the coming-together of clay, a fast wheel, a kiln, a skilled potter and many other things (see Box 3.4).

Box 3.4 Making a Pot

Lambos Malafouris has explored the issue of how a potter makes a pot, drawing on **material engagement theory**, which argues that to understand artefacts, we cannot divide them into two parts: physical properties on the one hand and human agency on the other. This is to reproduce the Cartesian split between mind and matter, nature and culture. Instead, we need to look at the interaction between human and object, at the space in between them. Let us examine this through his example of a potter at the potter's wheel. If you ask a potter how they make a pot, you may not get very satisfactory answers; it is often easier for them to show than explain it. This is because a great deal of what they do is unconscious, it resides in muscle memory; it is the potter's hands you should be asking, not the potter. Acknowledging this, you might think that the potter still has a mental image in their head of what they are doing; even if they are not aware of it, and this image is transmitted to their hands. But this way of thinking is still too binary; it thinks of "making" as the conjunction of an active human on passive material. Many archaeologists adopted this view when thinking about artefact classifications; that a "type" somehow refers to some kind of mental template. But you only have to look at a potter at work to see how silly this is.

Watch a video on YouTube of a potter at work. What is going on? The wheel is spinning and just that action alone creates certain forces acting on the clay, and depending on where the clay is placed, it may even fly off the wheel. The potter's hands join this spinning lump of clay and guide it; they use the force of movement in the wheel and resistant properties of clay to shape it; water or slurry may be required depending on the plasticity of the clay. But the rotating lump of clay also acts back on those hands, and so it is a constant interplay between materials and forces. In short, to make a pot is all about the dynamic interactions of bodies of matter, human and non-human. This is not to say the potter has no image of what the final pot should look like, but this image of a final pot is based on other pots made before and even if there is great diversity in the range of forms one can make on a potter's wheel, any prior form will also have been a collaboration between the potter, the wheel, the clay and whatever other tools are involved. All of these elements contribute; alter one of them, and the possibilities will also change. A less skilled potter will make different pots to an expert, a slow wheel offers different forces than a fast wheel; different clays react differently to the temperatures in a kiln.

Figure 3.7 Making a pot: island of Sifnos, Greece (photo: Lambros Malafouris, ERC HANDMADE [No. 771997]).

> Material engagement theory argues that the divide between mind and matter – or more accurately, between brain, body and world, is not clear cut. That mental acts do not just occur in our heads, or even in our hands and fingers, but extend outward into the things around us. This has been called extended cognition. But for Malafouris, it isn't just about cognition but material agency. In this way, material engagement theory shares a similar outlook to ANT which views agency as distributed between entities, where the focus is not so much on individual actors as collectives or assemblages.

The most recent work within the phenomenological tradition has moved away from a relational ontology to reflect on what things are apart from their relations, most notably in the work of philosopher Graham Harman and his promotion of an object-oriented ontology. Harman's phenomenology argues that things always hold something in reserve, that they exceed their relations. Consider Heidegger's jug or hammer: what relations they have, whether to humans or to other things like wine or nails, the jug or hammer, cannot be fully reduced to these relations. That is, if you take all these relations away, they will still have some kind of autonomous existence. In some ways, what is at stake here is the choice between what is called an essentialist versus relational ontology; the former argues that things *in addition* have some kind of existence outside of any relations with other things, whereas the latter suggests that all things are ultimately defined by their relations. Archaeologists differ on which side they fall. What do you think?

Animism and Indigenous Ontologies

For many of us, the mental is a property only of humans, or at most, other sentient beings. More narrowly, we also tend to associate it with a very specific quality of being sentient or human, one which is not reducible to any of our body parts, even if we acknowledge that it clearly seems to have a corporeal basis (i.e. in the brain or nervous system). Which is why we don't think of a shoe or even our hair or nails as having this property. A shoe might be said to *reflect* a mental process (such as a desire to look "cool"), but in itself, it is not conscious, sentient or even animate. Indeed, this invokes another deep division of our ontology: things that are alive (and can die) and things that are inanimate (they cannot die because they can never be alive in the first place). A shoe is inanimate (even if it is made in part of once-animate matter, such as the skin of an ox) and my nails, while animate in part, become inanimate once clipped off.

And yet many archaeologists have argued that these divisions are closing us off from recognizing past ontologies that were different from our own. What happens if we consider that a shoe or my nail clippings might actually be animate? Actually, this is not as hard as it sounds. Within European society, even as recently as the last century, folk beliefs existed around the use of items associated with the body which had power to ward off evil, misfortune or witchcraft. Witch bottles containing human hair, nail clippings or urine have been found concealed in many

Figure 3.8 The Holywell witch bottle (photo: Andy Chopping/MOLA).

houses dating from the seventeenth century right into the early twentieth century, as have shoes and other items of clothing (Figure 3.8). These inanimate objects were obviously regarded as having some power and agency which many of us today no longer attribute to them. One way to express this is to argue that this agency is derivative from the person they came from; that the power *really* comes from the person and that the objects are merely acting as conduits or "secondary agents". This is an approach that was also proposed by anthropologist Alfred Gell, one of the scholars who had a big influence in archaeology in the early 2000s. But another way to express this is to argue that these things are autonomous agents, that they act independently of their human donor and actually have the potential to resist the donor's intentions or even work against them. Such objects now appear to be not simply animate but even sentient.

Many of us don't exist in a world where shoes can be animate, let alone sentient – although we clearly enjoy toying with these ontological divisions in fiction where cars are alive or dolls become serial killers. But in archaeology, we tend to stick firmly to these divisions. We might recognize that artefacts *reflect* the conceptual structures of their makers or that humans can *delegate* or *extend* agency to objects, but in themselves such things remain ultimately inert, inanimate, non-sentient. But some scholars have suggested that we do go further, that we entertain the animacy of matter, which in part is about forcing us to confront our ontological boundaries. What does it mean to be alive? The same spirit drives those archaeologists who encourage us to take indigenous ontologies seriously, where shamans *do* transform into bears or eagles, not just *think* they do. The latter is our normal attitude: we can accept that different cultures see the world differently, what is called **cultural relativism**, but ultimately, there is just one reality: one world, multiple viewpoints. But for anthropologist Viveiros de Castro, we should rather invert this formula: many worlds, one viewpoint. Thus while for us, humans, jaguars and tapirs all exist in one world as stable entities, for Amerindian groups, being is more fluid and changes depending on what kind of being you are; when a tapir sees a human, they really see a jaguar, while when a jaguar sees a human, they really see a tapir, and when jaguars and tapirs see their own kind, they only see humans. Archaeologists like Benjamin Alberti and Yvonne Marshall who have taken up de Castro's ideas which are known as **perspectivism** (to distinguish it from cultural relativism) argue that we should take seriously the possibility that reality is literally different in different places and periods. They are not necessarily asking us to believe what shamans believe but simply to suspend our own beliefs and see what happens – to be open to a world which is otherwise than our own.

Box 3.5 Artefacts or Belongings?

Many years ago, I was excavating an abandoned lot in a small town in South Africa; I was interested in understanding the early history of the town as it started life as a mission station for former slaves in the post-emancipation period. We found a household dump dating to the early twentieth century associated with the foundations of a house that had been built in the mid-nineteenth century and torn down in the 1980s. One day, we were visited by a neighbour who asked us what we were planning to do with all the broken pottery, glassware and other objects we had dug out of the dump – did we perhaps intend to return them to their owner? I didn't know what to say and I am ashamed to say, this possibility didn't even occur to me. Although their owner was long dead, their daughter still lived in the town as we had interviewed her about the property. I saw these objects purely as artefacts, as historical evidence. In the end, after analysis, we returned them to their resting place in the ground.

As archaeologists, we typically view finds and artefacts as inert matter, things which provide evidence or data for understanding the past. But for many indigenous peoples, calling something an artefact is potentially hurtful and disrespectful, where the term "belonging" is considered more apt. The same applies to burial sites where what archaeologists call skeletons, descendant communities think of as ancestors. Names matter, especially in contexts where archaeology is working with descendant communities for they reveal a very different attitude to archaeological remains. Such concerns have, for example, been enshrined in a document entitled *Recommendations for Decolonizing British Columbia's Heritage-Related Processes and Legislation*. Archaeologists Julie Hollowell and George Nichols working with First Nations in British Columbia contrast a typical archaeological perspective with an indigenous one, where "[o]ne emphasizes responsibilities to *objects from the past* in the present; the other focuses on *obligations to people*, both past and present".

Even though all of us can understand objects in terms of personal or collective belonging, as archaeologists we tend view the objects we deal with as removed from such associations because of the way we separate past and present. And yet archaeologists do still have a tacit sense of artefacts as belongings, but this is somehow partitioned into a different box. Artefacts become the "property" of the state or nation or humanity as a whole. Debates about cultural property in European and North American Museums have been conducted for decades now, such as the famous case of the Parthenon or "Elgin" Marbles, a sculpted frieze that was taken from the Parthenon in Athens and now resides in the British Museum. More recently, Dan Hicks has explored the sad history of the Benin Bronzes, which are scattered across various museums in the global "north" but all of which derived as plunder after a British naval attack from 1897. Questions of "ownership" and "belonging" are undoubtedly thrown in sharp relief when the deep connections between colonialism and the history of archaeology are exposed. Increasing demands for **de-colonizing methodologies** in archaeology are part of an attempt to acknowledge this history and as such can we ever say an artefact is not also a belonging?

From Representational to Performative Recording

We have come a long way from the archaeologist sorting out their bag of finds, so it is time to try and bring this discussion back to the main topic of this section: the relation between data and classification. Recording objects in archaeology, creating data, always involves some form of classification or categorization, whether these manifest in explicit typologies and taxonomies or through more generic (ontological) terminological and conceptual divisions and categories. Archaeologists have long been aware that these systems of classification and conceptual divisions which affect how we sort out stuff are archaeological constructs. For some, these constructs capture something of the way past peoples also ordered their reality, whether specifically in terms of ethno-taxonomies or more generally through conceptual structures. For others, all that matters is that these constructs conform to observed and demonstrable patterning in the material remains and whether they related to mental or conceptual schemes or more general behavioural and social processes was beside the point. However, both positions tended to operate under an assumption that the world was split into a mental and material realm, even if there was some reciprocal relation between the two. What we have seen developing since the turn of the millennium is a position where this division is increasingly under attack, where different systems of classification are not superimposed on an underlying, singular reality, but where what is real – the ontological – cannot be disentangled from what is perceived.

The way this is often expressed is that we have moved from a **representational** to a **performative** model of knowledge production. Under a representational model, our recording systems, our classifications, are attempts to *represent* our archaeological material to mirror natural cleavages, to follow the materials own "seams" as closely as possible. This presupposes such divisions are latent in the objects themselves. This is a very natural assumption. Yet as we have seen, there are many ways to cut the cake, and the first cuts we make often end up determining subsequent divisions and analysis in a way that makes it even harder to work with alternate classifications. The point is, the way our data are coded and classified is actually the product of concrete, real-world actions (like separating pot and bone in a finds bag) and instead of seeing classification as a *representation* of our archaeological material, we rather see it as *emergent* from a performative interaction between the archaeologist and her material. As soon as we do this, we also see how the nature of reality, of things themselves and their properties are also emergent at the same time; classification and ontology co-emerge as part of a performative model of science. In fact we saw exactly the same thing happening in the last chapter on fieldwork; that a site plan or section/profile drawing is not simply a representation of what you see in the ground, but that the archaeologists' intervention in the ground – the way they trowelled the surface or cut the trench edge – enabled both the site itself and the record we make of it, to co-emerge (see Box 2.3). These ideas place notions of performance and interaction at the centre; by this same token, we might define recording in performative rather than representational terms.

Yet surely a bone is still a bone; whether we put it in a pile with other bones or place it with other finds (say artefacts associated with food preparation), it doesn't magically change appearance. Yes and no. On the one hand, a bone certainly looks different among a pile of other bones as opposed to when it is in a pile of artefacts; different qualities of it will probably catch your eye. On the other hand, taken in isolation, of course the bone remains the same. But remember Heidegger and how the hammer can change its existential status depending on its relation to us? Because of the way archaeologists specifically interact with bones, what matters about it are how it is transformed from being that physical object dug out of the ground to a bit of data in an archive; it is in this process of transformation that the question of ontology becomes connected to that of classification. As data, the bone now exists in a very specific and different way to before. It helps to think about this in relation to how someone different – not an archaeologist – might interact with a bone and how they will transform it in a different way. Consider a craftworker who may take it and physically work on it, cutting off an end, drilling a hole there, polishing this section. Now the bone has physically transformed so ontologically, a new object has been born: a bone handle. The craft person hasn't just created a conceptual category of "bone handle", they have also altered reality with a new object. The point here is that the archaeological operation is no different: it also entails both an ontological and conceptual re-ordering simultaneously. You may think the bone remains unaltered, but actually it has changed; it has been cleaned of dirt, it has been sorted and grouped with other objects and likely placed in a bag and/or box with numbers and codes written on them. And most importantly, it has become a string of text and numbers in your database. The bone in an archaeological archive is a different object to the bone buried in the soil, just as that is a different object to the bone as part of the skeleton of a once living animal. It undergoes ontological as well as classificatory transformations.

> **Box 3.6 Digital Collections and Archaeological Prosthetics**
>
> How often do you get to handle real artefacts in your studies? I am sure this varies between institutions and programmes; for some of you, it may happen rarely if at all, for others there may some parts of your study that put great emphasis on first-hand experience. But in the wake of the recent coronavirus pandemic when many of us had to move to online and virtual platforms, even the most practical of courses faced severe challenges. At the University of Lund in Sweden, experimental work with using 3D digital collections for teaching in the context of the pandemic found there were both benefits and costs with such collections. On the one hand, students had access to a much larger corpus of material, 24/7, wherever they were; they could see stuff not normally visible with the naked eye, could alter lighting, angles and even annotate the objects, and their capacity for manipulation was greatly enhanced over artefacts that were more sensitive to handling. On the other hand, interaction overwhelmingly emphasized the visual engagement with objects at the expense of other senses (e.g. touch, sound, smell) and it is generally clear that such collections can never replace handling real objects, but as a complimentary resource, they have great value.
>
> But then we have always found "translations" of our objects as a major source of potential, whether these are traditional paper plans and drawings or textual descriptions and databases. One of the key points of this chapter is that we are always re-working the stuff we encounter, making new things (e.g. records) from them and then interrogating and manipulating these products. In that respect, 3D collections are just the latest incarnation

of a process we have been carrying out for more than 150 years. At the same time, each new form of translation, each new media, brings with it new possibilities for working and the digital "revolution" has certainly done this. This potential of digital collections has been explored by Monika Stobiecka through her concept of archaeological prosthetics.

Prosthetics in vernacular usage refers to artificial limbs, but within theoretical discourse, it has taken on a broader meaning to encompass almost all material culture, as extensions of the human body which not only compensate for disabilities but also enhance "normal" functions. Glasses compensate for poor eyesight, but a microscope or telescope enhances our visual capabilities. Almost any object can be seen as a prosthetic in this sense, which is why philosopher Andy Clarke has called humans natural-born cyborgs, extending Donna Haraway's original identification of the cyborg as a key metaphor to rethink what it means to be human (see Chapter 7 for further discussion of this). But Stobiecka takes this notion of prosthetics to suggest that we also rethink archaeological collections as potential hybrids of the physical and digital. As an example, she cites a project on statues scattered around Paris where missing limbs had been replaced by digitally produced prosthetics, so that a replica of the Venus de Milo was given two artificial limbs. This was not an archaeological project but a promotional campaign to raise awareness for the global need of prostheses. But Stobiecka argues it has wider relevance for the role of digital collections in archaeology. Instead of seeing digital media as a means to replace or even complement physical collections, we see what potential they might have if we work to fuse the two together in more substantial ways – that we prostheticize archaeology.

In our story of the pottery class at the start of this chapter, it ended with our student pondering the complexities of naming things and whether the way we categorize pottery should not match the way people in the past did. Usually archaeologists don't know how people in the past categorized stuff, let alone what they called them unless they are lucky to have written documents. But even then, we cannot be sure either how widely used such terms were or how consistently. Indeed, if we think about this further in light of what we have talked about in this chapter, when archaeologists classify objects and even invent names for them like "Bell Beaker pottery", it is so they can do something with these categories, like plot them on a distribution map or compare their ratio to other objects. Classifications and names are a way of putting objects to work. And in fact the same is almost certainly true of any names or classifications that one might find in written sources; "china" when it appears in shop account books or probate inventories is a different object to the one the customer may buy or drink tea from. In documents and records, objects take on a new lease of life, a new form of existence when rendered as inscriptions, whether this is in archaeological records or historical archives.

Exercises for the Classroom

1. Look at a range of different records that archaeologists routinely make and discuss their relation to the concepts of data and fact.
2. Create a simple classification from a group of everyday objects or archaeological data; discuss what attributes were selected to base the classification on and how might this change if different qualities were chosen? What kind of questions does the classification allow and what does it exclude?
3. Take an archaeological object and divide the class into two debate teams: one argues that the object has certain essential properties than cannot be explained by reference to relations with other things and the other that any definition of an object can be reduced to such relations.

Further Reading

Recording Technologies

For a general discussion about the difference between data and facts, see Rosenberg (2013); for a discussion of small and big facts, see Leonelli (2011). On maps as more than representational records as discussed in Box 3.1, see the important volume by Gillings et al. (2019) and also papers by Hacigüzeller (2012, 2017), Wickstead (2009) and Witmore (2013). For a good example on the analytical potential of 3D GIS, see Dell'Unto et al. (2016). General discussion about the theoretical implications of big data in archaeology are addressed in the work of Jeremy Huggett (2012, 2015, 2020), Cooper and Green (2016) and Gabriele Gattiglia (2015), while papers in Huvila (2018) explore some of the epistemological issues around digitization in archaeology. On ARIADNE, see Meghini et al. (2017), while for recent work on visual recognition software as discussed in Box 3.2, see, for example, Gualandi et al. (2021) and Pawlowicz and Downum (2021). For a recent review of data sharing in archaeology, see Marwick and Pilaar-Birch (2018) and Kansa et al. (2019).

Sorting Out Stuff

Good discussions of the phenomenological approach to ontology can be found in Olsen (2010, esp. chapter 4), Witmore (2014) and Edgeworth (2016). ANT has become pervasive in archaeology and was a key influence behind symmetrical archaeology (Witmore 2007); a useful account can be found in Dolwick (2009), while Knappet and Malafouris (2010) offer a variety of case studies which are variously inspired by ANT, including Malafouris' paper on the potter discussed in Box 3.4. For assemblage theory and archaeology, see Jervis (2019) and the papers in Hamilakis and Jones (2017). Issues of indigenous ontologies are addressed in a variety of publications; useful references include Alberti and Bray (2009), Alberti et al. (2011) and also various papers in Harrison-Buck and Hendon (2018). An important book which showcases both streams is Crellin et al. (2021). In relation to issues of nomenclature and artefacts as belongings, see the papers by Hollowell and Nichols (2009) and Schaepe et al. (2017; also 2020). The literature on cultural patrimony and restitution is huge but see, for example, Robson et al. (2006); for the recent study of the Benin Bronzes, see Hicks (2020).

From Representational to Performative Recording

On documentation as performance, see Huvila and Sköld (2021). For the Lund study on digital collections, see Ekengren et al. (2021) and on digitization of collections in general, see Newell (2012). Stobiecka's prosthetic archaeology can be found in Stobiecka (2020).

References

Alberti, B. & T. Bray. 2009. Animating Archaeology: Of Subjects, Objects and Alternative Ontologies. *Cambridge Archaeological Journal* 19(3): 337–43.

Alberti, B., S. Fowles, M. Holbraad, Y. Marshall & C. Witmore. 2011. "Worlds Otherwise": Archaeology, Anthropology and Ontological Difference. *Current Anthropology* 52(6): 896–912.

Austin, D. & J. Thomas. 1990. The 'Proper' Study of Medieval Archaeology: A Case Study. In D. Austin & L. Alcock (eds.), *From the Baltic to the Black Sea. Studies in Medieval Archaeology*. London: Routledge, pp. 43–78.

Beaudry, M.C. 1988. Words for Things: Linguistic Analysis of Probate Inventories. In M. Beaudry (ed.), *Documentary Archaeology in the New World*. Cambridge: Cambridge University Press, pp. 43–50.

Beaudry, M.C., J. Long, H.M. Miller, F.D. Neiman & G. Wheeler Stone. 1983. A Vessel Typology for Early Chesapeake Ceramics: The Potomac Typological System. *Historical Archaeology* 17(1): 18–43.

Cooper, A. & C. Green. 2016. Embracing the Complexities of 'Big Data' in Archaeology: The Case of the English Landscape and Identities Project. *Journal of Archaeological Method and Theory* 23: 271–304.

Crellin, R., C. Cipolla, L. Montgomery, O. Harris & S. Moore. 2021. *Archaeological Theory in Dialogue. Situating Relationality, Ontology, Posthumanism, and Indigenous Paradigms*. London: Routledge.

Dell'Unto, N., G. Landeschi, A-M.L. Touati, M. Dellepiane, M. Callieri & D. Ferdani. 2016. Experiencing Ancient Buildings from a 3D GIS Perspective: A Case Drawn From the Swedish Pompeii Project. *Journal of Archaeological Method and Theory* 23: 73–94.

Dolwick, J. 2009. 'The Social' and Beyond: Introducing Actor Network Theory. *Journal of Maritime Archaeology* 4: 21–49.

Edgeworth, M. 2016. Grounded Objects. Archaeology and Speculative Realism. *Archaeological Dialogues* 23(1): 93–113.

Ekengren, F., M. Callieri, D. Dininno, Å. Berggren, S. Macheridis & N. Dell'Unto. 2021. Dynamic Collections: A 3D Web Infrastructure for Artifact Engagement. *Open Archaeology* 7: 337–52.

Gattiglia, G. 2015. Think Big About Data: Archaeology and the Big Data Challenge. *Archäologische Informationen* 38: 113–24.

Gillings, M., P. Hacıgüzeller & G. Lock (eds.). 2019. *Re-Mapping Archaeology. Critical Perspectives, Alternative Mappings*. London: Routledge.

Gualandi, M.L., G. Gattiglia & F. Anichini. 2021. An Open System for Collection and Automatic Recognition of Pottery Through Neural Network Algorithms. *Heritage* 4: 140–59.

Hacıgüzeller, P. 2012. GIS, Critique, Representation and Beyond. *Journal of Social Archaeology* 12(2): 245–63.

Hacıgüzeller, P. 2017. Archaeological (Digital) Maps as Performances: Towards Alternative Mappings. *Norwegian Archaeological Review* 12(2): 245–63.

Hamilakis, Y. & A. Jones. 2017. Archaeology and Assemblage. *Cambridge Archaeological Journal* 27(1): 77–84.

Harrison-Buck, E. & J. Hendon (eds.). 2018. *Relational Identities and Other-than-Human Agency in Archaeology*. Louisville: University Press of Colorado.

Hicks, D. 2020. *The Brutish Museums. The Benin Bronzes, Colonial Violence and Cultural Restitution*. London: Pluto Press.

Hollowell, J. & G. Nichols. 2009. Using Ethnographic Methods to Articulate Community-Based Conceptions of Cultural Heritage Management. *Public Archaeology* 8(2–3): 141–60.

Huggett, J. 2012. Lost in Information? Ways of Knowing and Modes of Representation in E-Archaeology. *World Archaeology* 44(4): 538–52.

Huggett, J. 2015. Digital Haystacks: Open Data and the Transformation of Archaeological Knowledge. In A. Wilson & B. Edwards (eds.), *Open Source Archaeology: Ethics and Practice*. Berlin: De Gruyter Open, pp. 6–29.

Huggett, J. 2020. Is Big Digital Data Different? Towards a New Archaeological Paradigm. *Journal of Field Archaeology* 45 (sup1).

Huvila, I. (ed.). 2018. *Archaeology and Archaeological Information in the Digital Society*. London: Routledge.

Huvila, I. & O. Sköld. 2021. Choreographies of Making Archaeological Data. *Open Archaeology* 7(1): 1602–17. https://doi.org/10.1515/opar-2020-0212.

Jervis, B. 2019. *Assemblage Thought and Archaeology*. London: Routledge.

Kansa, S.W., L. Atici, E.C. Kansa & R.H. Meadow. 2019. Archaeological Analysis in the Information Age: Guidelines for Maximizing the Reach, Comprehensiveness, and Longevity of Data. *Advances in Archaeological Practice* 8(1): 40–52. Cambridge University Press.

Knappet, C. & L. Malafouris (eds.). 2010. *Material Agency. Towards a Non-Anthropocentric Approach*. New York: Springer.

Leonelli, S. 2011. Packaging Small Facts for Re-Use: Databases in Model Organism Biology. In P. Howlett & M. Morgan (eds.), *How Well Do Facts Travel? The Dissemination of Reliable Knowledge*. Cambridge: Cambridge University Press, pp. 325–48.

Marwick, B. & S. Pilaar-Birch. 2018. A Standard for the Scholarly Citation of Archaeological Data as an Incentive to Data Sharing. *Advances in Archaeological Practice* 6(2): 125–43.

Meghini, C., R. Scopigno et al. 2017. ARIADNE: A Research Infrastructure for Archaeology ACM. *Journal of Computing and Cultural Heritage* 99, Article 1.

Newell, J. 2012. Old Objects, New Media: Historical Collections, Digitization and Affect. *Journal of Material Culture* 17(3): 287–306.

Olsen, B. 2010. *In Defence of Things. Archaeology and the Ontology of Objects*. Lanham: AltaMira Press.

Pawlowicz, L.M. & C.E. Downum. 2021. Applications of Deep Learning to Decorated Ceramic Typology and Classification: A Case Study Using Tusayan White Ware From Northeast Arizona. *Journal of Archaeological Science* 130: 105375. https://doi.org/10.1016/j.jas.2021.105375.

Robson, E., L. Treadwell & C. Gosden (eds.). 2006. *Who Owns Objects? The Ethics and Politics of Collecting Cultural Artefacts*. Oxford: Oxbow Books.

Rosenberg, D. 2013. Data Before the Fact. In L. Gitelman (ed.), *"Raw Data" Is an Oxymoron*. Cambridge, MA: MIT Press, pp. 15–40.

Schaepe, D.M., B. Angelbeck, D. Snook & J.R. Welch. 2017. Archaeology as Therapy. Connecting Belongings, Knowledge, Time, Place, and Well-Being. *Current Anthropology* 58(4): 502–33.

Schaepe, D.M., G. Nichols & K. Dolata. 2020. *Recommendations for Decolonizing British Columbia's Heritage-Related Processes and Legislation*. Brentwood Bay: First People's Cultural Council.

Stobiecka, M. 2020. Towards a Prosthetic Archaeology. *Journal of Social Archaeology* 20(3): 335–52.

Wickstead, H. 2009. The Uber archaeologist: Art, GIS and the Male Gaze Revisited. *Journal of Social Archaeology* 9(2): 249–71.

Witmore, C. 2007. Symmetrical Archaeology: Excerpts of a Manifesto. *World Archaeology* 39(4): 546–62.

Witmore, C. 2013. The World on a Flat Surface: Maps From the Archaeology of Greece and Beyond. In S. Bonde & S. Houston (eds.), *Re-Presenting the Past: Archaeology Through Text and Image*. Oxford: Oxbow Books, pp. 125–49.

Witmore, C. 2014. Archaeology and the New Materialisms. *Journal of Contemporary Archaeology* 1(2): 203–24.

4 Writing Up

> **Situation 4: At the Computer**
>
> *The student is sitting at her desk, staring at the blank screen. The cursor blinks at her, impatiently waiting for her to start typing. Nothing. Maybe a cup of coffee will solve it . . . or a quick check of email. Before she knows it, an hour has passed. Time to get on with it. She brings up the empty word document, clicks back to her files with charts, tables, and images and tries to think again how to start. Glances at her handwritten notes next to her keyboard with ideas and even a skeleton structure. She knows her data inside and out. If this were a simple lab report, it would be no problem – introduction, methodology, summary of the key the results. There are templates for this kind of stuff. But not this; not writing a paper for a high-ranking journal which will get her work more widely known and appreciated, not to mention earn her important academic credits. No one teaches you how to do this. Of course, she knows the general rules about scholarly writing, referencing and can adopt the standard structure used in many papers; that's not the problem. She even has a title – Fisherman's Friends: fishhooks and eel-traps in the Medieval Fens. The problem is how to turn her data into a meaningful account: what is the angle here? What is the story behind all this? What is it that she really wants to say?*

Writing and the Archaeological Process

Archaeology as Literary Production

When I was a student, I remember being told that one of the worst sins you could commit as an archaeologist was not to publish your fieldwork. It was almost on a par with not making a record of any excavation or intervention that would irreversibly alter a site; the record, and by extension the publication, was the ultimate rationale and justification for the fact that excavation was also destruction. In acting

DOI: 10.4324/9781003098294-5

as a justification or compensation for "destroying" a site through excavation, the written record and publication also became the ultimate end point or goal of fieldwork; once the report is written or published, your obligation as an archaeologist to that site is fulfilled and you can be guilt-free about digging up another one. In reality, of course, archaeologists often run several projects concurrently and even if they are back-to-back, the post-excavation and writing up phases invariably overlap with the next project. But regardless of this, or the length of time it might take, writing up is commonly seen as the end point of a long archaeological process that started with an encounter, a question or a project design brief.

One way to see this is that archaeology is all about the conversion or translation of physical things into words. Remember in the previous chapters how we examined the construction of facts and data in the field: they are coded abstractions, inscriptions which represent a physical, sensual reality. That "5Y 7/10" or "honey brown" are words which attempt to convey the sensual experience of the colour of soil. From notebooks to *pro forma* sheets, the conversion to words happens right at the very start of an archaeological intervention. When we start writing up our report, we draw on these field texts (and images such as plans and photographs, matrices, etc.) to construct another text – this time, one more "readerly" and then, if we think the project deserves wider dissemination through publication as a journal article or monograph, we use that grey report as a basis to write up the publication, also probably drawing on other reports or publications to contextualize it. In short, there is an over-riding impetus towards textualization, and especially "readerly" textualization as it moves from the field into the world of publication. Not only is writing up the end point of the archaeological process, it suffuses the whole process where writing up, though present from the start, becomes increasingly removed from the physical stuff and more entangled with other texts.

To some extent, this is a useful way to think about what archaeologists do, but there are some problems with it; two in particular I would like to focus on. One concerns the dominance of text over other forms of representation and dissemination; the other relates more generally to the linear way in which this model depicts the archaeological operation. Let's start with the first issue. In many ways, the dominance of text is curious because in the field, the production of images are as prevalent as texts, from site plans to photographs and even videos, not to mention sketches on context sheets, notebooks and even labels. But as one moves out of the field and into working on a grey report, the images start to take second place as text takes over, a pattern which is largely reinforced in publication. Images increasingly become supplemental to text and are either used purely as "dressing" or when they have a more critical role to the narrative or argument, it is because they somehow act to validate a claim or statement made through the text. The text is what frames the relevance of the image so that a site plan, a graph or a photograph often work as form of evidential support.

Archaeologists have long criticized this marginalization of images. There are many aspects to the discussion surrounding visualization in archaeology, but in terms of the role images play in the construction of a fieldwork report, I would like to return to the discussion we made of images in Chapter 3. Recall that one of the features of archaeological images, especially ones produced through fieldwork and lab work like site plans, artefact drawings and photographs, is the burden of representation they often shoulder, over and above other data types like numbers and texts. Because of their sensory (specifically visual) nature, they somehow seem to be "closer" to the thing itself, whereas words and particularly numbers are obvious abstractions. This illusion of proximity is ironically also what keeps images marginalized; they come to stand in for the thing itself, so their role in a report is to be evidentiary support, a silent witness. As a result, they can never stand alone but only always take meaning and relevance from the text which frames this relevance. However, this is not inevitable and in fact there are other ways of engaging and thinking of images which give them much more agency, as we will see throughout this chapter. But to see how, we need to move on to address the second issue I mentioned: the linearity of the archaeological process.

In many ways, the idea of archaeology following a linear path makes a lot of sense; we formulate a research plan, go into the field to conduct our excavation or survey, come home and process the data and finally write up the results. There is a temporality to the process that makes it hard to do one, without previously having done the other. One can hardly write up the report before the fieldwork! Although . . . I once met an archaeologist working in CRM who proudly told me that they more or less did do this all time. What they meant, of course, is that their reports had a set template or structure where the introduction and methodology sections could be already pre-written and the results and conclusions simply slotted in quickly after the fieldwork. Although an extreme example, to an extent it shows how the linearity is closely connected to a notion of the archaeological process as highly routinized and repetitive. And in fact, because the reality of engaging with the world often subverts one's expectations, in real life, the archaeological process is much less linear than on paper.

For a start, as soon as you go into the field, you frequently end up returning to your research plan and modifying it, a process which probably continues right through the whole project. Also, on many projects, field data begin to be processed almost simultaneously even if it continues after the fieldwork. Moreover, there will be critical differences between projects which have a single fieldwork phase (e.g. often the case in commercial or development-led work) as opposed to research projects which run over several years; in the latter case, the processing phase can loop back and feed into fieldwork. The same goes for annual progress or interim reports which might be published or produced during the lifetime of the project. In short, the linearity is often presented as an ideal, whereas in reality, different stages of archaeological work will overlap, loop back and generally be more blurred.

Such recursiveness and mixing is, on the whole, a good thing. One should always be adaptable and flexible when it comes to a research plan, especially if your data turn up something very unexpected. And having site data processed while you are still doing fieldwork can be hugely beneficial. At Çatalhöyük, archaeologists studying the animal bones or plant remains were working on site at the same time as the excavation and would make regular tours to discuss with the diggers what each was finding. This near synchronous feedback clearly benefits everyone. But in terms of the main topic of this chapter, it is the question of writing up that is perhaps most intransigent here as there is something that makes it a bit different to these other issues. One can write interim reports, even interim publications, just as one can give talks or site tours which also help to disseminate the results of the project so far. But the expectation is that a *final* report or publication is still necessary to close a project. Writing up provides *closure*, and it is this closure which ultimately also constitutes the linearity of the process in the ideal. Writing up is the *telos* or ultimate goal of an archaeological project. This is how linearity is linked back into the issue with which I opened this chapter, on fieldwork (specifically excavation) as destruction. It relates to this sense of fulfilling the obligation we have towards the archaeological remains; the final report or publication acts to repay the debt incurred to our peers, to society, the moment we decide to intervene with those remains. As long as fieldwork is viewed like this, writing up will remain both the ultimate end of the archaeological process and its ultimate rationale or justification. It comes at the end precisely because it provides closure; it provides closure because it is the "end" (i.e. goal) of the process.

Box 4.1   Honouring Ambiguity and Dealing With Doubt

In many instances, certainty is a virtue; if we get on board a plane, we want to feel certain it will go up and come down again without falling out of the sky. Every day, we do things on the assumption that things will work: our computer will turn on when we press the power button, the car will start, the shop will be open when it says it will. Yet as we know, all of these certainties are really just probabilities. Sometimes planes and computers crash, sometimes cars don't start and that shop is closed. Certainty is better thought of as a continuum than an either/or. Yet when it comes to science, there is often an expectation that certainty is black and white. If an archaeologist is asked: *How can you be certain that this really happened?* The answer is, of course, they cannot. But this doesn't make them a bad scientist. No scientist is infallible, and it doesn't matter how certain one may be about something, there is always room for doubt or ambiguity. Yet despite this acknowledgement of "room for doubt", archaeology on the whole, remains wedded to a view which endorses certainty and values unambiguous knowledge. Archaeologist Joan Gero critiqued this stance from a feminist perspective. She identified three important ways in which ambiguity needs to be acknowledged in archaeology: first, archaeological evidence is never enough to guarantee proof of any interpretation. This is a well-known facet of any philosophy of science. Second, the variables involved in most archaeological problems are too complex in their number and relations for our evidence or interpretations to fully encompass. Third and finally, archaeological evidence is intrinsically fragmentary and partial, so it can never hope to offer certitude.

Yet despite these often-acknowledged limitations, archaeologists carry on as if certainty was still a goal. They do this because, as Gero argued, they have adopted various "mechanisms of closure", which act to plug these gaps and holes in our knowledge-making practices and create a false sense of certainty. Gero describes various strategies that archaeologists use as mechanisms of closure such as "data cleaning", where data are packaged into neat categorizations and coding that create uniformity. Artefact typologies are common examples of such. Another strategy involves "pushing the data" which is when a "possible" quietly turns into a "probable", where early on in an interpretation "such-and-such *may* be the case" transforms into "*was* the case" by the end of paper, but without really any supporting change. These strategies and more create an inflated sense of confidence which Gero linked to a masculinist style of thinking; from a feminist perspective, "honouring ambiguity" means resisting interpretive closure which certainty carries in its wake; it means leaving open an interpretive space for novel and different views on the past.

At the same time, the equivocation that many scientists do have around their interpretations has been exploited by some groups for political purposes. The most prominent example of this in recent times has been the early discourse around climate change, where, even if many scientists were fairly sure that human-induced greenhouse gases were responsible for global warming, any disagreements among scientists and ambiguity was used by other groups to deny climate change was real. Similar strategies were used to cast doubt on claims linking smoking to cancer. Although these "merchants of doubt" seem to be using similar arguments to Gero (but for a completely opposite purpose) and indeed espousing a long western tradition of scepticism, there is an important difference. In exploiting ambiguity to discredit climate scientists, they are relying on a public's inherent sense that science is *supposed* to provide certainty, so when they don't offer this, we *should* be sceptical. But science can never do that, and it is for this reason, Gero's argument is all the more important. It is perhaps telling that today, climate scientists have become more certain in their interpretations precisely as a response to this backlash. Climate change is now a fact. Although the evidence to support this has increased and by any standards this interpretation is fully warranted, one cannot help also see it as an inevitable rhetorical counter-strategy to those merchants of doubt: certainty is what matters.

A revival of such certainty has also followed in the wake of the resurgence of archaeological science, prompting Tim Flohr-Sørensen to revive Gero's argument, but with added nuance. Flohr-Sørensen makes a distinction between ambiguity and vagueness, where ambiguity is about the uncertainty between two or more interpretations while vagueness is about a more intrinsic uncertainty. For example, whether to categorize artefact X as Type A or B may be ambiguous, but the assumption is often there is a correct attribution. But maybe the difference between Type A and B can never be clear cut and is inherently blurred, so in this case, the uncertainty

> relates to an intrinsic vagueness. Flohr-Sørensen points out that even if science admits ambiguity, it generally does not like vagueness: it needs clearly defined entities, attributes and processes, whereas in reality, vagueness is a real property of the world or at least our experience of it. Indeed, he argues that the very fragmentary and partial nature of archaeological remains that Gero highlighted as a central dimension of our ambiguity and which is usually seen as a limitation should be realized as an opportunity to explore vagueness as a productive aspect of past and present realities.

Archaeology as Excavation

Yet there are different ways to think about the archaeological process – but to do that, we need to recognize what is driving this idea of archaeology as a linear trajectory. When you ask almost anyone what they think about, when they think about archaeology, it will probably involve excavation. Most of the students in my university want to go on digs; some may like working with finds, but when it comes to other fieldwork like survey, few seem as enthusiastic. Excavation is a master trope of archaeology. As Julian Thomas has argued, excavation sets up a model premised on verticality and depth; we work down to get to the past, we dig deep to retrieve and understand what happened centuries and millennia ago. The excavation metaphor here is closely bundled with notions of a buried or past truth which one can also see at work in psychoanalysis and textual interpretation to get to the real meaning which is buried beneath the surface layer of memories or writing. However, it's not simply that it has almost become a metonym for the whole discipline; it also influences the way we conceptualize the archaeological process as a whole. It achieves this in a very specific way.

We have already mentioned the familiar refrain "excavation is destruction". If one takes excavation as the role model, its implicit or explicit association with destruction conjures up notions of irreversibility. Excavation is irrevocable or irreversible – one cannot go back and excavate the same site twice, not exactly and literally, even if in some senses this view can be qualified (see Box 6.3 on the unrepeatable experiment in Chapter 6). It is this irreversibility that puts a burden on the record and publication and thus helps to establish the idea of archaeology as a linear chain of events, triggered by the act of fieldwork and only completed upon publication, which acts to repay the obligation created through the destruction of a site in the wake of excavation. However, this "destruction" is never unruly – quite the contrary, it is highly organized. We try and decompose a site into its constituent elements (layers, deposits, features); we separate finds from soil and of course separate different types of finds from each other, as we discussed in the last chapter. All our fieldwork revolves around the process of physically disaggregating a continuous mass of ground into layers, cuts, flints, bones, stones and potsherds. This fragmentation continues in the post-excavation stage as the different "fragments" are then taken off by different specialists for study, each of whom will write their own specialist report.

As Andy Jones has argued though, this fragmentation is offset by another process: that of synthesis or re-connecting the fragments (Figure 4.1). This we do by connecting those layers into a stratigraphic matrix, grouping deposits or features together which seem to relate functionally or spatially, re-organizing finds by material or functional categories. In short, we reconstitute the fragments and we do this most effectively through textualization. Let's consider a typical post-excavation process; one gathers the field notes and *pro forma* sheets and starts to build a master matrix from the individual relations given on sheets; one starts to pull related textual descriptions together and build up a narrative or account of a building or site over time. The fragmentary notes are used to reconstitute a more coherent text. It is the same with images; individual plans are overlaid and co-ordinated to create "phase plans" or composite plans which are neatened up, maybe showing only selected features to create a coherent image. Whether this is done digitally or the old-fashioned way with hand-drawn plans, the process is the same. Artefact drawings are inked up, scanned (or scanned and traced on computer) and arranged on a page; photographs are touched up, cropped and reworked. You can always tell the difference between a report where someone has put effort into cleaning up images and others which more or less dump semi-processed or field images straight in. The former always looks more "finished". But perhaps more crucially, it is also at this stage that the ratio of text to image might start to shift; a field archive might contain as many images or more than text; in the report, text will start to dominate but not as much as it will do in other publications and relates to the issue of marginalization discussed earlier.

These dual processes of fragmentation and synthesis are also intimately connected to a hierarchical organization, both of knowledge and labour. For example, an excavator might be responsible for digging, recording and interpreting their layer or feature, but a supervisor will have the job of interpreting the trench or area and making sure the site is being disaggregated "correctly" as well as interpretively re-connecting all those fragments through their diary, fieldnotes or trench/

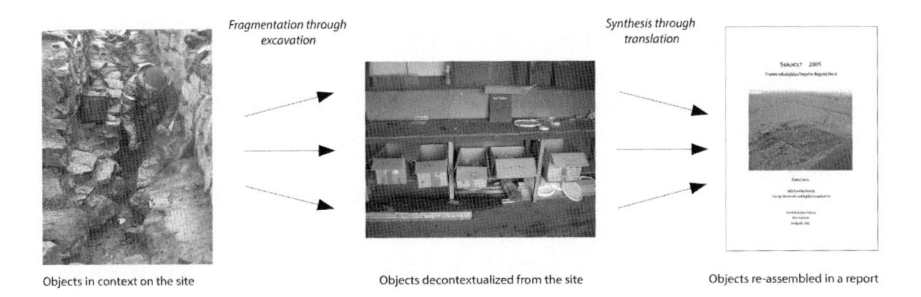

Figure 4.1 The fragmentation and synthesis of the archaeological process (adapted from Jones 2002).

area report (see discussion in Chapter 2 on the separation of intellectual and manual labour). At the apex is the site director who does the same but at the widest scale of the project itself, drawing together not only the work of the field team but also the various specialists such as zooarchaeologists, ceramic and lithic experts and so on. The role of writing plays a fundamental part of this process, especially the synthesis; specialists will attempt to create coherence and order over the bags of separated finds in their reports, just as the director will attempt to create a coherent whole from the atomized archive of notes, sheets, finds and samples through writing up the final report. This epistemological hierarchy is reproduced in a political hierarchy of labour and vocality; pick up any excavation monograph and it will usually be the director's name as the lead author or editor, with contributions by specialists and perhaps supervisors, while most of the field team are relegated to the acknowledgements. Although there are some good examples of projects which buck this trend, they are the exceptions that prove the rule.

In summary, one of the reasons we continue to view writing up as the final or end point of any archaeological project is that we take excavation as a role model for the whole archaeological process. Excavation as an irreversible act of destruction through fragmentation, where writing serves to simultaneously *atone* for and *reconstitute* the "wholeness" or "intactness" of a site which is lost through the act of excavation.

But the question we now need to ask is this: what happens if we displace excavation from its position as master trope? Even if excavation is a central part of what we do as archaeologists, it is not the only thing we do. It is not even the only kind of fieldwork we do. A lot of archaeological work does not have these qualities of destruction through fragmentation; fieldwork through remote sensing and earthwork survey or assemblage analysis can be re-enacted over and over again, on the exact same sites or material without incurring any such debt or duty because such interventions leave the stuff as it was. In this vein, Rodney Harrison has urged archaeologists to consider a different metaphor for archaeological practice, to replace excavation by surface survey as the paradigm of our working method. What Harrison means by this is an approach to fieldwork and archaeology in general which sees our work as one of moving across a surface to find connections rather than digging down to uncover buried truths – that we use the metaphor of seeing spatial connections between earthworks or finds scattered across a field, rather than vertical superposition of upper layers concealing lower ones. Harrison has argued that archaeology is less about the retrieval of buried pasts, but the exposure of contemporaneous surfaces and working within a horizontal field of assembling and re-assembling elements. Building on Harrison's distinction, we can perhaps also rethink what we mean by discovery. Discovery is also a key trope of archaeology and one linked usually to excavation, and although discovery is also a component of field surveys, given the etymology of the word, the association of discovery with exposing or revealing something covered up clearly resonates much more with excavation. However, given its common meaning of simply learning about something, discovery is in fact something that happens all the way through the archaeological process; discovery doesn't just happen in the field, it also happens when you are working on archives or finds, it happens when you are reading a journal article which enables you to make a connection. In other words, discovery too is best thought of as a lateral or horizontal process, not a vertical one of uncovering some concealed truth.

Moreover, if we adopt the "horizontal" field survey as our metaphor instead of the "vertical" excavation, the function of writing also shifts. In such contexts, because destruction through fragmentation is not an issue, closure or finality is also less of an issue; because we are not digging down, we can never get to the bottom. By staying on the surface, it is much easier to see all writing up as in effect, *interim*. The interim or provisional nature of archaeological writing in general is something the discipline has long acknowledged. All our statements or interpretations, however plausible or well-researched, remain contingent and subject to revision. The idea that any interpretation could be final, that an issue was closed or resolved, was heavily critiqued in the 1980s, and few if any archaeologists today would contest this. Even an excavation report that purports to be the final word can be re-interpreted, and the history of our discipline offers many examples. Given this, it surely makes sense then to think about the role of writing in the archaeological process as also interim – as something always "in between", "in the meantime". This may sound difficult, especially with excavation, yet new digital technologies are making this more possible while at the same time, also more complex in what Ruth Tringham has called the "afterlives" of a project.

Recent work on digital platforms for fieldwork and other project archives is suggesting a complete change in how we conceptualize the writing up of projects. Online access has certainly had a big impact on academia and scholarship as traditional print formats – whether journals or monographs – become increasingly more available in an online format, sometimes with no print version made (e.g. Internet Archaeology; https://intarch.ac.uk/). Moreover, digital dissemination and storage of so-called grey literature and even project archives has also extended the accessibility and reach of much archaeological reporting and online sites like the ADS and Digital Archaeological Record (tDAR) as discussed in the last chapter, are providing invaluable archiving services for the field. However, the transition to a digital platform for archaeological projects is more than simply about accessibility; for many archaeologists, it is also an opportunity to rethink the traditional publishing model.

At a minimum level, making archives and grey reports available online arguably circumvents the need for costly, final print publication, especially of excavation and fieldwork monographs. More fundamentally, however, by exploiting the capabilities of a digital platform for a project archive, the very need for a "final" publication becomes up for debate. A "final" publication of, say an excavation, in its traditional format could be seen to have two major drawbacks. First, no matter how detailed it will be, it will always have to summarize and condense the data; for a scholar wanting the detail, they might still have to consult the original archive. In order to address this, older monographs might have included microfiches or later CD-ROMs as appendices which would contain primary databases and technical reports. With the arrival of the internet, some may have even provided links to online databases. But in all these cases, the print format remains the primary "interface" to the project, which leads me to the second drawback. The print or published text is always the view of data as seen through the eyes of its main author(s); even if an interpretation of the site is given as a separate chapter or section at the end, it informs the structure and selection of data throughout the text. Moreover, even if the text offers multiple interpretations of the data, as a text it is static and fixed. Any further interpretations will have to be published in a separate text.

Yet by presenting one's project digitally as its primary interface, both of these drawbacks can be avoided. By using the capabilities of a digital platform to "publish" all the data, there is no need to condense or select; by drawing on the capabilities of a digital platform to organize this data in interactive and non-linear ways through hyperlinks/hypertext, multiple versions or layers of data can be offered, from condensed to primary data. A good example of this is the publication of a building in Gabii, Italy by Rachel Opitz, Marcello Mogetta and Nicola Terrenato which includes a hypertext-linked report with associated database and interactive 3D model (www.fulcrum.org/concern/monographs/n009w229r; for a different example, see Box 4.2). Moreover, being on a digital platform, any interpretations of the data can be modified, updated so that the project is never really closed but always open for new angles, fresh insights. It reinforces the ideas of interpretation as an ongoing process that, in principle at least, need never be closed. Moreover, the source of these interpretations no longer need be the preserve of the main author/excavator, because the reader has full access to the whole archive, they also have greater agency to interpreting the site in their own way, without being bound to the "official version" of the author. To an extent, a digital platform allows a DIY approach to the site report, one which subverts the epistemological and political hierarchy of the traditional print format with a vocality which privileges its lead author/director.

Box 4.2   Rigny Excavation: An Online Excavation Report

Reports of excavations are becoming more and more accessible online these days, whether through national databases like the ADS (archaeologydataservice.co.uk) or institutional websites like the Museum of London Archaeology (mola.org.uk). But in most cases, these are traditional reports which are downloadable as pdf documents and do not really exploit the capabilities of a digital medium for rethinking the excavation report. Yet one example of the latter is the excavations at the medieval settlement and church of Rigny in France, where an online interface has been built to allow the site to be presented in ways that conventional "print" media could not achieve. The project draws inspiration from French archaeologist Jean-Claude Gardin, who argued for such developments at a time when computers were only

94 *Writing Up*

just entering archaeology in the 1970s. The goal was to produce an excavation report that was both minimalist in how it conveyed the information, yet at the same time, preserved all the relationships between the data, both contextual and inferential in such a way that a reader could quickly retrieve what was needed. The diagram in Figure 4.2 shows how the "architecture" of the site works; a user can choose to read a simple narrative of the site (block 1) or opt for a more synoptic reading, which means either following the chains of reasoning used to make inferences (block 2) or examining the chronological relations between different features (block 3). All three of these rapid summaries of the site can then be explored in more detail by going into the detailed arguments which underly them (block 4), which in turn is based on the primary data, stored in a central database called *Archives du Sol* (Archives of the Soil).

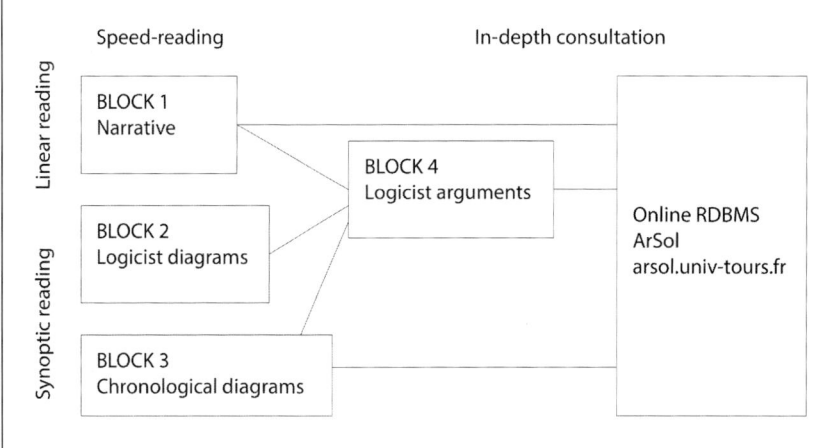

Figure 4.2 The architecture of the Rigny excavation archive (redrawn after Marlet et al. 2019).

These are of course ideal scenarios. In reality, the impact of digital publishing may not be as revolutionary. For one, very few people will actually devote the time and energy needed to go into an online archive in such detail to re-interpret a site; some will of course, but then the numbers are perhaps no greater than those who in earlier decades, would have gone back to original fieldnotes and records. People have enough to do just working through their own project data. Nonetheless, one should not dismiss the facility digital archives have to offer, especially as working with legacy archives may increasingly be a realistic option for postgraduate projects rather than generating original material. But even if such accessibility opened the floodgates to multivocal interpretation, there is another side to this we must not forget. No matter how much primary data are made available online, no matter how much multiple interpretations of such data are facilitated or made easier through a digital platform, we must not forget the lessons of the last chapter. That data remain coded in a certain way, which means it will always be pre-interpreted in a certain way. No digital or online project archive can offer raw data, because as has already been emphasized, there is no such thing. And in fact however much freedom of interpretation such an archive might claim to offer, the imprint of its producers will always put limits on that freedom.

Again, this is not to suggest there is no difference between a traditional, printed report of a project and an online archive; there clearly is and in fact calling the online archive an "archive" is misleading. The point of much of the new work is to blur or even break down the boundaries between archive and publication. These online projects are neither archive nor publication but something else altogether, something which we lack a good term or word for. Indeed, returning to the original issue of interest here, it is how digital publishing, especially of projects and project data, upsets the traditional notion of linearity in the archaeological process. By making projects fully and primarily digital, it also undercuts the notion of finality and closure of the traditional print format. But not just finality and closure; as we have seen, a digital platform also offers a different way to articulate the relation between fragmentation and synthesis. Where a traditional, print publication was supposed to offer a textual synthesis of the fieldwork data, the archive is supposed to offer that data in a more fragmented state. What these new digital platforms also do is disrupt this opposition, where both atomized data and synthesis are possible in the same medium.

All of which brings us back to the dominance of text over image. It is in these digital environments that visual data can start to take on a role that was previously suppressed and offer what has been called a multimodal publication; that is a form of publication which incorporates different types of media and modes of expression which is not possible in print format. While in traditional print publication, text dominated the medium of expression, the digital format highlights the performativity of images and indeed all data. Whether in the form of numerical tables, textual descriptions or images, data are no longer confined to a role of evidential support whose relevance is framed by the text. Now they can be active tools for reading and navigating a site. This is especially obvious in two of the more prominent digital developments, GIS and VR. With GIS, images are no longer static but dynamic, layers can be turned off and on, spatial queries and operations can be conducted because of the way image and other data forms (texts, numbers) can be worked together, where the image (as map interface) takes on the central role. With VR, although often done as a computerized version of the traditional reconstruction, increasingly it is being seen and used as a tool to explore and think about the site in a way that would previously be hard to do. In such cases, realism again, is not necessarily relevant; rather it is what opportunities it offers for interacting with and learning about the site in a new medium (Box 4.3).

There are perhaps two key aspects here to highlight. One concerns the dynamic nature of images in such a context. Both GIS and VR are *dynamic* media, where an image can change, where time becomes a key dimension. Reading and looking at images involves time too of course, and there is certainly an added complexity to this when the two are combined which often demands a back-and-forth rhythm between text and image. But with dynamic images, yet another layer of temporal complexity is added, which can be achieved even with a simple. gif. Seeing images as dynamic also questions the idea of a finished image; this has been particularly relevant in the context of reconstructions, where John Swogger has argued against the "tyranny of monumentalization". By this, he means the concern for reconstructions to be polished and perfect rather than incorporating a sense of the ephemeral; he suggests that we see reconstructions as always interim and that this can be articulated through the style of drawing. But images are not only increasingly dynamic, they are also linked to other media in a much more complex way than texts. Thus whereas a text might be accompanied by an image as in a traditional print format, images generated through GIS, for example, engage multiple media – images, texts, even video and audio. Think of Google Maps and how you can swap background maps, shift from aerial to ground views, filter for certain locations like restaurants, link to their website or when you are using Google Earth, even upload your own photos. What makes GIS so productive is that it merges what were previously different types of data and media which had to be handled separately: images, numbers and text are now all bundled together. More generally though, what the digital environment achieves is an inversion or at least a levelling of the prior dominance of text over image.

Box 4.3   Virtual Reality at Çatalhöyük

Digital 3D reconstructions of archaeological sites are becoming more common now as they not only bring a site back to life, they also allow one to fly through a site and experience it in a way that a static reconstruction can never achieve. Such forms of "telepresence" are of course familiar to us from other contexts like gaming or flight simulators, although the immersive aspect of VR in archaeology has perhaps not been too successful. Of more importance is what Colleen Morgan calls the conceptual aspect of VR, that is, using VR as a tool to "think through" the site. Adopting tools used in the popular Second Life platform, a virtual world of Çatalhöyük called Okapi Island was constructed by Ruth Tringham at the University of Berkeley to explore the potential of Second Life as exploring alternative forms of education and civic engagement. Morgan entered this world and set about doing various "virtual" tasks such as plastering the walls. In the process, all kinds of questions were raised about how the original inhabitants of the site went about their daily tasks and the experiences gained in the virtual world of Çatalhöyük could be used to understand aspects of the "real" site.

Figure 4.3 In the Virtual World of Second Life, Ruth Galileo stands on top of Okapi Island, aka the East Mound of Çatalhöyük, Turkey, surveying her team's construction in 2007–2008 of Neolithic houses (based on the South archaeological area) and, on the right, the shelter over the BACH archaeological area (image: Ruth Tringham).

For Morgan, three important conclusions could be drawn from this "experiment". First, being actively involved in the construction of the virtual world is an important part of learning; this is not something that should just be left to the computer geeks. Second, accuracy was not that important. The point of VR reconstructions is not about fidelity or tying to recreate the "lost world of Çatalhöyük" as truthfully as possible. What matters is the process, not the final product; it is what is learnt through the process of interacting with virtual materials. Third and finally, avatars matter. Just as in real life, in the virtual world, experience is altered depending on your body size, gender, what clothes you are wearing, and all of these can also be used as way to reveal how experience and understanding is always situated and framed in relation to human difference.

Although one can use GIS or VR as part of the post-excavation phase of analysis and leave them behind in favour of a traditional print-style publication, the capacity of digital publication for incorporating these kinds of programs means that the conventional lab or fieldwork report might well disappear over time and with it, the hegemony of writing. However, not all archaeological writing is about reporting the results of fieldwork or lab work. More than 30 years ago, French archaeologist Jean-Claude Gardin suggested that computers would/should transform archaeological writing (see Box 4.2), that (conventional) publications should be preserved for highly interpretive texts, syntheses and so on (which he called explanations), while all primary data collection and data-processing projects should be confined to digital archives (which he called compilations). What this means in practice is that things like excavation or fieldwork reports would slowly be phased out, that empirical studies or results of fieldwork would stop being published and journals and books would rather be more selective and focus only on more interpretive studies. To some extent, this has happened. Many journals will no longer publish site reports and only accept papers of more general relevance. On the other hand, there are still many local/regional or period-specific journals which do publish essentially site reports, and as with the genre of site monographs, they remain strong. At the same time, both kinds of texts – empirical results and interpretive essays – have been migrating onto digital and online media, so the issue of print versus digital media is perhaps not the distinction here. Rather it is about the diversity of archaeological texts, whatever their medium.

While we might question how strong a divide there should be between empirical and interpretive texts along the lines Gardin suggested (think how this relates to the discussion of interpretation and description in chapter 2), there is no denying that there is more to archaeological writing than reporting on the results of fieldwork or lab work. The whole discussion in the first half of this chapter has explored the role of writing primarily in relation to fieldwork and a linear model of the archaeological process. In the second half, we need to broaden the scope of enquiry and consider the diversity of archaeological texts and writing and particularly reflect on how different genres and styles of composition relate to archaeological knowledge.

Archaeological Texts

Archaeological Genres

How do archaeologists write? Well, you can find some books out there which will offer advice on how to do it, but our goal here is not to provide a masterclass in archaeological writing but rather to survey the field and investigate the theoretical dimensions of writing. Let us start by asking what kind of texts archaeologists produce. Perhaps the easiest examples to start with are textbooks, like the one you are reading now and those you use in other courses. Textbooks belong to a broad genre of writing, which aims to offer an overview or synthesis of current state of knowledge on a topic or branch of study. All scholars benefit from such overviews, not just students, and that is why textbooks can be seen as just a specific sub-genre within this broader type as they are often written slightly differently. Indeed, if we think of such overviews as a genre, they can differ quite radically from each other. Some can be journal articles, others edited volumes, and yet others single-authored works. They can also vary a lot in terms of how they are written; some might be more intended as reference works to be used for mining information while others might be written more in an instructional mode, with exercises and case studies. These latter are closer to the traditional idea of a textbook, especially as they are used in secondary education and first year tertiary education courses.

What emerges from this, is that a key way to think about texts is in terms of their function: what purpose are they serving, what do they do? Textbooks of course are there to help students learn the basics of a topic or branch of study and do this by providing key information/sources and examples of how to work with this information. Other archaeological texts do different things. Let's take another example, the excavation report or monograph which we discussed in the last section. This is one of the most paradigmatic genres of archaeology, not surprisingly given the paradigmatic role fieldwork – especially excavation – has in defining the discipline. But what does the excavation monograph do? What function does it perform? At a rather obvious level, it presents the results of fieldwork – it is a report on what was found and what it means. Like overviews, excavation reports can appear as journal articles, books and even edited volumes. In terms of its function, the form in which it appears is not relevant so long as that form has a primarily written character. With the migration of such genres to a digital and online platform however, this written character is changing as we discussed, and as such, as a genre, the excavation monograph might conceivably disappear to be replaced by a website.

Besides overviews and fieldwork reports, there are of course still other genres in archaeology and here, I will just mention one more: the case study. Case studies, like overviews, are a common genre across many disciplines and might be broadly defined as a focused study of a particular place, object or type of thing from which broader conclusions are made – or implied. As such, a case study might draw on an excavation report (e.g. it might focus on one excavated site), but it is not the same kind of text as the excavation report. Where an excavation report will go into detail about the features, stratigraphy and finds, for example, a case study will summarize this and focus on aspects which relate to a more interpretive or thematic question. For example, I used a site I had excavated to work through issues of periodization and time; this was a case study because the focus is not so much on the specific site as the issue or problem which the site is used to illustrate. A case study is, in effect, a way of working through a problem by taking a single example. As such, one might contrast case studies with comparative studies, where the goal is to look for similarities and differences in multiple data sets or cases in order to identify broader patterns. Comparative studies often – though not necessarily – use statistical means to achieve this. However, the line between case studies and comparative studies might not always be clear, though often a hard distinction is made between the in-depth, concrete analysis of a single case in the former and a more abstract, comparative analysis of multiple cases in the latter.

These examples don't exhaust all the possible genres of archaeological writing, and furthermore as we saw in the last example, sometimes the distinction between them might not be very sharp. Fieldwork reports can blur with case studies, while

100 *Writing Up*

```
Disciplinary core ← | Overviews (e.g. textbooks, topical reviews, period/area syntheses) | Reports (e.g. excavation monographs, lab reports) | Case studies (e.g. thematic monographs or papers) | → Disciplinary cutting edge
```

Figure 4.4 Principal genres in archaeology and their relation to disciplinary knowledge.

case studies might incorporate overviews and so on. Like always, reality is always messier than the tidy categories we try and impose upon it. But thinking about writing in terms of genres is still helpful because it helps us to focus on what it is a text is trying to do. Different texts serve different functions, and it is important to recognize this in relation to how we go on to understand their role in the production of disciplinary knowledge and identity. So let's revisit the three genres just discussed and think about what role they perform in light of this issue (Figure 4.4).

The overview – whether in the form of a textbook or a publication intended for peers – has a critical role to play in the reproduction of the discipline and disciplinary knowledge. As a survey of the state of knowledge, it acts to codify and legitimize a specific range of topics, concepts, methods and facts. It tells the student and scholar, that this is what the discipline is – and by implication *ought to be* – working on. There is a usually implicit normative or prescriptive dimension to overviews insofar as, while they purport to try and describe the state of art on a particular field, they also inevitably help define it too. The distinction between these two is blurred and in fact in many ways, they are simply two sides of the same coin. But given that, it is thus important to understand that no matter how comprehensive a textbook or review is, it will always be selective, not only in terms of what it includes and excludes but also in terms of how it structures and organizes this overview. Different approaches will result in foregrounding and marginalizing different things; as an example, just compare different textbooks on archaeological theory. Indeed, the less consensus there is on a topic or within a discipline, the more variability there is likely to be between such textbooks or reviews, though on the whole, the less consensus there is, the less likely a textbook or review will exist in the first place.

Moving next to the field report (or lab report), this also plays a critical role in archaeology but somewhat differently to the overview. These texts are in a sense, the discipline's primary sources, its empirical foundation, much like manuscripts and official documents are for historians. Of course, one could argue that the field notes and remains themselves are primary, but few of us can examine these original sources ourselves, due to limitations on time, funding and access. These reports thus frequently become the primary sources for other genres like overviews and case studies. Indeed, the field and lab reports offer a more processed version of these sources, one that is more immediately usable. If I want to know about the ceramics from a site, it will be a lot quicker and (usually) better to go to the ceramic report than back to the bags of pottery, especially if I am not a ceramic specialist. In a sense, the field or lab report acts as a kind of eyewitness or expert testimony in a trial; they are documents that implicitly embody a pledge that these data are real, that it took the form it did and that you can trust it. We all know the common picture of science is one where you are supposed to trust nothing, to test everything and be critical of everything; but no scientist can be there to observe or participate in all experiments, just as no archaeologist can take part in all excavations. As a discipline, we work on trust: trust in our colleagues and in the veracity of their reports which present field or lab data. This is one of the reasons why field reports are also so focused on detail and convention; such trust needs to be embedded in protocols that we all follow. This should not prevent us from questioning field or lab reports, especially if we see the protocols have not been followed or if there is ambiguity in the results. Indeed, occasionally we do "go back to the original", and so another important quality of these reports – and academic scholarship in general – is traceability: the ability to re-trace the path from the ground to the page. But like overviews, such reports act in a way to legitimize aspects of the discipline, particularly its working methods and the form its primary sources should take; even if our field or lab notes might constitute the actual primary record, they may not be something we can easily share with the discipline, even if we want to – which of course we should. Moreover, although such primary records can be perfectly respectable, they can also be messy, incoherent and incomplete. As we saw in the last section, the original archive remains fragmentary; it needs ordering, cleaning so that it can act as a reliable witness, one you can trust.

Finally, we turn to case studies. In many ways, these embody the cutting edge of the field, the explorers, texts which work at the frontiers or edges of the discipline. They seek to tackle a pre-existing problem or issue or raise a new idea or topic that has not been addressed before. This is not to say that all case studies are ground-breaking, radical or revolutionary; just that on the whole, they tend not to work on topics for which there is widespread consensus. Rather than legitimize current methods, forms of data and knowledge, case studies seek to legitimize a future or potential direction for the discipline. If case studies are successful, they generate more research and papers and collect followers and imitators; if not, they tend to wither away and are forgotten. A good case study thus acts as an exemplar or model solution to a problem, one which other scholars pick up and work with or develop in new directions themselves. But what makes a successful case study? This is not easy to define, but one of the common pitfalls of a poor case study is where the relation between the general issue and concrete example is ill-fitting. A common critique, for example, of theoretical case study papers is that while they might outline the theoretical framework and issues beautifully, when they come to give an archaeological example to illustrate the theory, it falls flat. It doesn't quite live up to the promise or hype in the first part of the paper. More general critiques of case studies have been made from within the social sciences which touch on the same issue of relationality; indeed, some have even argued that you cannot make generalizations from case studies, that at most they offer food for thought, initial ideas for subsequent development. But this is fundamentally to mistake the nature of generalization that case studies make. It is to evaluate the case study as if it was a comparative study, where generalization is purely a quantitative process that gathers credit through the power of numbers. But qualitative generalization is still possible through a single example – the trick is choosing the right example. Or, to put this more symmetrically, what makes a good case study is that the example selected to explore an issue, "gels" with the problem so fresh and productive insight on the problem emerges.

What I have tried to get across in this brief survey of archaeological genres of writing is that different texts perform different jobs in relation to the formation of disciplinary knowledge and identity. At one end, you have overviews including textbooks which act to legitimate the current consensual or mainstream views around a topic or branch of study. At the other end, you have case studies which work on the frontiers of disciplinary knowledge, attempting to forge new directions for the discipline. In between, you have field and lab reports; on the one hand, these legitimize current standards and protocols of empirical research, on the other, they present new data and results which can feed into case studies. What this sketch depicts is an image of a discipline with a stable core (overviews and reports) which changes only slowly, surrounded by a more dynamic outer layer (monographs and case studies). But this dynamic outer layer is in fact much richer than I have portrayed here and tying a text down to a genre is not always obvious – or satisfying. In many ways one needs to go deeper into the process of writing to see this richness, which includes more creative aspects like the use of fiction and narrative, dialogues and conversations. In short, we need to explore the world of archaeological composition.

Archaeological Composition

In the last section, we explored some different genres of archaeological writing and related them to the function they served within the discipline, especially in connection to the consolidation or creation of archaeological knowledge. In this section, we will delve even deeper into the question of how archaeological texts are related to the production of knowledge by examining a different facet of them, namely their composition. One can assess a text in many different ways: how enjoyable or boring it is, how easy or hard it is to follow, but in terms of archaeological writing, and scholarly or scientific writing in general, arguably a key outcome is that you want the reader to find what you are saying believable. Whether the reader likes or agrees with what you are saying is another matter; at least it has to have a degree of plausibility. Plausibility is certainly aided by following certain conventions; as we suggested earlier, conventions engender trust because it suggests you are operating under the same rules as your reader. With all archaeological texts, we usually expect a certain minimum in terms of convention in scholarly writing: proper referencing, correct use of language and grammar, clarity and originality of expression and so on. All the kinds of things a teacher expects of student essays and other written projects and also peers expect of their colleagues when they submit papers and books for publication. Sloppy and inconsistent citations, poor grammar and plagiarism are all issues that are important and common to all academic writing. But many of these things are not as straightforward as they first appear and that is what I will be exploring in this section.

For example, if you were to open a book or journal paper and see lots of graphs and tables with quantitative data, what might that tell you? Does it perhaps give an impression that this is a very scientific text? Similarly, if you turn to another example and see only text, perhaps with the occasional photograph, what kind of unconscious expectations might you have of the kind of paper it will be? One crude but not entirely inaccurate way of looking at this is to see how different traditions of working with archaeological material affect the type of writing and vice versa. For example, we might make a rough distinction between what are called STEM disciplines and their associated publications and those produced in the humanities. The STEM disciplines include (natural) science, technology, engineering and mathematics while the humanities include history, literature and philosophy. As we shall see, archaeology typically straddles this divide, often uncomfortably so (see Chapter 7).

STEM texts tend to be journal articles and multi-authored (reflecting the teamwork in labs); they are heavy on methodology and usually are peppered with quantitative and statistical data, usually in the form of tables and graphs. They also tend to be fairly short texts. Humanities texts on the other hand are often much longer as journal articles (and more commonly produce books), are single-authored and tend to stress more the theoretical context than methodology. They also put greater stress on textual sources, which is why their bibliographies are also often much longer. Now of course this is somewhat of a caricature, especially as it applies to archaeology and some social sciences where the division is much more blurred. Not only do you see both styles of publication (even in the same journal), sometimes you see both styles mixed within the same paper or book. Nevertheless, many archaeologists will lean more towards the STEM side, while others are more comfortable in the humanities, and as a rough division, it still has some value. Even if the divide is somewhat artificial, one would be hard pushed to say it has no basis in reality; just think about how the education system continues to perpetuate these two channels as a fork in the road as one moves through secondary and into tertiary education.

Whatever kind of shadow this old division between science and humanities still casts on our discipline today, there is no intrinsic reason why our writing should feel the need to perpetuate this divide. In many ways, we should consider it a challenge and novelty to explore and experiment with forms of writing that try to break free of it, to relish the diversity of our materials and find ways for them to work together. In the following sections, we will look at composition in less polarized way and address a number of different dimensions common to all texts: standpoint, mode of address, citation and imagery.

Standpoint

To begin, consider what we might call standpoint or point of view. From what position is the text written? Many academic texts are written in the third person and passive voice. For example, consider this sentence: "The dating of this feature was based both on C14 and the typological characteristics of associated finds". The archaeologist is absent from this statement, it is rather presented as matter of fact, attributable to no one in particular. As students, you may have been told to avoid or limit the use of the first person (e.g. "I think that . . .") in your essays and this is because a lot of academic writing wants to promote and encourage a detached, impersonal point of view. It does this because such detachment helps to create a sense of neutrality, an absence of bias and thus give the impression of being more credible. At the same time though, all academic writing has identifiable authors which partly contradicts the rhetoric of detachment. Indeed, often the credibility of a text is enhanced by knowledge of who the author is; in older antiquarian accounts, one sees this connection made more explicit as the text is more commonly written in the first person and active voice, especially when dealing with reports of fieldwork or observations. The credibility of these reports is bound up with the status of the witness and so who is talking has a bearing on how believable it is. Under contemporary academic norms, we aspire to sever that link, illustrated, for example, in the process of blind reviews; but the fact is, the status of the author inevitably influences the reception of texts.

But adopting the first person and active voice is not simply a matter of "owning up" to authorship; it is also about acknowledging the concrete connection you, as the author, have, towards the material you are discussing. Writing a description of an excavation in the first person underlines the role you played in that work. Moreover, the difference between the first person/active voice and third person/passive voice standpoints is caught up in the ambiguities around our attitude to our data. On the one hand, we recognize that what makes an expert or specialist credible is their deep familiarity with their subject matter. They know it intimately and such proximity is regarded an epistemic virtue. What gave Gordon Childe his command over European prehistory was that he was writing about things he had first-hand knowledge of. His syntheses were based on hours, days and weeks spent in museums and collections around Europe. He knew his stuff, as we would say today. Yet he still mostly wrote about it in the third person. And he did so because paradoxically, distance and detachment was also an epistemic virtue; appearing too close could suggest bias, blinkered vision, a lack of objectivity. Ultimately, there is no simple equation here between standpoint and a proper scientific attitude. The tension between intimacy and detachment towards one's data should perhaps be seen as a productive one, rather than a problem; we need both, and the trick is making them work in a way that enhances our disciplinary goals.

Mode of Address

Another aspect of composition relates to the way it structures our understanding of the archaeological object. For many, language might be seen as a neutral medium for communicating about or representing reality. Yet during the later 1980s and 1990s, archaeologists grappled with the problem of what has been called a "crisis of representation", where issues of how language was not a neutral medium for representing reality but rather structured that reality. Much of this debate was played out through the concept of **narrative**, which sometimes was taken to refer to a particular style of writing common to the humanities, and sometimes inflated to refer to all kinds of writing, from site reports to historical fiction. Some archaeologists suggested that the particular mode of writing actually dominated and determined representations of the past, either through its particular style of rhetoric or because it followed a basic plot form. Misia Landau's famous analysis of early twentieth century accounts of human evolution showed how they followed a classic form of the European folktale: within an initial state of calm (pre-human ancestors living in the trees), a different future is anticipated for the main character or "hero" (pre-humans were different from other primates); then something happens to alter the calm (environmental or evolutionary change) resulting in the hero leaving (humans leave their forest to spread out over the globe). This journey includes various tests and trials (predators, extreme environments) over which the hero triumphs through the acquisition of special powers (intelligence) to find their true self (civilization). Even if we are sceptical that most archaeological accounts cannot be so easily mapped onto a fairy-tale structure like this, there are more simple plot structures that do often match our accounts, such as the three-stage rise, peak and decline of empires or "cultures".

One of the problems that such approaches faced, however, was that the discussion inevitably got tangled up with the extent to which any archaeological narrative was fictional and therefore raised the problem how any notion of truth or credibility could be maintained. Such problems can be avoided if we pull back from seeing all writing as a form of narrative and acknowledge that narrative is just one form of writing among others and that even narrative itself incorporates quite diverse genres. Traditionally, for example, composition studies recognizes four different types of writing: narration, description, exposition and argument (Figure 4.5). This classification is based, for some scholars at least, on what a text intends to do. It defines a text by its performative function, and as a result, this alters the way a text is written and the conventions it uses. Texts are, after all, media of communication, and just as we can use different modes of address to each other (lecturing, conversing, imploring, commanding), so in archaeology we can use different modes of writing to communicate with the reader. Narrative, for example, is defined by its intention to tell a story – it has events and actors and a plot which unfolds over time. An argument on the other hand is better defined by its advocacy of a claim or thesis: it provides justifications or warrants, it offers up evidence. Because of these differences, each kind of text also carries somewhat different sets of epistemic criteria for "truthfulness"; that is, you cannot judge a narrative on the same criteria you would an argument or vice versa.

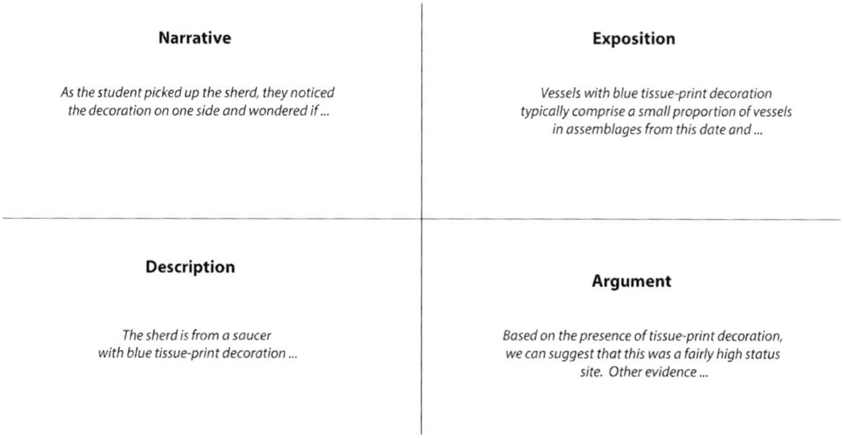

Narrative	Exposition
As the student picked up the sherd, they noticed the decoration on one side and wondered if ...	Vessels with blue tissue-print decoration typically comprise a small proportion of vessels in assemblages from this date and ...
Description	**Argument**
The sherd is from a saucer with blue tissue-print decoration ...	Based on the presence of tissue-print decoration, we can suggest that this was a fairly high status site. Other evidence ...

Figure 4.5 Principal modes of address in writing with hypothetical examples.

Archaeology makes use of all four types (and no doubt, more), and reducing all archaeological writing to forms of narrative is very limiting. A report on C14 calibration curves is hardly the same kind of text as a theoretical reflection on agency. In this textbook, I make use of all modes of address; the vignettes which start each chapter, for example, use fictional narrative to create a concrete and relatable situation, but one which has implications which are drawn out in the rest of the chapter through exposition, description and argument as well as autobiographical narratives of my own experiences in archaeology. Moreover, even within the narrative form, there is important variation. For example, there is a great difference between a fictionalized narrative such as that Janet Spector used to great effect in her study on an awl found at an archaeological site linked to the Eastern Dakota/Sioux tribe and Carmel Schrire's autobiographical approach to writing about her excavations of a Dutch colonial outpost in South Africa. Only one of these purports to be fictional in the sense we ordinarily understand it yet both are narratives. Creating fictional narratives can be a very productive way to engage with the archaeology, but so can an autobiographical narrative. There is also a great difference between narratives that appear in the medium of print and text and are fixed, and narratives that emerge through the interaction of the "reader" and the "text", as in, for example, Ruth Tringham's recombinant histories which are based on "users" creating their own narrative through their navigation of a website or in museums and heritage sites (see Box 4.4). Arguably, archaeological gaming is also all about the user-creation of a narrative. The museum visitor, the web-browser or the gamer are all creating or interacting with forms of narrative in the way they navigate through these spaces, especially if they are designed for such immersive engagement. In all of these narrative examples, the nature of truth is configured differently and perhaps more to the point, archaeological writing is never about representing the past but rather about (re-)presencing it. Clearly most texts are referring to things absent for the reader – stone tools, building remains, living communities. But if we see writing as a form of presencing these things, rather than representing them, then we also shift our perspective on how such texts might be evaluated.

Box 4.4   Storytelling on the Acropolis

It is almost ironic that most of the time, archaeologists are communicating about things through the medium of texts and images – especially to each other and to their students, when museums are full of actual stuff. But even museums make use of text and images and today, of course, digital media are becoming ever more important through interactive screens, personal audio guides and so on. Just having cases of objects on their own would not satisfy most visitors, who come to museums wanting to engage with its exhibits but need guidance. One of the most fruitful ways to provide this guidance is through storytelling. An innovative and experimental project was developed at the Acropolis Museum in Athens among others in Europe by using interactive digital technology to develop this idea in exciting ways.

The CHESS project (Cultural Heritage Experiences through Socio-personal interactions and Storytelling) aimed to enhance visitor's experiences at museums and cultural heritage sites in two ways. First, by personalizing the information about objects and displays to the specific visitor or group. Museums have for a long time now confronted the problems of being elitist or serving a small section of society; recognizing the diversity of its visitors was an important element of what became known as the New Museology from the latter part of the twentieth century. But catering to such diversity is not always easy, which is where the personalization that digital technologies allow, opens up huge potential. The second way in which digital technology is used is to maintain or revive a sense of wonder and discovery in the museum visit. Most of us have probably experienced museum fatigue, where gazing at endless cases and exhibits soon dulls our senses and exhausts our spirit. Keeping the visitor engaged is another key challenge for most curators. How can digital technologies help tackle these two challenges?

Based on research, the CHESS project identified six "visitor types" or persona, defined by certain characteristics. In addition, there were five key topics based on the museum exhibits, such as "animals and monsters" or "gods and humans". Storytellers then crafted narratives around these topics, tailoring it to the characteristics of the individual persona. On (or even before) arriving at the museum, the visitor fills out a questionnaire which will identify their persona; from then on, using a pad or smartphone, they are guided around the museum by an audio narration (or textual for the hearing-impaired) with interactive multimedia links. The potential for both addressing the diversity of visitors and keeping them engaged will probably always be a challenge for museums, but using digital technology by connecting storytelling to the walking path of a visitor through a museum is clearly one fruitful way to meet this challenge.

Another good example of this is from Poland at a recent exhibition called *Treasures of Peru: The Royal Tomb at Castillo de Huarmey*; this exploited one of the key aspects of archaeology – discovery – by creating in one of the exhibition rooms a series of boxes and wooden structure set up to resemble the mud-brick architecture of the site. Visitors climb into the structure, as into the tomb and search for QR codes that would link them to information about the site. As Monika Stobiecka points out, this double process of physical searching in the boxes and structure and virtual searching through digital content captures the spirit of archaeology for many people: "What could be a better means to show archaeology than to motivate the public to uncover artifacts and information?" For Stobiecka, exhibitions like this challenge us to exploit the full capabilities of digital technologies in rethinking storytelling in museums, especially when in so many cases, the use of digital media simply reproduces older, analogue forms of narrative.

Citation

The third element of composition I want to discuss is citation: the various sources cited by a text in its notes and bibliography. Superficially, citation shows you have done your homework – that you are quoting all the relevant literature and thus it exhibits your scholarly credentials. In many ways, this function dominates a lot of academic work, even if it is perhaps more implicit than explicit. At a deeper level though, thorough and exhaustive citation is an acknowledgement of one's dependence on other people's work, that archaeology, like any discipline, is a communal enterprise and you couldn't say what you are saying in a text without relying on this prior work. As a form of acknowledgement, it also helps the reader situate your own text with respect to others, avoiding potential charges of plagiarism. But more importantly, in acknowledging other's work, you are drawing on the credibility of sources which have already been "approved" by the discipline insofar as they have been published and using that credibility to enhance the reception of your own work. This does not imply such citation is purely for show; some citations will do this, but when they work honestly, they are citing another text as a means of helping to validate a point without having to reinvent the wheel and thus enable discussion to move forward. A text which cites an excavation report or lab analysis is using this citation as a shorthand to show that you can trust assertions or statements made, because these statements are backed up by other texts which you can consult. Similarly, a text which cites a theoretical or philosophical work is using that to support its usage of a concept or theory in the context of its own discussion. Citations are like chains of custody – they allow you to follow the credibility of statements (should you choose) by going back to a (usually) more detailed source.

Yet citation practice also reveals the politicization of knowledge, for *who* you cite and who the discipline *expects* you to cite are caught up in contemporary valuations of authority. Zoe Todd, an indigenous (Métis) anthropologist from Canada, has described her concern over the way the scientific discourse of climate change and human-environmental relations is a closed circle of scholars citing each other and Euro-western academic traditions, ignoring the rich vein of indigenous ideas and knowledge. Similar criticisms have been made within feminist positions for a long time, about how mainly male archaeologists or scholars might dominate a bibliography and how something as seemingly "marginal" as citation actually carries quite central, political and epistemological implications. Todd's critique, however, raises even deeper problems. For even though a lot of contemporary archaeological and anthropological theory might foreground indigenous ideas, such as the "ontological turn" and the recent interest in animism as discussed in Chapter 3, it still runs the risk of marginalizing indigenous voices because it appropriates and repackages these ideas for an academic audience. It uses such ideas as a well or resource upon which to draw; rather than actually engaging with and citing indigenous scholars, we cite their "Euro-western" interpreters. The politics of citation are evident everywhere, and so you should look at the reading lists attached to the chapters of this book and ask yourself what my citation practices tell you. You can be sure there is clearly a bias towards Anglo-American authors but maybe others too.

Imagery

The fourth and final aspect of composition I want to discuss is the non-textual aspect of a text, an issue that we also raised at the beginning of this chapter. Graphs, diagrams, plans, photographs and statistical summaries are all examples of in-text features which, though sometimes can be purely decorative, are usually meant to lend support or credibility to statements within the text. They are like little windows into the primary research and work that might lie behind a text, acting to condense or presence aspects of that primary research and show that what you are saying is based on actual research. In one sense, they act a bit like citations discussed in the last section, but there is a difference. This role of visual and numerical imagery as a kind of evidential support is something we raised earlier in the chapter; we also pointed out that in such a role, images tend to be relegated to a secondary position vis-à-vis text as they are there as supporting cast, not the principal actors – even if their role is nonetheless vital. Yet many archaeologists have argued for giving images a more central role, and while we have discussed some of the ways in which this is achieved through digital platforms and field reports, in terms of more traditional print publications this has taken a different direction.

Here, the function of the photo essay is perhaps the most important. Photo essays are "texts" which are essentially dominated by a series of photographs or montages with minimal textual input which occurs in the form of an introduction and sometimes text embedded within the image (in contrast to the usual form of embedding images within text). The whole point of foregrounding images is to resist the quality of indexicality I discussed previously. As many archaeologists have argued, rather than see photographs as representative or indexical of something – a site, an artefact – we regard them rather as actual material presences or traces of a place or event. Photography then becomes not a mode of documentation, but a mode of presencing and its effects are not to be measured by their fidelity of representation but their power of evocation. This clearly resonates with what we pointed out previously in relation to the nature of certain forms of writing such as description and narration. Moreover, to read visual essays may require a different sensitivity; you need to flick a mental switch and engage with them in quite different ways. Indeed, rather than think of them as texts at all, it is more helpful to relate them to your experience of visiting a site or museum, which in a similar way offers up a montage of images and texts.

Although photo essays are perhaps the most well-known genre, appearing in otherwise conventional journals and books, there are other formats used by archaeologists such as the cartoon strip while other examples such as the conference poster or infographic has been around a long time. In short, although traditional text remains the dominant form of material dissemination in archaeology, the importance and function of images cannot be ignored, and as I have discussed throughout this chapter, images remain in constant tension with text in terms of their positioning. As always, there is no right or wrong here; diversity is what matters.

For our student with writer's block in the vignette which opened this chapter, the problem was eventually solved when she recalled what started her on this journey: an old man who visited the site where they had found several iron fishhooks regaled the digging crew with fishing stories from when he was a boy. She realized she had her own story to tell, one that connected fishhooks to fishbones, fishbones to food, and food to communities. Outlining the structure of the paper on her blank word document, the elements of the plot, the major characters suddenly started to come together with ease, as she shifted between pdfs of journal papers, the excel file of her data tables and graphs, and jpegs of the excavation and artefacts. As her fingers typed, she paused for a moment to wonder how on earth people did all this before computers.

Exercises

1. Compare a website and a traditional printed monograph of an archaeological project; discuss the pros and cons of each.
2. Look through some journal papers or books in your library and try and identify what archaeological genre they belong to; also try to identify particular styles of composition such as narrative or exposition. Is there any relation between the style of composition and the genre?

3. Using an object as a foil, divide into groups and make a short presentation about it, each group using one of the four major modes of composition (narration, description, exposition and argument).
4. Look at the bibliographies of a paper and see if there is any gender or other bias in the ratio of authors. Can you say anything about the topic or type of paper based solely on its citations?

Further Reading

Writing and the Archaeological Process

For a critique of the general marginalization of images in favour of text, see Cochrane and Russell (2007). For a general discussion of closure in interpretation and the issue of ambiguity and vagueness, see Gero (2007), Sørensen (2015) and Marila (2017). On "merchants of doubt", see Oreskes and Conway (2010). On the dominant trope of excavation as guiding the archaeological process, see Harrison (2011), while issues of surface and depth are discussed in Thomas (2004, chapter 7). Andy Jones discussion of fragmentation and synthesis can be found in Jones (2002, esp. chapter 3). A discussion of the role of digital media on excavation reporting can be found in Buccellati (2017, esp. Part IV) although the seminal work of Jean-Claude Gardin (1980) remains deeply relevant. For the Gardin-inspired example of Rigny, see Marlet et al. (2019), while for the Gabii house project, see Opitz et al. (2016). For an early, pioneering work using hypertext (or "living text") in archaeology to encourage active reading, see Holtorf (2000–2008), while an important paper exploring the interpretive potential of hypertext in a feminist context, see Joyce and Tringham (2007). On the digital afterlives of projects, see Tringham (in press). The role of VR in archaeology is explored both by Morgan (2009) and Harrison (2009), while John Swogger's discussion of reconstruction drawings can be found in Swogger (2000).

Archaeological Texts

For a discussion of genres in archaeology and writing in general, see Lucas (2019, especially chapter 3). The case study as a particular genre is discussed in more detail by Lucas and Olsen (2022) while for its contrast to the comparative study, see Ribeiro (2019). For standpoint, Hodder's (1989) discussion of the historical changes in writing site reports remains a seminal text, while for narrative, the key text is Pluciennik (1999). Joyce (2002) addresses both standpoint and narrative in her major work on the languages of archaeology, which foregrounds dialogue. For more recent discussions of narrative, see van Dyke and Bernbeck (2015), Lucas (2019) and van Helden and Witcher (2020). For the examples of narrative plots in archaeology, see Landau (1991) and Rudebeck (1996); for examples of diversity in narrative in archaeology, compare Spector (1993), Schrire (1995) and Tringham (2015). For the failures and possibilities of digital storytelling in museums, see Copplestone and Dunne (2017). The CHESS project discussed in Box 4.5 is presented by Pujol et al. (2012), while Stobiecka's study of the Polish exhibition can be found in Stobiecka (2020). Lucas (2019, chapter 4) discusses different modes of address in archaeology. For the issues around citation from an indigenous and feminist perspective, see Todd (2016). Seminal work on traditional conventions of archaeological illustration was established by Moser (1998, 2012, 2014), while general reflections on visual media include Perry (2015) and Shanks and Webmoor (2010) and Opgenhaffen (2021). Useful collected volumes include Molyneaux (1997) and Smiles and Moser (2005). For photography, see Shanks (1997), Shanks and Svabo (2013), Hamilakis et al. (2009), McFadyen and Hicks (2020); for artefact drawing, see Lopes (2009). On the notion of "presencing" instead of representing in photographs, see Hamilakis et al. (2009) and Pétursdóttir and Olsen (2014), while in relation to writing, see Olsen and Pétursdóttir (2021).

References

Buccellati, G. 2017. *A Critique of Archaeological Reason. Structural, Digital, and Philosophical Aspects of the Excavated Record*. Cambridge: Cambridge University Press.

Cochrane, A. & I. Russell. 2007. Visualizing Archaeologies: A Manifesto. *Cambridge Archaeological Journal* 17(1): 3–19.

Copplestone, T. & D. Dunne. 2017. Digital Media, Creativity, Narrative Structure and Heritage. *Internet Archaeology* 44. https://doi.org/10.11141/ia.44.2.

Gardin, J-C. 1980. *Archaeological Constructs. An Aspect of Theoretical Archaeology*. Cambridge: Cambridge University Press.

Gero, J. 2007. Honoring Ambiguity/Problematizing Certitude. *Journal of Archaeological Method and Theory* 14: 311–27.

Hamilakis, Y., A. Anagnostopoulos & F. Ifantidis. 2009. Postcards from the Edge of Time: Archaeology, Photography, Archaeological Ethnography (a Photo Essay). *Public Archaeology* 8(2–3): 283–309.

Harrison, R. 2009. Excavating Second Life. Cyber-archaeologists, Heritage and Virtual Communities. *Journal of Material Culture* 14(1): 75–106.

Harrison, R. 2011. Surface Assemblages. Towards an Archaeology in and of the Present. *Archaeological Dialogues* 18(2): 141–61.

Hodder, I. 1989. Writing Archaeology: Site Reports in Context. *Antiquity* 63: 268–74.

Holtorf, C. 2000–2008. *Monumental Past: The Life-histories of Megalithic Monuments in Mecklenburg-Vorpommern (Germany)*. Electronic Monograph. University of Toronto: Centre for Instructional Technology Development. http://hdl.handle.net/1807/245.

Jones, A. 2002. *Archaeological Theory and Scientific Practice*. Cambridge: Cambridge University Press.

Joyce, R. 2002. *The Languages of Archaeology. Dialogues, Narrative and Writing*. Oxford: Blackwells.

Joyce, R. & R. Tringham. 2007. Feminist Adventures in Hypertext. *Journal of Archaeological Method and Theory* 14(3): 328–58.

Landau, M. 1991. *Narratives of Human Evolution: The Hero Story*. New Haven: Yale University Press.

Lopes, D. 2009. Drawing in a Social Science: Lithic Illustration. *Perspectives on Science* 17: 5–25.

Lucas, G. 2019. *Writing the Past. Knowledge and Literary Production in Archaeology.* London: Routledge.
Lucas, G. & B. Olsen. 2022. The Case Study in Archaeological Theory. *American Antiquity* 87(2): 352–67.
Marila, M. 2017. Vagueness and Archaeological Interpretation: A Sensuous Approach to Archaeological Knowledge Formation Through Finds Analysis. *Norwegian Archaeological Review* 50(1): 66–88.
Marlet, O., E. Zadora-Rio, P-Y. Buard, B. Markhoff & X. Rodier. 2019. The Archaeological Excavation Report of Rigny: An Example of an Interoperable Logicist Publication. *Heritage* 2: 761–73.
McFadyen, L. & D. Hicks (eds.). 2020. *Archaeology and Photography. Time, Objectivity and Archive.* London: Bloomsbury.
Molyneaux, B. (ed.). 1997. *The Cultural Life of Images: Visual Representation in Archaeology.* London: Routledge.
Morgan, C. 2009. (Re)Building Çatalhöyük: Changing Virtual Reality in Archaeology. *Archaeologies* 5(3): 468–87.
Moser, S. 1998. *Ancestral Images. The Iconography of Human Antiquity.* Ithaca, New York: Cornell University Press.
Moser, S. 2012. Archaeological Visualisation: Early Artifact Illustration and the Birth of the Archaeological Image. In I. Hodder (ed.), *Archaeological Theory Today* (2nd edition). Polity Press, pp. 292–322.
Moser, S. 2014. Making Expert Knowledge Through the Image: Antiquarian Images and Early Modern Scientific Illustration. *Isis* 105(1): 58–99.
Olsen, B. & Þ. Pétursdóttir. 2021. Writing Things After Discourse. In B. Olsen, M. Burstrom, C. DeSilvey & Þ. Pétursdóttir (eds.), *After Discourse. Things, Affects, Ethics.* London: Routledge, pp. 23–41.
Opgenhaffen, L. 2021. Visualizing Archaeologists: A Reflexive History of Visualization Practice in Archaeology. *Open Archaeology* 7: 353–77.
Opitz, R., M. Mogetta & N. Terrenato. 2016. *A Mid- Republican House from Gabii* (Final edition of epub, 2018). Ann Arbor: University of Michigan Press. Doi:10.3998/mpub.9231782.
Oreskes, N. & E. Conway. 2010. *Merchants of Doubt.* New York: Bloomsbury.
Perry, S. 2015. Crafting Knowledge with (Digital) Visual Media in Archaeology. In R. Chapman & A. Wylie (eds.), *Material Evidence. Learning from Archaeological Practice.* London: Routledge, pp. 189–210.
Pétursdóttir, Þ. & B. Olsen. 2014. Imaging Modern Decay: The Aesthetics of Ruin Photography. *Journal of Contemporary Archaeology* 1(1): 7–23.
Plucienik, M. 1999. Archaeological Narratives and Other Ways of Telling. *Current Anthropology* 40: 653–78.
Pujol, L., M. Roussou, S. Poulo, O. Balet, M. Vayanou & Y. Ioannidis. 2012. Personalizing Interactive Digital Storytelling in Archaeological Museums: The CHESS project. *40th Annual Conference of Computer Applications and Quantitative Methods in Archaeology (CAA)*, Southampton, UK, 26–29 March, pp. 77–90.
Ribeiro, A. 2019. Science, Data, and Case Studies Under the Third Science Revolution. *Current Swedish Archaeology* 27: 115–32.
Rudebeck, E. 1996. Heroes and Tragic Figures in the Transition to the Neolithic: Exploring Images of the Human Being in Archaeological Texts. *Journal of European Archaeology* 4: 55–86.
Schrire, C. 1995. *Digging Through Darkness. Chronicles of an Archaeologist.* Charlottesville: University Press of Virginia.

Shanks, M. 1997. Photography and Archaeology. In B. Molyneaux (ed.), *The Cultural Life of Images: Visual Representation in Archaeology*. London: Routledge, pp. 73–107.

Shanks, M. & C. Svabo. 2013. Archaeology and Photography: A Pragmatology. In A. González Ruibal (ed.), *Reclaiming Archaeology: Beyond the Tropes of Modernity*. London: Routledge, pp. 89–102.

Shanks, M. & T. Webmoor. 2010. A Political Economy of Visual Media in Archaeology, in S. Bonde & S. Houston (eds.), *Re-Presenting the Past: Archaeology Through Image and Text*. Providence, RI: Brown University Press, pp. 87–110.

Smiles, S. & S. Moser (eds.). 2005. *Envisioning the Past: Archaeology and the Image* (New Interventions in Art History). Oxford: Blackwell.

Smith, M.E. 2017. Social Science and Archaeological Enquiry. *Antiquity* 91(356): 520–8.

Sørensen, T.F. 2015. In Praise of Vagueness: Uncertainty, Ambiguity and Archaeological Methodology. *Journal of Archaeological Method and Theory* 23(2): 1–23.

Spector, J. 1993. *What This Awl Means: Feminist Archaeology at a Wahpeton Dakota Village*. St. Paul: Minnesota Historical Society Press.

Stobiecka, M. 2020. Farewell to Tradition? Presenting Archaeology After the Digital Turn. *Advances in Archaeological Practice* 8(3): 313–18.

Swogger, J. 2000. Image and Interpretation: The Tyranny of Representation? In I. Hodder (ed.), *Towards Reflexive Method in Archaeology: The Example of Çatalhöyük*. Cambridge: McDonald Institute for Archaeological Research, pp. 143–52.

Thomas, J. 2004. *Archaeology and Modernity*. London: Routledge.

Todd, Z. 2016. An Indigenous Feminist's Take on the Ontological Turn: 'Ontology' Is Just Another Word for Colonialism. *Journal of Historical Sociology* 29(1): 4–22.

Tringham, R. 2015. Creating Narratives of the Past as Recombinant Histories. In R.M. Van Dyke & R. Bernbeck (eds.), *Subjects and Narratives in Archaeology*. Boulder: University Press of Colorado, pp. 27–54.

Tringham, R. in press. On the Digital and Analog Afterlives of Archaeological Projects. In K. Garstki (ed.), *Critical Archaeology in the Digital Age*. Los Angeles, CA: Cotsen Institute of Archaeology Press.

van Dyke, R.M. & R. Bernbeck (eds.). 2015. *Subjects and Narratives in Archaeology*. Boulder: University Press of Colorado.

Van Helden, D. & R. Witcher (eds.). 2020. *Researching the Archaeological Past Through Imagined Narratives. A Necessary Fiction*. London: Routledge.

5 Building a Case

> **Situation 5: Submitting a Paper for Publication**
>
> *A doctoral student recently submitted their first paper for publication in a peer-reviewed journal and has just had the reviewers' comments back with a decision from the editor that they will accept the paper but pending major revisions. The student is a little confused and not sure whether to feel happy or dejected. Reviewer #1 was brief and generally very positive but offered little in the way of constructive feedback. Reviewer #2's comments covered 5 pages and was very detailed, offering lots of specific points but seemed to rip the paper apart to such an extent, our student didn't know where to start. Reviewer #3 was more mixed, being generally supportive but raising several critical points which also seemed to question the whole basis of the paper. After reading the reviews, the student feels exhausted and somewhat unsure on how to proceed. Sometimes it felt as if the reviewers simply didn't get what it was they were trying to do – yet these are presumably scholars who know better, so surely they must have a point? When they submitted, the student felt very proud of their paper and felt sure it would meet with only minor comments; what went wrong? What makes for a successful paper and why do they feel so clueless?*

On Archaeological Jigsaws and Crosswords

In this chapter I want to explore the issues around how archaeologists make convincing arguments when writing an essay or monograph; what is needed to make an account believable or plausible? Recall in the last chapter that I identified a number of different genres of archaeological writing, including fieldwork reports and literature reviews, but I singled out the case study as one of the dominant formats for developing disciplinary knowledge in new directions. These kinds of texts can be contentious, but at the very least, they make claims which often require

DOI: 10.4324/9781003098294-6

some kind of support or substantiation. Often, these texts take the compositional structure of an argument, a mode of address or rhetoric which we also touched on in the last chapter, though they can also incorporate other modes such as narrative, description and exposition. Generally speaking, a student thesis or dissertation mimics this genre insofar as it tries to tackle a research question or problem and thus introduces the student to the most valued type of writing in academia: an original piece of research. But what is it that makes a good research paper? As a student, you might be given templates to follow on how to structure and organize the layout and chapter breakdown of a thesis such as IMRAD (Introduction, Methods, Results and Discussion), and you also know by now the various protocols of citation and referencing, but this doesn't really tell you how to pull off a successful argument.

There is, of course, no simple answer to this, no easy recipe to follow. Part of it is choosing the right question or problem, part of it finding the right methodology. I will discuss both of these aspects in more detail in the next chapter. But here, I want to focus more on the way all these elements come together and to think about what it is that helps us build an argument and makes an argument convincing to others. To do that, I will explore a number of different models of reasoning that archaeologists have proposed over the years, models which share some features in common and some not; each has their benefits and drawbacks and each are probably better suited to certain types of problems and questions more than others. In order to discuss these models though, we first need to provide some background.

Many of the approaches I will go on to discuss in this chapter, directly or indirectly, begin from a position of opposition to a very simple model of reasoning called **induction**. Think of induction as the scapegoat or fall-guy: the kind of approach that is so hopelessly useless that no one in their right minds would really endorse it. So what is it? In very simple terms, induction says that knowledge is based on the accumulation of observable facts; the more we dig, the more data we gather, the better our understanding of the past. To some extent, this sounds perfectly reasonable – why would I call it useless? Pick any spot on earth and run a "before and after" scenario; before we investigated this spot, we knew nothing about the human presence here in the past; afterwards, having surveyed surface ruins, test-pitted artefact scatters and so on, we now know something about people who once lived here. Something is more than nothing, *ergo*, induction works! The problem here is not that the accumulation of information does not increase knowledge; it is just not enough. In this example, identifying the nature of the ruins or artefacts is what really matters, otherwise all we really have is a bunch of stuff testifying to human presence. What kind of knowledge is that? How do we date these finds, how do we know what kind of activities were going on, what were people doing there and when and for how long? This is where induction starts to break down, because it assumes the answers to these kinds of questions will emerge once you have enough data.

Two North American archaeologists, Gordon Willey and Philip Phillips criticized this approach in the 1950s, calling it the "jigsaw hypothesis": when you have enough pieces of the puzzle, the picture will emerge. But how will having more pieces do this? How will having one thousand ruins tell you more than ten if you cannot identify what those ruins are or when they date to? Having a larger dataset can be productive, but only if that data is framed by a context which enables you to draw connections within the data or to other data from elsewhere. Another way to put this is that facts or data, in themselves, are meaningless without a broader context. Part of this relates to questions of coding and classification that we discussed in chapter 3; but it is not quite the same. For example, let's say you are walking down the high street and you observe some objects along the way – cigarette butts, chewing gum, sweet wrappers, a coin, etc. These are observations about that street which we might record as data or facts. But what do they mean? What do they tell you? That (some) people are untidy? That the street cleaners have not been recently (if they exist)? But these conclusions imply a previous question, even if it might not be explicitly stated: these things are evidence of discard practices. To interpret something means treating these observations as more than facts or data but as *evidence*.

As evidence, the *same* data or facts can often mean different things. For example, I might have formulated a more explicit question: do objects found on a street pavement reflect the presence or density of shops? Now, these same objects – cigarette butts, chewing gum, sweet wrappers and coins – become evidence not of discard practices but of the density of shops along the street. Is there more litter where there are more shops? It is the same with our archaeological data; those ruins and find scatters are not just facts or data, they are evidence and so have significance in relation to a particular question or set of assumptions. Our knowledge of the past is as much dependent on our questions and assumptions as it is on the amount of data we have; they are what turn these data and facts into evidence. As evidence, it then needs to fit with our questions and assumptions. If we want to see the density of litter as evidence for the density of shops, we need to show that the two densities are correlated: where you have more of one, you have more of the other and vice versa. In other words, the evidence has to be coherent with each other and our interpretation.

Philosopher Susan Haack used the example of a crossword to illustrate this dual aspect to knowledge; to successfully complete a crossword you need not only to guess the right word from the clue ("evidence"), you also need to make sure some of the letters in a word fit with those of others ("coherence"). Instead of a jigsaw puzzle then, it is better to think of archaeological knowledge construction as a crossword puzzle (Figure 5.1). In reality of course, the archaeological record is like neither; both are just metaphors for visualizing the nature of work we do, and if you push the analogy too far, they don't work anymore. The most obvious limitations of both jigsaws and crosswords is that they are finite and can be "finished"; working with archaeological evidence is never like this. Nonetheless, as metaphors, they are useful to help us characterize what it is we think we are doing when trying to build an interpretation or explanation for our facts or data. But even within this broad metaphor of the crossword, there are different ways of characterizing this process when it comes to the details, especially in how "coherence" is defined. In the first part of this chapter, I want to outline three approaches which stress the robustness of the logical links in an argument; coherence for all three is largely about structural integrity in the final product. Towards the end of the chapter, I will discuss three other approaches where coherence is more of a work in progress, it is about the process not the product where coherence and integrity come through how the reasoning unfolds over time.

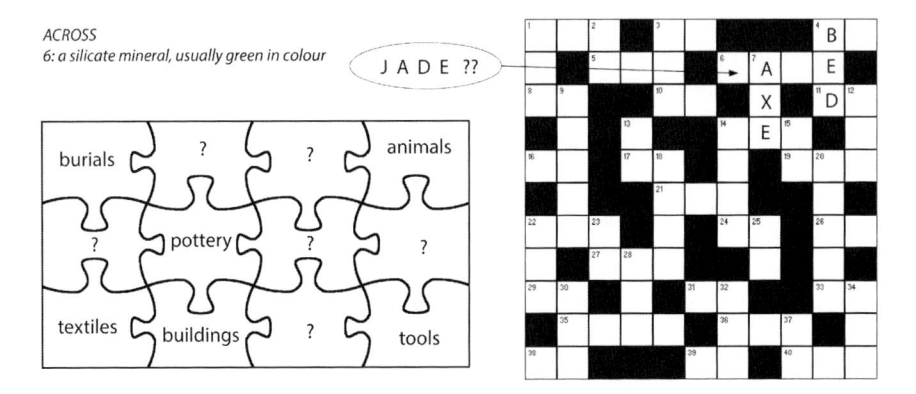

Figure 5.1 Two views of archaeological knowledge. Left: jigsaw model, where the goal is to fill in the blanks by simply accumulating more pieces (induction). Right: crossword model, where the goal is to fill in the blanks by ensuring coherence between the pieces and correspondence with the clues.

Accounting for the Evidence

The three approaches to be discussed in this first section are: hypothesis testing, inference to the best explanation and evidential reasoning. All three involve slightly different procedures for accounting for the evidence.

Hypothesis Testing

The first approach I want to discuss sounds the most scientific – and that's because it emerged in archaeology in the 1960s as part of an attempt to make archaeology more scientific. Hypothesis testing is, as it sounds, a procedure where you come up with a hypothesis and then test it against the data. When it first emerged in archaeology in the 1960s, it was linked with a desire to formulate laws in archaeology, rather like in the natural sciences, but nowadays it no longer has such associations. If we go back to the example of the litter on the street, my hypothesis might be: density of litter increases in proportion to proximity of shops. To test that hypothesis, I need to go out and collect two types of data: distribution of litter and distribution of shops and then compare them. Now, one of the original ideas behind hypothesis testing is that it didn't really matter where the idea for the hypothesis came from; you could have dreamed it, it could be a gut instinct or you could have carefully worked it out from prolonged observation. None of this really mattered, because in the end, all that counted was that it withstood testing. The stress here is really on the quality of the test, not the source of the hypothesis and in that regard; there are two key things that most archaeologists who use hypothesis testing emphasize.

The first is that the test is best viewed not as an attempt to prove a hypothesis but refute it. This sounds crazy, but one of the reasons why hypothesis testing emerged was because it needed to get around one of the major problems of induction that I did not mention earlier: that no matter how many data or observations you have supporting a particular inference, it will never be enough to prove it. No matter how many times the sun rises every day, there is no guarantee it will happen tomorrow. It is likely of course, indeed very likely (thankfully!) – but there is always a chance it won't happen. It only takes one instance to refute the generalization that the sun rises every day. The same applies to our hypothetical example of street litter; maybe in our study, the hypothesis was borne out, but there is no guarantee that if we tried the study again on a different day or a different street, it would still show the same correlation. Testing is not infallible then; testing a hypothesis is not the same as proving it. No archaeologist would argue that just because a test supports the hypothesis, it must be true; no, all they would say is that it has been shown to be *probably* true. How do we evaluate this probability though? Well if you go about testing a hypothesis purely in order to confirm it, there is a chance you will focus on data that will do only this and ignore potentially contradictory data. This is known as confirmation bias. But if you set out looking for data that will refute your hypothesis, but the hypothesis still stands up to such testing, then it is generally considered much stronger than a test which is only set up to confirm it. In practice, it may not always be easy to know how the archaeologist has devised the test but usually it is enough that the results of the test will either support or contradict the hypothesis.

If seeking to refute a hypothesis is generally considered to increase the probability of it being correct, can we measure this increase? Some archaeologists might not worry about needing to quantify this – they might just rely on the force of corroboration and leave it at that. For many though, this is a matter that can be subject to numerical qualification, using statistical tests which return measures of probability. Indeed, when you put the two things together – the emphasis on refutation and quantifying probability – you get what is often the most common way of conducting hypothesis testing: excluding the null hypothesis. The null hypothesis simply expresses the likelihood of a hypothesis *not* being true. What is the probability that the distribution of litter and shops are *not* correlated? If this probability is extremely low, then we can say the null hypothesis has been excluded. Alternatively, there are also other tests which quantify the probability of a correlation and then one would say the hypothesis has been corroborated. Although often scholars will use other terms like "proof" or "confirmation", it is better – and more accurate – to think in terms of negatives; that is, the inference has not been refuted.

> **Box 5.1 Hypothesis Testing and Mayan Household Rituals**
>
> Lisa Lucero used hypothesis testing to explore the connection between cosmological beliefs and household space in pre-Columbian Mayan settlements. Based on her observations of recent Mayan ceremonies she identified three distinct practices which had specific material signatures. One

120 *Building a Case*

Hypothesis
Pre-Columbian Maya practiced dedication, ancestor veneration, and termination rites in the home

Testable implications

1. *Caches should be found beneath floors (e.g. jade or obsidian artefacts, pottery)*

2. *Burials should be found under house floors*

3. *Deposits should be found on floor surfaces consisting of broken and burned items (e.g. pottery)*

Actual observations

Obsidian blades, grinding tools, bone needles, spindle whorls, and many other objects found under floors

12 burials found inside houses

Deposits of smashed and burned pottery vessels found on floor surfaces

Hypothesis refuted?

Yes

No

Figure 5.2 Diagram showing the structure of hypothesis testing in Lucero's example.

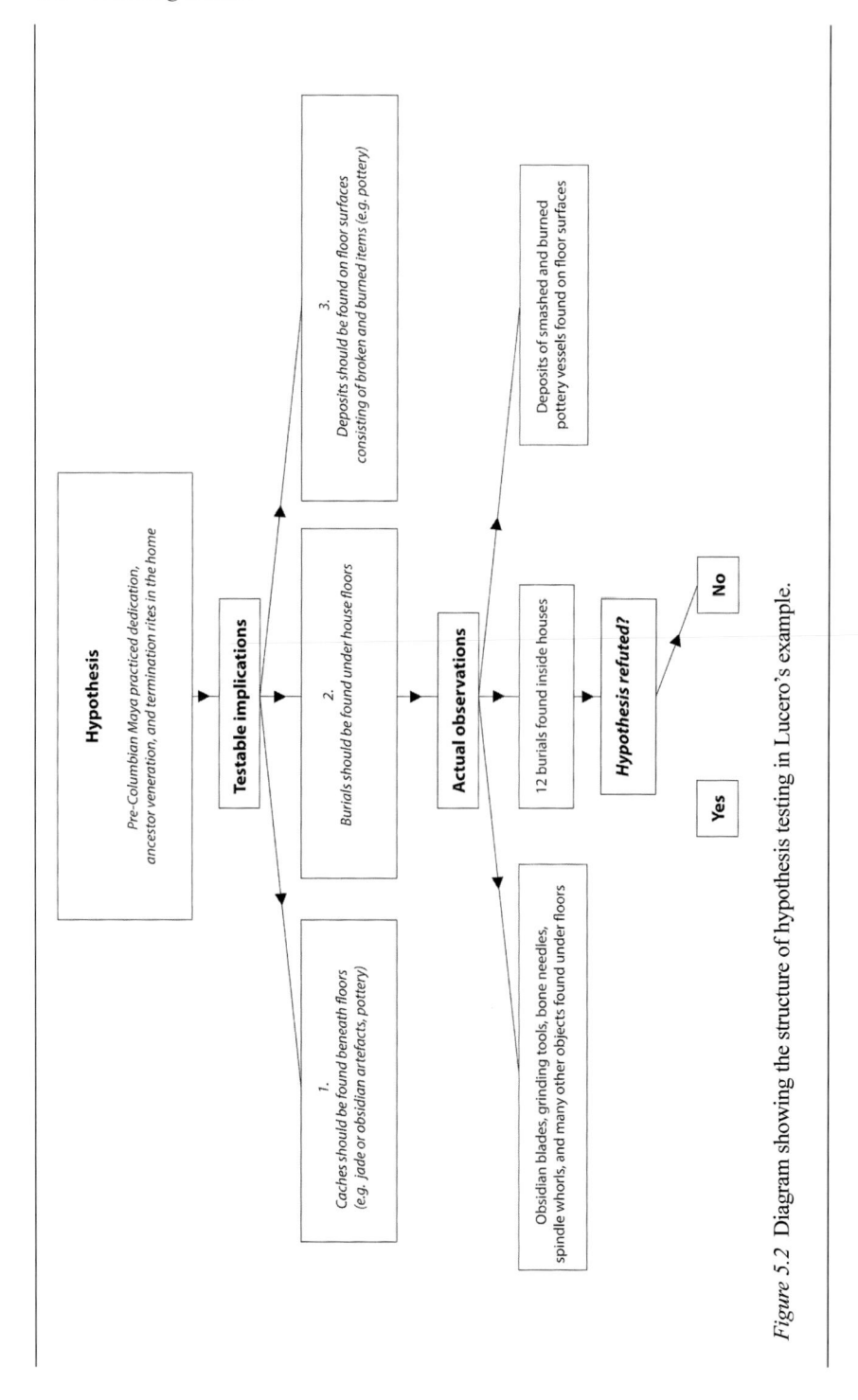

concerned dedications made to "activate" the house which involved the placement of caches under the floor; another was ancestor veneration rites which entailed burying the dead under the floors; and the third was termination ceremonies which de-activated a house whose practice involved breaking objects or partially destroying a house. Based on these ethnographic observations, she formulated the following hypothesis: if pre-Columbian Maya practiced dedication, ancestor veneration and termination rites in home, then we should find caches, burials and broken artefacts in home. Critical to this hypothesis is the assumption of continuity in traditions.

Given the very specific way the hypothesis has been framed, very specific test implications are established: 1) caches should be found beneath floors (e.g. jade or obsidian artefacts, pottery); 2) burials should be found under house floors and 3) deposits should be found on floor surfaces consisting of broken and burned items (e.g. pottery). Lucero then set about testing this hypothesis at the Mayan site of Saturday Creek in Belize, dated c. 900–1500 CE. What did she find? Under the floors were obsidian blades, fragments from grinding tools, bone needles, spindle whorls and many other objects. Also, 12 burials were found in the commoner houses, while several deposits of smashed and burned vessels were found on floor surfaces. In short, she concluded that the evidence supported the hypothesis that the pre-Columbian Maya practiced dedication, ancestor veneration and termination rites at home.

Characterizing inferences as "not refuted" rather than "confirmed" is better for another reason too. Because even if the hypothesis seems to withstand testing, it doesn't mean there are no other explanations for the same patterning. This is why you might often hear people say, "correlation is not causation". For example, let's say our litter on the street hypothesis has withstood very stringent statistical testing and not been refuted so far; how safe are we in assuming that the reason for this is that discard practices are related to proximity to shops? That people going into shops are discarding cigarettes or those coming out dropping candy wrappers and coins? What if there is something else we are missing here? What if, perhaps there is a close connection between density of shops and density of bus stops – and what if the real correlation is not between litter and shops but litter and bus stops? Suddenly, all the effort that went into testing starts to seem pointless if another hypothesis might fit the situation just as well. It is as if we have a line of cells in our crossword and two words will fit equally well, both with the clue and other words which use some of the same letters; which do we choose? This problem is known as equifinality, which states that different processes or causes can result in the same effects or outcome. It is precisely problems like this which leads us to consider the second approach adopted by archaeologists: inference to the best explanation.

Inference to the Best Explanation

Inference to the best explanation (hereafter IBE) is a mouthful but expresses the crux of the approach rather well; it assumes there are always multiple, competing explanations for a certain set of data or facts and that our job is to find the best one. Like hypothesis testing, IBE ideally is all about trying to refute hypotheses, only instead of hoping the hypothesis stands up to testing, the hope is that most of them won't. In effect, IBE works on a process of elimination to get to the "last man standing". Once again, the final "victor" does not constitute a proven hypothesis, only that it is the best in a bunch, and quite possibly, there is always the chance a hypothesis that has not been considered might be better still. Yet simply by virtue of considering more than one hypothesis, IBE is often considered superior as it at least starts to take account of equifinality. Moreover, because IBE is testing at least two, if not more, competing hypotheses, it can also adjust the scope of its evidence and data.

Let's say we have two hypotheses and both of them are supported by the same data; in our example of street litter, both the shop and bus stop hypotheses are supported by the litter distributions. How do we decide which is better? There are two things we can do. The first is, we can focus on those cases where bus stops are not positioned close to shops and see which pattern seems to hold out better. Sometimes though, this may not be possible; maybe shops and bus stops shadow each other consistently so there is no room to explore this. So the other thing we can do is think about what makes shops and bus stops different and whether those differences might account for other aspects of the litter distribution. Bus stops are located close to the street side of the pavement while shops are located on the opposite side; what if the distribution of litter clusters is slightly towards one side of the pavement rather than the other? This new bit of data, which before we might not even have considered, now becomes evidence to adjudicate between two hypotheses.

Box 5.2 A Process of Elimination: Modelling Neolithic Farming Practice in Central Europe

Although a lot is known about the "when" and "how" of the spread of farming into Neolithic Europe, the "what" is often quite contentious. What kind of farming was it exactly? Amy Bogaard decided to compare four different models or hypotheses about the nature of early farming in Europe and assess which of the four best stood up against the variety of available evidence. The four models were: 1) shifting cultivation, 2) extensive and cultivation, 3) floodplain cultivation and 4) intensive garden cultivation.

Each of these models had certain, testable implications and Bogaard went through them, one by one, comparing them against the evidence until she

Hypotheses	Evidence of permanence: annuals, low numbers of tree species	Evidence of intensity: garden weeds predominate over field weeds	Evidence of seasonality: presence of autumn weeds
H1: Shifting cultivation	X	X	X
H2: Extensive ard cultivation	✓	X	X
H3: Floodplain cultivation	✓	✓	X
H4: Intensive garden cultivation	✓	✓	✓

Figure 5.3 Diagram showing the structure of IBE in Bogaard's example. Four hypotheses (H1-H4) are tested against three strands of evidence. Ticks indicate the presence of evidence showing only one hypothesis (H4) withstands all three tests.

found only one model remaining, using not only general archaeological evidence but also weed ecology and weed taxa associated with crops remains recovered from archaeological sites. Shifting cultivation was the first to go as it implied temporary or transient settlements which straightaway made it untenable given the presence of permanent plots in the archaeological record. It also didn't help that ethnographically, livestock tended to not be part of this agricultural package whereas animal domesticates are well attested archaeologically. But crucially, the dominance of annual weeds and low woodland species suggested forest clearance and permanent plots. The second model to go was extensive ard cultivation; although this does imply fixed plots, it also generally implies a much more hierarchical social division of labour, something we don't see archaeologically until much later. More concretely, a method of discriminating between garden and field weeds suggested that most crops were being grown in small horticultural plots rather than extensive fields. The third model of floodplain cultivation on the other hand both uses fixed plots and is intensive rather than extensive, meaning it relies on smaller fields cultivated by small households. But so does the fourth model, intensive garden cultivation. So how to choose between these two? Seasonality is the answer: floodplain cultivation can only work with spring-sown crops, while garden cultivation works also with autumn-sowing or even both spring and autumn-sowing. Bogaard found that the weed evidence on the whole supported the fourth model as autumn-sown crops seem to have been favoured – and so by a process of elimination, she argues this is our best model to date.

In other words, IBE exploits the differences between hypotheses to broaden the scope of what you use as evidence. Ideally, the more hypotheses you have to compare, the better. Moreover, because the goal is to find the "best of the bunch", the issue of quantifying the probability of any given hypothesis is less important, and testing using statistical means is rare. Furthermore, the construction of a hypothesis now becomes rather more important than it did for hypothesis testing, because in principle, one could imagine hundreds or thousands of hypotheses to account for a set of observations, but we don't want to waste time testing all of them. We need to narrow them down to the most plausible number and then test those. For this reason, the construction of hypotheses is considered fairly important, even if it remains largely untheorized; but the assumption is a better hypothesis is one that has been drawn from familiarity with the context of the data. That it is, what you might call, an educated or informed guess, not a wild speculation. Imagine trying to construct an hypothesis to explain your data with only a very superficial familiarity with that data; it won't be easy and in fact the chances are, you will come up with something either very vague or even non-sensical.

This process of hypothesis construction is often called abduction because it has been drawn from the same data which it will be then tested against. It is also why IBE is also sometimes called abduction, but this is perhaps confusing, so such conflation will be avoided here. Abduction is mostly about hypothesis construction, whereas IBE is about hypothesis justification. Think of it this way: imagine looking at a collection of artefacts to get a sense of what the variability is before constructing a formal typology (abduction); this typology is then tested on the same data but also compared against competing or existing typologies to see which fits best (IBE). For some archaeologists, using the same data to construct a hypothesis as to test it is regarded as circular; it will just lead to a self-fulfilling inference. However, this ignores the effect of having multiple hypotheses which act to counter such circularity by the (often slight and subtle) different empirical implications each hypothesis has. Abduction was a term used by philosopher Charles Sanders Peirce to distinguish it from deduction and induction, which both carry connotations of being connected to a more idealized form of reasoning, whereas for Peirce, abduction was a better representation of practical reasoning and fuzzy logic. It was partly all about making the best guess from the available evidence – although there is another dimension to abduction, we will address later in this chapter, concerning novelty. However, in many ways, Peirce's notion of abduction as practical reasoning has a lot in common with the third and last model we will explore, evidential reasoning.

Evidential Reasoning

Both hypothesis testing and IBE share in common a model of reasoning which is somewhat idealized; it presents the testing of one or more hypothesis as well-thought out and carefully planned, with a strict order in which to do something. First you line up your hypothesis, then you go about testing it; they both operate on a clear separation and distinction between what is called hypothesis generation and hypothesis justification, even if IBE grants the former a little more importance. In this, they are quite different to the third approach. Recent work on evidential reasoning, inference networks and the structure of argument try to account for the more informal aspects of "logic in use" yet with still enough formality to allow an explicit evaluation of the strength of an interpretation. They do this by breaking an interpretation down into three components: the claim, the evidence and the warrants, taking inspiration in part from legal argumentation.

Most research papers make some kind of claim: some statement or assertion which is the major point of the research. This might take the form of an explicit hypothesis, but just as easily it might not. Returning once more to our street litter example, it might be something like "People are more likely to litter when entering and leaving shops/bus stops". To support a claim like this, the research will cite evidence – in this same example, the distribution of litter and shops/bus stops. Now so far, this sounds very similar to hypothesis testing, though in this case, the evidence is not presented as a test of the hypothesis but as support for a claim. Is this just a case of wordplay though? Is it not really the same thing dressed up in different words? Not really, though admittedly there are similarities. The difference is due to the role of the third element: warrants, which are what really distinguishes this fourth approach. Warrants are what link the evidence to the claim; they are often the unspoken assumptions and background theory which help the evidence act to support the claim. In my street litter example, the warrants here would include the fact that litter on the street is in its original location and has not moved, that my identification of shops or bus stops is accurate and not subject to bias (e.g. based on a map or street directory that is out of date). Warrants are essentially what makes the connection between evidence and claim stand or fall, because in most cases, the evidence is unlikely to be presented unless it was fairly convincing. It is possible, for example, that the correlation between density of litter and density of shops is very high and this evidence therefore supports the claim; but if it turns out that litter actually gets moved around – kicked and swept by wind, so that it tends to concentrate around shop entrances – then this argument can be shown to break down. Not because the evidence is weak but because one of the support assumptions or warrants is invalid.

Box 5.3 Networks of Trade and Networks of Inference: the Case of the Copper Ingots

Bob Chapman and Alison Wylie, who have been principal figures in promoting models of evidential reasoning in archaeology, used a case from the Mediterranean Bronze Age to illustrate how archaeological arguments hold up – or in this case, break down. They analysed this case by breaking the argument down into three parts: the claim, the evidence and, most importantly, the warrants which acted to hold the claim and evidence together. They cited a study which used lead isotope analysis of copper ingots to suggest a Cypriot source of ingots found in Sardinia, because the isotope profiles matched. This might sound fine, but its implications were quite broad as it had repercussions for the extent and scale of trade in the Mediterranean at this time. Consequently, many archaeologists disagreed with this

126 *Building a Case*

DATUM

LEAD ISOTOPE RESULTS

Oxhide ingots from Sardinia have the same LIA profiles as Cypriot copper ore deposits

INITIAL WARRANTS

Lead isotope chemistry control samples from known sources

REBUTTAL 1

Probable overlap of ore profiles given similar geology

CONSTRUCTIVE RESPONSE

Refinement of LIA profiles for Cypriot ore deposits

REBUTTAL 2

Re-mixing and re-smelting of metals

DEFLECTION

No evidence of re-smelting no necessity for re-cycling

EVIDENTIAL CLAIMS

PROVENANCE CLAIMS

LIA values of Sardinian ingots match Cypriot ore profile suggesting Cyprus as a source for Sardinian ingots

IF rebuttals 1 and 2 can be shown to be false

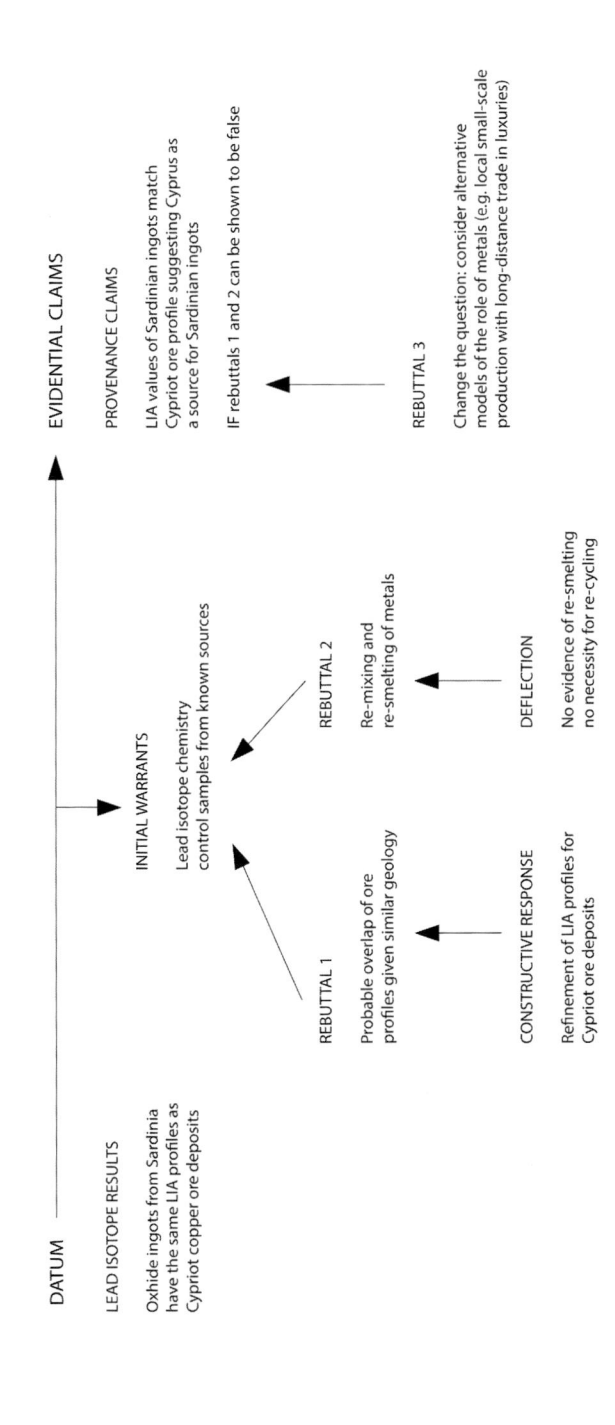

REBUTTAL 3

Change the question: consider alternative models of the role of metals (e.g. local small-scale production with long-distance trade in luxuries)

Figure 5.4 Diagram showing the structure of arguments adapted from an example in Chapman and Wylie (2016). A claim of provenance is made on the basis of specific data linked by warrants; note the criticisms (rebuttals) which largely focus on the warrants as the weak link in the argument.

inference even though the claim was based on the well-established science of lead isotope chemistry. How so? They argued that the profiles of Cypriot and Sardinian copper ores were not distinct enough to tell apart; moreover, given the possibility that metals were commonly re-cycled and mixed, the profiles anyway could be misleading. In response, the supporters of the original claim argued that there was no evidence of re-cycling and in fact these ingots represented primary smelting bars. But they did acknowledge the need for more work on differentiating the different ores and after doing so, felt their original inference was upheld. But for some archaeologists, the whole question was poorly framed as it presupposed a simple model of discrete centres of production and distribution, whereas the reality was probably more complex. Chapman and Wylie usefully sketch out their analysis of the argument in the form of a diagram (Figure 5.4).

This way of looking at archaeological interpretation is interesting because in its focus on warrants, it displays a concern for often hidden, background knowledge and the role it plays in building interpretation. It accepts that one cannot easily separate "theory" from "data".

Having reviewed the first three approaches, which one should you choose? There is no right answer here; each has its merits and drawbacks, and to some extent, it depends on how you want to define your research objective. Any method – whether of reasoning or excavation strategy – can only really be judged on the basis of the aims or purpose to which it is attached. One might say that all research starts from a problem or question, and the aim is to find some kind of "solution" or answer to that problem or question. But how you go about doing that depends in part on the nature of the problem or question and the kind of solution you choose to adopt. Sometimes, framing it as a hypothesis to be tested is the most appropriate, sometimes comparing multiple competing hypotheses is the best way to go, while in other cases, it might be more fitting to use the evidence to make a general claim. Part of this though comes down to where you want to put the stress: on *testing* hypotheses or on *supporting* an inference. To some extent, these differences may be matters of rhetoric – how we choose to compose or present an interpretation, regardless of the actual process involved.

Working With Evidence

The three approaches discussed in the last section – hypothesis testing, IBE and evidential reasoning – all presuppose a certain way of working and writing, more specifically, a certain mode of rhetoric: argument. But as we saw in Chapter 4, argument is just one style of composition. There are other ways to frame or build a case, ones that put less stress on accounting for some evidence or set of facts through the structural integrity of testing or warrants but more on the process

128 *Building a Case*

of working through/with the evidence. In many ways, a narrative style is more suited to this form of reasoning and in fact it is no surprise that these alternative approaches derive from philosophies of history and textual interpretation. In this section, we will discuss three more varieties of reasoning: **hermeneutics**, diagnosis and nomadic thinking.

Hermeneutics and Reading the Past

Instead of speaking of the construction of hypotheses and their testing, or of claims and warrants, an alternative view is to talk about the recursive interplay between prior assumptions and present experience. Overall, these two mutually reinforce each other: present experience helps to substantiate prior assumptions and prior assumptions inform present experience. Think of the sun rising every day; this is a continual process. This mutual reinforcement is known as the hermeneutic circle. It might sound like a vicious circle, but the fact is, it can and does get broken; perhaps not often in everyday life (or with the sun rising!), but sometimes and in contexts of scientific research, you might argue that "brokenness" is what is actually being sought for. So how is it broken? By present experience suddenly not matching prior expectations.

Let's return to our example of street litter to see how this works more concretely. Let's say you are walking down the street and you are used to a certain amount of litter because this is how the streets usually are where you live. But then you turn a corner and suddenly the litter has increased noticeably – now your prior assumptions about a general background quantity of litter have been challenged; you need to revise them. Why is there more litter here than on "your" street? Is my street unusually clean or is this street unusually dirty? I might formulate all kinds of explanations for this as I walk down the street, and it occurs to me that my street has less shops and this might account for the difference. Happy with my explanation I walk on, but then realize there are also bus stops on this street which are lacking on mine and in fact I even notice that the litter seems to concentrate closer to the road edge of the pavement. Perhaps this explains the litter – people getting off and on buses, not coming in and out of shops. This "breaking" of the cycle by a mismatch of prior assumptions and present experience results in a "forward" movement of interpretation, which is why some archaeologists preferred to call it a hermeneutic spiral than a circle – that with each turn, there is also some displacement.

Box 5.4   Hermeneutics at Haddenham: Evolving Interpretations of a Neolithic Causewayed Enclosure

Ian Hodder presented a classic case of hermeneutic interpretation in his reflections on fieldwork at an early Neolithic causewayed enclosure in eastern England. The first season of excavations at the site of Haddenham

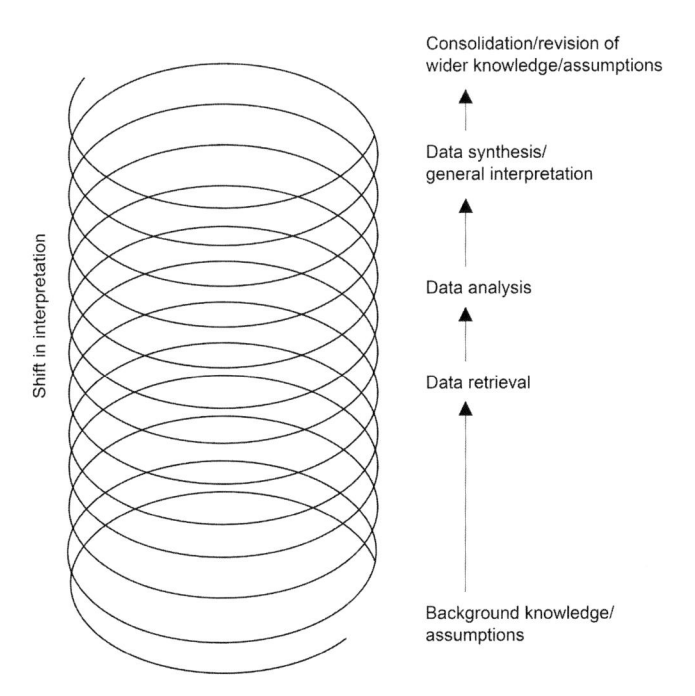

Figure 5.5 The hermeneutic spiral (redrawn from Hodder 1992).

uncovered a ditch, filled with animal bones, stone tools and prehistoric potsherds – all kinds of things they would have expected of such a site. Only there were two problems: they had also expected to see a smaller inner ditch but could not find it, and more troubling, some of the bones turned out to be horse bones, which shouldn't be there as horses didn't appear until the end of the Neolithic. Was this a new discovery? Or could they have got something wrong? A closer comparison with other features on the site suggested that what they thought was the whole ditch turned out to be just its upper fill. In fact they hadn't reached the bottom but were still only in the upper layers of the ditch which was later dated to the Iron Age. This not only accounted for the presence of horse bones, it also explained why they didn't locate the inner ditch – it was further in than they were expecting because of their preconceptions about the size of the main ditch.

During subsequent seasons, more cases like this emerged. For example, they expected to see some patterning in the distribution of finds within ditches around the circuit of the enclosure based on what had been found at other sites. But this patterning never emerged until they started to look at finds distribution in relation to things like the number of times a ditch segment had been recut or how long a segment was. Once they took this into

> account, the variability of finds started to make more sense, but it also added something new to our understanding of Neolithic enclosures. In short, prior assumptions about this type of site informed expectations during its excavation, but through the excavation of this particular site, new ideas about such sites were also produced, such as interpretations of competitive social display. Hodder captured this recursive process of interpretation in the form of an hermeneutic spiral (Figure 5.5).

This account does sound very similar to IBE, but there is a difference. IBE presented this manner of reasoning as all planned out in advance, where all the hypotheses were lined up and then tested, whereas the hermeneutic approach situates this process as drawn out, as embedded in a constant process of back and forth. One way to think about this is in terms of a continual dialogue of question and answer; you ask a question, and in answering it, you find new questions emerge and so on. It is not that one is more realistic than the other; archaeologists operate in both ways. But with IBE and even hypothesis testing, interpretation is always presented as a singular, one-off event, and even if these events can be added together to create a sense of broader "progress", the focus remains on the individual test. With hermeneutics, there is no clear division between the test and the hypothesis because this process is always ongoing. More significantly though, the relation between prior assumptions and present experience is not directly translatable into hypothesis and test. Prior assumptions include a wide range of unspoken presuppositions as well as explicitly formulated conjectures; in effect, they include the whole spectrum of background knowledge that relates to that present experience. When there is a mismatch between the two, either you end up incorporating present experience into that background knowledge, subtly altering it, or you find a way to discount or account for the anomaly of your present experience.

This may sound far less scientific, but the fact is, archaeologists who operate with hypothesis testing or IBE do exactly the same thing; when a hypothesis doesn't seem to pass a test or when an anomalous case shows up, they will still often "save the theory" by invoking unusual or extraneous circumstances (known technically as the *ceteris paribus* clause – i.e. all things being equal). Let's say I have one street out of a sample of ten where the correlation between litter density and shop/but stop distribution completely breaks down; strictly speaking, this one case is enough to refute the hypothesis. In these circumstances, rather than give up what seems to be a useful theory, archaeologists usually play their "get out of jail free" card and suggest something unusual was happening with this street – some extra factors that don't apply on the other streets, such as the presence of more bins, a more environmentally friendly community or whatever, what might also be called *auxiliary hypotheses*. Ideally, one would try and identify what these other factors are, but it is just as likely it will remain unformulated. In short then, there is nothing especially unscientific about working with the data as described by hermeneutics. What it does is underline the fact that you cannot separate any specific interpretation from the wider body of experience and knowledge that make up archaeology, and this back and forth between prior assumptions and present experience is equally a back and forth between the specific case you are dealing with and the larger whole of disciplinary knowledge. It sees reasoning as a process of tacking back and forth between elements and a wider context, part and whole, not a test between "theory" and "data" as the earlier approaches largely characterize it as. It can be useful also to think about this difference in relation to the issue of certainty and ambiguity which we discussed in the last chapter, where a focus on the process as more open-ended encourages more room for ambiguity (Box 4.1).

Detection, Diagnosis and Discernment

Although such reasoning is largely considered as something on analogy with textual interpretation, it can be aligned with a much broader tradition of reading signs and traces. Just as trackers infer the movements of their prey by "reading" broken vegetation, scat, smells; or a doctor infers an illness from its symptoms; or a detective "reads" a crime scene from its clues; so an archaeologist "reads the past" from traces of long passed human activity. All these activities share a very similar method which some historians have characterized as being very different to a conventional scientific model. Although there is clear affinity with textual interpretation, there are some important differences; with textual interpretation and hermeneutics, the emphasis is on reading signs as carriers of meaning, where the relation of the part (the sign) to the whole (language) is what frames the operation. With this other method – for which we lack a good generic name, but we might call "tracking" the evidence – the emphasis is on seeing traces as residues or "memories", where the relation of an effect (the trace) is linked to an antecedent event (action). Overall, archaeologists have written much more about reading as hermeneutics than as detection or diagnosis, though one can find scattered references to the latter through the literature. Yet in some ways, detection and diagnosis are much more appropriate given the non-textual and non-representational nature of most archaeological remains. Moreover, this method of working with traces shares something in common with last approach in the previous section on evidential reasoning: it starts with the evidence and works outward from there. It is why one historian – Carlo Ginzburg – called this method the evidentiary paradigm.

Box 5.5   Bodies of Evidence or Silent Witness?

The idea of seeing archaeological interpretation as a process of "reading" – whether of signs or traces – connects archaeology to the whole field of forensics. Forensic archaeology is of course a specialist field on its own, one where traces are regarded more specifically as evidence of a crime. Signs and traces become clues to solving a case. Zoë Crossland has explored these connections through her work on how scientists have approached the dead body since the nineteenth century, particularly highlighting the recurrent tension between seeing the dead body as both evidence to be read and as an active agent bearing witness to who they were/are. Indeed, regarding how the corpse is capable of a kind of postmortem speech can be extrapolated more broadly to attribute animacy to facts and evidence. Thus forensic experts often talk about the dead body acting as a "silent witness", "talking from the grave", and thus minimizing their role in interpretation. As such, the dead body comes to have agency and speak for itself. At the same time, the same experts will also refer to bones as evidence, turning the body into a more passive "thing", requiring the intervention of the scientist to elicit its story.

What is really interesting here is to see how the attribution of agency for interpretation shifts between two different places – sometimes with the dead body, sometimes with the scientist. The question is: is this simply a case of rhetorical slippage or is it telling us something more important about how interpretation happens? Unlike the other approaches discussed in this chapter – even hermeneutics – Crossland's argument suggests that interpretation is a process that emerges not between the reader and the text, or the archaeologist and their evidence, but from a more dynamic interplay *between* the evidence. Crossland's later development of these ideas in relation to "forensic afterlives" captures this much better, where the whole notion of "reading" evidence becomes somewhat inadequate, once the evidence itself starts to take a more active role.

For example, consider how fingerprinting works in forensics; a print taken from a crime scene remains only potential evidence until it is matched to a fingerprint taken from an identified suspect. Crossland highlights two key evidential relations here: indexical and iconic. An indexical relation is where evidence is based on a causal or physical relation between two things: fingerprints, like footprints and fossils are evidence of something by virtue of being directly caused or connected to the thing they are evidence of. An iconic relation is one of resemblance between evidence, that the pattern on the surface of a fingertip resembles the pattern on a fingerprint. Because the resemblance is so close, we may not think of this as iconic at all, but you only have to consider other kinds of forensic evidence to see the importance of iconic relations in evidence. Think about a cut mark or blunt force trauma to a corpse; we know there is an indexical relation to a weapon, but the particular nature of that weapon may be subject to doubt: what kind of knife or object caused this wound? In this case, the iconic relation between the edge or surface of the weapon and the scar left on the body is more problematic, so more foregrounded. Yet when matching a potential weapon to the injury, it involves exactly the same kind of process as matching a crime scene fingerprint to one in a database or taken from a potential suspect: it is purely iconic, there is no indexical relation involved, except the one inferred (Figure 5.6).

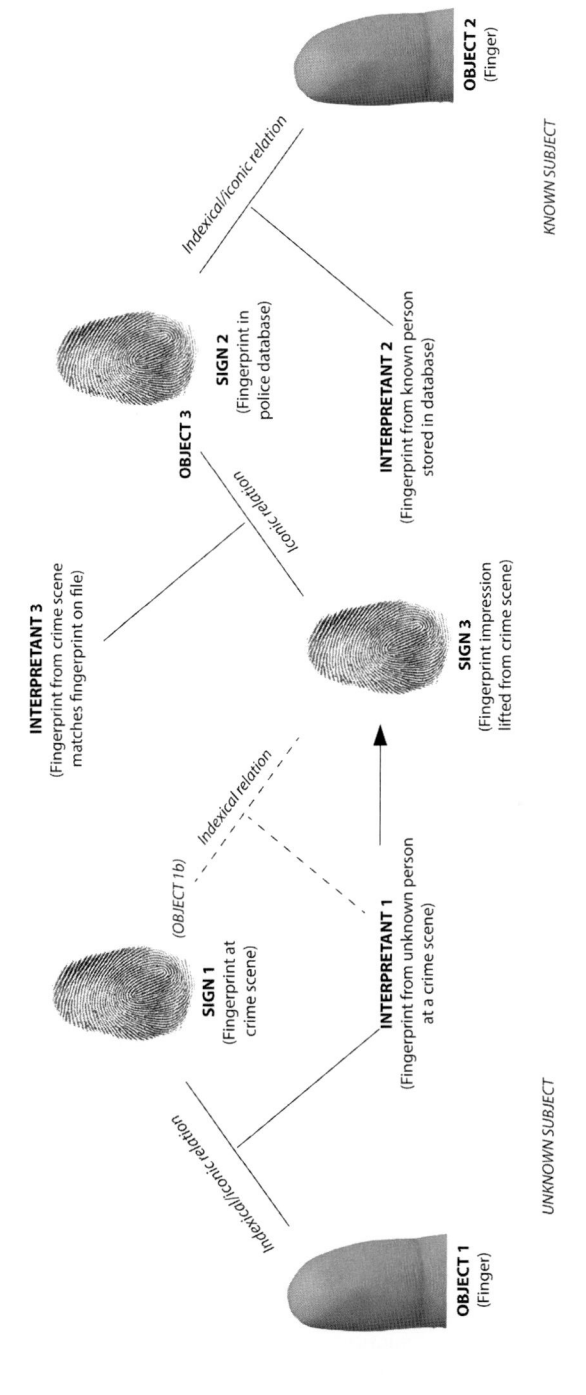

Figure 5.6 The evidential relations and Peircean semiotics of fingerprints.

> The archaeological record is full of both indexical and iconic relations: a grave is indexical of burial, an artefact is indexical of its production and so on. Similarly, the typological resemblance between two artefacts is iconic; where an artefact is dated based on association with a coin or radiocarbon date, and then when the same type of artefact is found on another site, we assume a similar date. Understanding evidence as a composite of indexical and iconic relations foregrounds the active role evidence has in shaping interpretation, even if these relations are always mediated by the context in which they occur – and for who they act as evidence. Although I have not contextualized this, Crossland's approach draws on philosopher Charles Sanders Peirce whom we met earlier in the context of abduction. In particular, his theory of semiotics identifies three modes through which signs relate to objects (indexical, iconic and symbolic) and argues that this relationship offers the ground for interpretation so that that sign relations are irreducibly tripartite (sign, object and interpretant). These ideas underpin the way Crossland approaches evidence and evidential reasoning (Figure 5.6). I will not discuss Peirce's ideas any further here, but for those interested, references are given in the further reading section at the end of this chapter.

Abduction, Speculation and Nomadic Thinking

We met abduction earlier in the section on inference to the best explanation. If you recall, the term has sometimes been conflated with IBE, but on the whole most scholars are careful to separate the two. Abduction is partly about generating hypotheses or theories from available data, and when archaeologists have used the term in this way, it is usually seen as part of hypothesis testing. However, some archaeologists have argued that abduction be given a more autonomous and leading role, especially when it comes to injecting novelty into our archaeological accounts. Marko Marila has drawn on Peirce's writings on abduction as a form of reasoning distinct from induction and deduction, characterized by the fact that it introduces something new. For example, with both induction and deduction, the conclusions are always implicit in the premises, but with abduction, an inference or conclusion involves a sideways leap, a speculative jump that goes way beyond what is contained in any initial premises of observations.

Marila's characterization of Peirce's concept of abduction owes a lot to another concept called transduction, which he derives from philosophers Henri Lefebvre and Gilbert Simondon, where reasoning works from the actual to the virtual or possible. Given *actual* evidence such as a distribution of litter along a street, we speculate about the *possible* events and processes which might have resulted in it. In itself, this may not sound too revolutionary, but the problem is we have become so used to viewing speculations like this as a hypothesis to be tested that we ignore what is truly powerful about them: their ability to say something about the world, which is not visible or present in the material from which the hypothesis has been drawn. As Marila suggests, what is valuable about speculation and abduction is not to provide fodder for testing but to prepare us for the unexpected – to keep interpretation open and alive to future possibilities. To understand the creative dimension of interpretation, we need to treat speculation far more seriously than we do. But there is another aspect to abduction and speculation that comes across clearer when we use the term transduction: a kind of sideways or lateral process of reasoning that is quite different to the vertical reasoning of many of the accounts discussed in this chapter.

We can turn to Michael Shanks characterization of this in terms of what he called tree-thinking and rhizomes-thinking, drawing on ideas of Deleuze and Guattari. Tree-thinking involves a hierarchy which moves from the data (roots) up to theory and interpretation (the canopy); the DIKW pyramid we discussed in Chapter 3 is a perfect example of this, but Shanks argues the basic idea has formed the template for much of archaeology. Two prominent ways debate has been framed shows how resilient tree-thinking is. One is when archaeologists talk about levels of theory (see Box 1.3) or bottom-up versus top-down theorizing. The other is when archaeologists talk about the relation between the particular and the general, typically manifest in both induction and deduction but also in hermeneutics. In all these cases, the arboreal metaphor is at work. But there is more to this than a hierarchy; tree-thinking also implies a logic of division and unity, like a trunk which splits into branches. Classification and typologies are obvious examples, but so is any kind of binary logic which creates dualisms such as nature/culture, mind/matter, including dialectics of thesis/antithesis and synthesis (see Box 5.6). In contrast, Shanks argued for rhizomes-thinking; rhizomes are subterranean plant stems that send out horizontal shoots and roots, and when applied to thought, it refers to a way of thinking which cuts across the neat classification and categories of tree-thinking and there is no impetus towards unity. If tree-thinking starts from a unity which subdivides, rhizomes-thinking starts from a multiplicity which seeks connections and conjunctions – but in such a way that does not forge an over-arching unity.

Shanks' discussion was in many ways three decades too early. Only now, as archaeology (and the humanities in general) embraces many of the ideas of Deleuze and Guattari within new materialisms and posthumanism, are some of these ideas becoming more prevalent. What philosopher Rosi Braidotti called nomadic thought (also after Deleuze and Guattari) is much the same thing as rhizomes-thinking. Nomadic thinking is also a powerful way to rethink theory itself; not as something rising above our data, but as a force that works through it. Yet its very wandering nature makes nomadic thinking a difficult thing to integrate into a science-like archaeology; by its very nature, it cannot be tamed or domesticated. This is not to argue against it – quite the opposite. Archaeology needs this kind of thinking, because like abduction and speculation, it remains one of the most powerful motors of innovation. The question is not whether we need nomadic thought; rather the question is whether in embracing it, do we need to abandon arboreal thought?

Box 5.6 Binary Thinking, Dualism and Dialectics

One of the most common criticisms you will find across a range of theoretical works in archaeology is the one directed towards dualisms: nature/culture, male/female, mental/material . . . these are almost resoundingly labelled as BAD. You will even find some evidence of that in this book, so what is going on? The main impetus behind this critique is its ontological implications; that is, the way it divides up the world and nature of existence into opposing categories which allow no mixing (see Chapters 3 and 7). We can see how this kind of thinking easily falls foul of our everyday experience: is a tree we bought in a nursery and plant in our garden nature or culture? How is a product marketed as 100% natural not cultural when it has been harvested and packaged? According to philosopher Bruno Latour, such dualisms are characteristic of modern, western thinking, and almost always, you will see the blame often attached to one poor philosopher: Descartes. That is why they are often called Cartesian dualisms or Cartesian thought.

The critique of dualisms is often lumped with another critique, that of binary thinking. Whereas dualisms often tend to be linked to universal, ontological divisions, binary thinking is just as likely to be strategic, contingent and contextual. Binary thinking involves a discernment or recognition of difference which typically marks out two concepts in some relation to each other. The distinction of nature and culture can be seen as an example of binary thought but so is up/down, hot/cold. One of the reasons why philosopher Peirce is so popular today is that he always worked in threes, not twos (see Figure 5.6). But one has to be careful here in how one understands binary thinking, because although it too has been heavily criticized in archaeology – especially in relation to **structuralism** – if you look closely, it is everywhere, even among those who critique dualisms. In simply rejecting dualistic or binary thinking, one implicitly *creates* a new binary: namely, non-binary or non-dualistic thought. In case you think this is somewhat disingenuous, think of Shanks' more positive distinction between tree- and rhizomes-thinking, the latter of which is supposed to reject the dualism of tree-thinking. Isn't this somewhat self-contradictory? And this is not just Shanks; the works of Deleuze and Guattari – the go-to philosophers for many in the humanities today – are replete with binary terms. How do we reconcile this?

The issue here lies not with binary logic *per se* but rather the question of how that binary logic plays out. What does that mean? Well, with tree-thinking, binary logic tends to operate in two main ways: reduction or subsumption. With reduction, of the two opposing terms, one is made equivalent to the other; for example, to overcome the mind/matter duality, we might say that the mental can be reduced to physical processes in the brain. In archaeology, many scholars tried to reduce culture to ecological and biological processes or vice versa: to turn nature into a cultural project. A crude example would be how explanations for gender difference are rooted in biology or the genes or conversely, how sexual difference is purely a cultural construct. With subsumption (or sublation, the German term is *aufheben*), instead of trying to reduce one term to another, both terms were subsumed within a third new term. This is the classic form of dialectical thinking commonly associated with Hegel and Marx, where tension between opposing ideas is resolved through a third idea. In Hegel's dialectic, the opposition between Being and Nothingness is resolved through Becoming, or to give another coarse yet more concrete example, the tension between feudal lords and serfs in medieval Europe resulted in the emergence of the bourgeoisie. As a basis for understanding the evolution of society, dialectical materialism exploited the dynamic potential of binary logic to fuel change. For the new third term of a dialectic always instigated a new round; in this example, the emergence of the bourgeoisie led to its opposing force, the proletariat and their conflict.

What reduction and subsumption share in common as ways of working with binary logic is that in both cases, a division or opposition is resolved

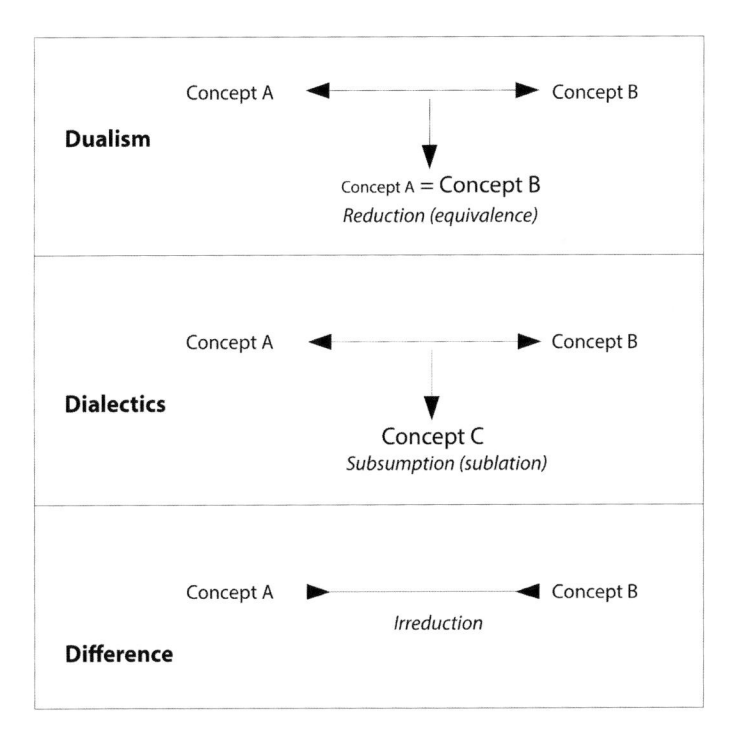

Figure 5.7 Three types of binary thinking based on the nature of the relation between two concepts.

through unity. In reduction, one term dominates and provides the means to understand the other, while in subsumption, a new third term enfolds the two older ones (Figure 5.7). If dialectics has a slight edge, it is in the fact that it recognizes this unity as short-lived, as it always results in a new contradiction. With nomadic or rhizomatic thinking, however, there is never any unity which dissolves the difference, however short-lived, but neither is there necessarily opposition or contradiction. What marks the relation between the two terms in the binary logic of nomadic thought is perhaps not one of opposition but attraction. Although there are some affinities between dialectics and nomadic thought, the main difference is that in the former, unity tends to prevail over difference whereas in the latter, the relation between two terms remains irreducible. These are admittedly difficult concepts, but the point here is that you should be careful when you hear someone bashing dualisms and binary thinking, because the more interesting issue is not the presence of two terms, but how the *relation* between those two terms is conceived and made to work.

Although this chapter has been devoted to discussing the way archaeologists create plausible or convincing accounts, we have seen there are a variety of ways in which this can be achieved. At one extreme, there are formalized approaches such as hypothesis testing and inference to the best explanation, at the other, more informal methods which draw on a hermeneutic model or evidentiary paradigm. How might this help our confused doctoral student whose confidence has taken a knock in the situation that opened this chapter? There is no easy answer to this; sometimes it is a case of submitting to the wrong journal or getting unlucky with a reviewer; different journals will have different "tastes" when it comes to styles of reasoning and argumentation informed by their history and editor, just as individual reviewers do. However, most archaeologists are aware of their own inclinations in these matters and try to be open; this is why it becomes important to spell out what your position is. Because ultimately the best way to evaluate an argument is in terms of what its goals or purpose is; some of the worst papers are those that claim to do one thing but then do something else. But it is also never that simple; part of the success of a paper also relates to issues of writing and composition that we addressed in the last chapter, but part of it is also about the basics of doing research, the topic of our next chapter.

Exercises

1. Take some journal articles and identify what kind of approach the authors use to build their case.
2. Look at some guidelines given to reviewers for a selection of peer-reviewed journals; how do they differ? If they do, why is that? Can you think of other guidelines you would write?

3. Take one journal article which has the form of an argument and analyse it in detail; how robust is it? What are its strengths and weaknesses? What assumptions does it make?

Further Reading

On Archaeological Jigsaws and Crosswords

The Willey and Phillips reference to the jigsaw hypothesis can be found in Phillips and Willey (1953), while Susan Haack's model of the crossword is in Haack (1993, esp. chapter 4). There has been a lot of ink spilt about archaeological reasoning and the work of Alison Wylie is central to much of this (Wylie 2002). For an historical overview, also see Lucas (2019, chapter 2).

Accounting for the Evidence

Of the three main approaches discussed here, hypothesis testing was heavily discussed in the later 1960s and 1970s; a classic paper is Binford (1967) while for a more recent case as summarized in this chapter, see Lucero (2014). For inference to the best explanation, a good summary is provided by Fogelin (2008), while for the example used here, see Bogaard (2015). Evidential reasoning is addressed by Chapman and Wylie, both in their co-authored study (2016) and in edited volume (2015) which includes a variety of important case studies.

Working With Evidence

Discussion of hermeneutics in archaeology can be found in Hodder (1991) and Johnsen and Olsen (1992), while Hodder's case study of the Haddenham enclosure can be found in Hodder (1992). The classic paper on the evidentiary paradigm can be found in Ginzburg (1990), while Zoë Crossland's work on the dead body can be found in Crossland (2009, 2018). More general discussions of the use of Peirce's theory of signs in archaeology can be found in Preucel (2006) and Crossland (2021). On Peirce's notion of abduction and its relation to speculation, see Marila (2020). For Shanks' discussion of tree- and rhizomes-thinking, see Shanks 1992, esp. part 1) while Braidotti (2014) discusses the issue of writing from a nomadic position.

References

Binford, L. 1967. Smudge Pits and Hide Smoking: The Use of Analogy in Archaeological Reasoning. *American Antiquity* 32(1): 1–12.
Bogaard, A. 2015. Lessons from Modelling Neolithic Farming Practices: Methods of Elimination. In R. Chapman & A. Wylie (eds.), *Material Evidence. Learning from Archaeological Practice*. London: Routledge, pp. 243–54.

Braidotti, R. 2014. Writing as a Nomadic Subject. *Comparative Critical Studies* 11(2–3): 163–84.

Chapman, R. & A. Wylie (eds.). 2015. *Material Evidence. Learning From Archaeological Practice*. London: Routledge.

Chapman, R. & A. Wylie. 2016. *Evidential Reasoning in Archaeology*. London: Bloomsbury.

Crossland, Z. 2009. Of Clues and Signs. The Dead Body and Its Evidential Traces. *American Anthropologist* 111(1): 69–80.

Crossland, Z. 2018. Forensic Afterlives. *Signs and Society* 6(3): 622–47.

Crossland, Z. 2021. 'Contextual Archaeology' Revisited: Reflections on Archaeology, Assemblages and Semiotics. In M.J. Boyd & R.C.P. Doonan (eds.), *Far From Equilibrium: An Archaeology of Energy, Life and Humanity: A Response to the Archaeology of John C. Barrett*. Oxford: Oxbow Books, pp. 85–102.

Fogelin, L. 2008. Inference to the Best Explanation: A Common and Effective Form of Archaeological Reasoning. *American Antiquity* 72(4): 603–25.

Ginzburg, C. 1990. Clues: Roots of an Evidential Paradigm. In C. Ginzburg (ed.), *Myths, Emblems, Clues*. London: Hutchinson Radius, pp. 96–125.

Haack, S. 1993. *Evidence and Inquiry. Towards Reconstruction in Epistemology*. London: Blackwell.

Hodder, I. 1991. Interpretive Archaeology and Its Role. *American Antiquity* 56: 7–18.

Hodder, I. 1992. The Haddenham Causewayed Enclosure – a Hermeneutic Circle. In I. Hodder (ed.), *Theory and Practice in Archaeology*. London: Routledge, pp. 184–207.

Johnsen, H. & B. Olsen. 1992. Hermeneutics and Archaeology: On the Philosophy of Contextual Archaeology. *American Antiquity* 57(3): 419–36.

Lucas, G. 2019. *Writing the Past. Knowledge and Literary Production in Archaeology*. London: Routledge.

Lucero, L.J. 2014. Hypothesis Testing in Archaeological Theory. In C. Smith (ed.), *Encyclopedia of Global Archaeology*. New York: Springer, pp. 3623–9.

Marila, M. 2020. *Introductory Notes to a Speculative Epistemology of Archaeology*. Doctoral Dissertation, University of Helsinki, Finland.

Phillips, P. & G. Willey. 1953. Method and Theory in American Archaeology: An Operational Basis for Culture-Historical Integration. *American Anthropologist* 55(1): 615–33.

Preucel, R. 2006. *Archaeological Semiotics*. Oxford: Blackwell Publishing.

Shanks, M. 1992. *Experiencing the Past. On the character of Archaeology*. London: Routledge.

Wylie, A. 2002. *Thinking from Things. Essays in the Philosophy of Archaeology*. Berkeley: University of California Press.

6 Doing Research

> **Situation 6: In the Supervisor's Office**
>
> *A Masters student has arrived at his first key meeting with his supervisor. His topic is early medieval spearheads in eastern England and he is particularly interested in exploring the relation between weapons and social identity. After a general chat, the supervisor starts to talk about the two most important aspects of the research design: "You need to decide on what theory you are going to use and how you are going to operationalize it; you have your dataset and you have a general question, but it needs to be made more focused, more concrete. What particular theoretical approaches to identity are you going to adopt and what methods will you use to link that theory to your dataset?" The student feels a little uncomfortable; he took theory and methods courses as an undergraduate and has read some "theoretical" papers on identity, but he had figured the answer to the question would emerge once he started working through his corpus. He doesn't want to "adopt a theory", he just wants to understand how spearheads fitted into early medieval society. Of course, some of this theory will help, but surely starting with the spearheads is more important than some abstract theory? The supervisor sees his confusion and tells him not to worry about this just yet. The first thing he needs to do is a background literature review and then they will have another meeting to hammer out the theoretical framework and methodology.*

Questions and Answers

Identifying and defining a research question is often the hardest part of any project, and then even if you have a question, finding a way to answer that can be equally challenging. So where do questions and answers come from? This is a very complex and layered issue and varies somewhat depending on the particular circumstances and situation you are in as an archaeologist. In the relatively controlled environment of student dissertations, the supervisor may even define the

DOI: 10.4324/9781003098294-7

question and methodology for you or at the very least, set strong guidelines. As you progress from undergraduate to graduate and doctoral studies though (if that is the path you take), more of this will be on your own shoulders and as a career scholar or researcher, you will be either entirely responsible for working this out or in collaboration with colleagues and other invested parties depending on the nature of the project. But however much freedom or guidance you have, there are a number of factors which play a role here. Let's have a look at some of them.

The first is about the current state of research. When conducting original research, one of the first things you do is make sure you know what work has already been done on this or related topics. Often, this will involve writing a literature review or state of the art, what is known in German as *Stand der Forschung*. Why is this important? Well, it stops you reinventing the wheel for a start; but more crucially, it enables you to identify what the current problems and issues are, where there is work still to be done and thus helps you to identify potentially fruitful research questions. These gaps or questions can range from the small and very local or specific to discipline-wide concerns. Let us then call this source of questions the "Swiss Cheese Situation"; it is about seeing disciplinary knowledge as some kind of general continuum but which has holes in it, which we can characterize either as gaps in our knowledge or questions in need of an answer. Such questions can vary depending on the extent and nature of existing research – they might be anything from gaps in the pottery sequence of a region to the mechanisms leading to social inequality.

Box 6.1   Research Agendas and Grand Challenges

In many ways, textbooks or literature review articles such as those published in the *Annual Review of Anthropology* are useful guides to both the current state of knowledge and the major topics or approaches in contemporary archaeology. However, sometimes there are publications which get more concrete and offer very specific suggestions for future research. In some countries or regions, a research framework agenda might be created, which helps to identify what is currently regarded as the most pressing issues or gaps, and such frameworks are especially useful in development-led or preventative archaeology where decisions have to be made on how to distribute often limited resources. While these might be appropriate for specific regions or periods, can the same be said for archaeology as a whole?

In 2014, a group of mostly North American archaeologists published a kind of manifesto, a set of 25 grand challenges for the discipline which, they suggested, could help to create a direction and sense of purpose for future research in archaeology. The challenges fell into five broad topics: 1) emergence, communities and complexity; 2) resilience, persistence and collapse; 3) movement, mobility and migration; 4) cognition, behaviour, and identity and 5) human–environment interactions. Each topic included several specific questions; for example, the first topic included questions around the development of inequality or markets while the last included issues of population dynamics and farming. The selection of topics and questions are themselves revealing of a certain mindset; they were generated first by a crowdsourcing initiative, which although global in its dissemination was dominated by responses from North America (79%). Participants of a follow-up workshop (who were also the authors of the article) were almost all from North America and though there was some theoretical diversity in the group, one cannot help but see the final list of challenges as a strong reflection of these filters.

Whatever your opinion of these 25 challenges, one of the problems with making any list is that it encourages uniformity, whether intentionally or inadvertently. Whether you are defining the most important research questions for the discipline or simply writing a research framework for preventative archaeology in your region, there is the danger that such lists act to obstruct innovation and penalize scholars for following a different path (see Box 2.8). And when this is written by a group of scholars occupying a hegemonic position within the discipline, this becomes doubly problematic. One of the recent criticisms of the large-scale European funding bodies is that it has privileged projects with a strong science element and thus helping to endorse a particular view of archaeology. For example, you are far more likely to get funded with a project which uses aDNA to trace prehistoric migrations than you are with a project exploring the political implications of such work. On a bigger scale, the same issues emerge in terms of heritage listings and what counts as worthy of being designated a World Heritage Site; Lynn Meskell's work here is especially relevant in uncovering the processes behind the manufacture of "internationalism" and problems of a "cosmopolitan archaeology".

How useful is it then to produce documents that aim to set out an agenda for disciplinary research – however well-intentioned they may be? At the same time, any work will inevitably carry certain connotations of what it considers to be the direction in which research should be headed; this textbook you are reading is an obvious example, framed by its own view of what theory is or should be. What is the difference then between such implicit prescriptions and more explicit agendas?

The second dimension which frames the nature of research is more personal. It is about drawing on your own, individual position and standpoint within the discipline, and within life and using that to shape your research goals and interests. For many, maybe most archaeologists, the reasons we become zooarchaeologists rather than palynologists or why we specialize in prehistoric India rather than medieval Europe are highly idiosyncratic. Maybe you had a really great teacher who got you into that topic; maybe you just have always loved the Vikings since you were a child. Of course, these kinds of choices are often very personal and specific, and indeed it is fortunate we each have our own passions and interests;

the discipline would be all the worse if everyone wanted to study Neolithic pottery! But there is more here to personal interest than simply the vicissitudes of specialization. It is fundamentally about how you see archaeology in the wider scheme of things: what is it good for, why are you choosing to spend several years of your life studying and maybe, the rest of your career in pursuit of it? Why does it matter? Maybe you don't reflect on this too deeply – it's simply fun or interesting. Isn't that a good enough reason? The same reason why you wear these clothes, like that music?

I certainly hope you do find archaeology interesting and fun; but just as your clothes or music is produced within a wider social and political context, so is archaeology. Just as your trainers may have been made in a sweatshop on the other side of the world, distributed to you by someone struggling to make ends meet, how is the archaeology you do implicated in making the world what it is – and whether that is a better or worse place? These are big questions that pertain to the relevance of a given research agenda, and to which I will return in the next chapter, but for many archaeologists, what they do is highly motivated by a sense of social and political justice. Feminist, Marxist and postcolonial or **de-colonizing archaeologies** are usually conducted by people who adopt the "personal is the political" approach to research. The kind of questions and answers they develop are closely entwined with their political beliefs. For a long time, archaeology promoted itself as a neutral science where political interests were seen to bias the course of research. Being explicit about how your politics intersected with your archaeology was usually regarded with deep suspicion. But all archaeology is in fact, politically biased (as we will explore later), and today, it is the adoption of a neutral stance that is more likely to be looked upon with suspicion than one which foregrounds politics.

Box 6.2 The Caring Archaeologist

"If a person can recognize why he or she is taking something on – disgust, awe, suffering, forbearance, endurance, love – there will follow a political or economic component. Although these sparks are emotional and personal, when they connect us to something we attempt to understand archaeologically, we are both satisfied and connected to a problem we see as worthwhile. Because we start with ourselves, we start with modern life and almost as inevitably with something political or economic or about justice, the functioning of our own society or of some other valued people or society. These ties get us to the heart of the social function of modern archaeology and may help to close the gap between archaeological goals and our own practice" (Leone 2003).

Mark Leone has been a central figure in historical archaeology in North America, well-known for his critical approach to capitalism through his decades-long fieldwork in Annapolis, Maryland. For Leone, it is important that an archaeologist knows why she or he decided to ask the questions they do: what drives them? For him, the answer was simple: he was deeply troubled by the gap between the rhetoric of American democracy and the reality of racial and class inequality and what historical archaeology was doing – or failing to do – to address this gap. This isn't about using archaeology for a political purpose so much as recognizing the politics in archaeology and the archaeology in politics. That this was an archaeological as much as a political question. Leone's work on exposing this gap – from critical studies of open-air museums like Colonial Williamsburg to his famous study of an eighteenth-century garden in Annapolis – reveals the ways in which matters of personal concern can become the basis for a lifelong research project. And what keeps such a project alive is precisely the emotional attachment – and the anger.

Leone has argued that all archaeologists get angry now and then, usually because of the gap between their expectations or goals and the reality of what they or the discipline actually achieves; such anger typically gets channelled through specific moments – and people – which for Leone is one way of seeing the various theoretical changes that have taken place in Anglo-American archaeology over the twentieth century. The key is to use such anger to feed our research and the questions we come up with. Yet care does not just need to be fuelled by anger; it can also be driven by love. A group of archaeologists have recently proposed seeing their work characterized by "heart-centred practice", one in part inspired by care-based professions like nursing and psychotherapy. That driving archaeology should be a concern for the well-being of other people for whom heritage and archaeological remains matter. Such archaeologies of heart have provided an umbrella under which to gather scholars who have long been driven by concern for the people whom archaeology impacts, such as those within indigenous and feminist archaeology.

Kishna Supernant, and indigenous (Métis) archaeologist based in Canada and one of those involved in developing archaeologies of the heart, has been active in promoting indigenous and feminist issues in the discipline. In an implicit reference to the 25 Grand Challenges (see Box 6.1), she invoked her own Grand Challenge No.1, which was how to decolonize and indigenize the educational curriculum in Canada. In a context where Native Americans and African Americans make up around or less than 1% of archaeologists, and where the political and colonial basis of archaeology is rarely foregrounded except in specialist courses, there clearly needs to be greater engagement and collaboration in archaeological pedagogy, despite

> the vast strides that have been made over the last few decades. History matters to people, and in caring for how indigenous views are incorporated into the curriculum, one is in effect, placing care at the centre of pedagogy – and that we teach others to care as well.
>
> Yet care can involve contradictory or at least competing interests. For Whitney Battle-Baptiste, an historical archaeologist of African descent who writes from an explicitly black feminist position, she acknowledges the different communities to which she belongs, especially to African Americans and to her fellow archaeologists. She confesses: "In reality, my identity as an archaeologist of African descent can at times be somewhat contradictory. For example, is it plausible to consider myself a part of the larger descendant community by birthright and simultaneously to be a member of the academy or research team that is interpreting a site?" She has described how her sense of responsibility at times became overwhelming yet at the same time, how the very contradictions between these responsibilities enabled her to tackle more critically, questions of race, class and gender that were relevant to all communities. Ultimately, care makes you a better archaeologist, as well as a better person.

Of course, whatever political stance you adopt, it is frequently informed by a wider body of writing and practice. The personal is never a purely personal position in the sense that it is your, unique angle on archaeology. All of which leads me to the third and final dimension: the broader historical context in which the discipline is situated. Although you might imagine that the history of archaeology is one of discoveries, the accumulation of new and improved information about the past, it is quite clear that throughout the history of the discipline, the kinds of questions and topics that have interested archaeologists have also changed. These changes are intimately connected to shifts in wider society. For example, the recurrent interest in human-environmental relations in the past has always been filtered through contemporary debates from the 1960s concerns with pollution through pesticides and fertilizers to the current anxieties about climate change and global warming. And archaeological studies of gender that emerged in the 1980s didn't happen in a vacuum; they were strongly influenced by the feminist movements of the preceding decades.

Traditional archaeological theory textbooks will sketch out these historical changes using what is known as the **paradigm** concept; a paradigm is generally considered to be a very general theoretical perspective or orientation, a bit like a world view but more local and specific to archaeology. Thus you might be told about the change from culture history to processualism to postprocessualism as the typical narrative of these changes as briefly referenced in Chapter 1 (Box 1.1). Another version paints a more generic image, where archaeology swings between periods of seeing itself as closer to the humanities and at other times, closer to the natural sciences (see Box 7.3). I have already mentioned why I think this kind of narrative is limiting, but even if we reject or qualify it, many archaeologists will still draw on this notion of the paradigm as rather loose and vague term to cover any general way of thinking, which guides the way a particular community of archaeologists work. For example, some might work within a paradigm of Darwinian evolution or dual inheritance theory; some might work within what today is often hailed as the new paradigm of object-oriented archaeology or new materialism. When you do operate within these frameworks, you inevitably focus on questions of issues which are often specific to them. For example, Darwinian archaeologists might be asking questions such as what context emerged to enable this artefact type to become so successful, thinking in terms of selection and "fitness"? While an archaeologist adopting assemblage theory might be more concerned with understanding the way an artefact acts to stabilize a particular assemblage of objects around it, that is how persistent associations between objects are made and maintained.

Essentially, these kinds of conceptual frameworks or paradigms are more or less synonymous with what many archaeologists think theory is. Such "theories" structure and guide the research process by defining what kind of questions we should be asking. Take a look at the topics listed in Box 6.1 again and think about how these questions are informed by particular theoretical orientations. Now while some archaeologists might stick with a particular theoretical orientation throughout their career, others will shift, maybe following whatever happens to be fashionable right now. Moreover, while some archaeologists will be very rigid in confining their focus to questions and issues that emerge from their chosen paradigm, others will be more flexible and explore continuities and connections between different perspectives. There are many different ways to think about how, as an archaeologist, you relate to these different theories and you will probably hear different opinions on what these mean. Some will be very critical of theory which constantly moves with whatever intellectual fashion happens to be "in", while others will be accused of being old-fashioned or reactionary; some will embrace theoretical eclecticism (i.e. mixing ideas from different, sometimes incompatible theories) while others will argue for conceptual rigour and purity. In most cases, these are stereotypes put up to support a particular argument.

Yet there is a real problem with characterizing theory this way and that is that it lends itself to a view of theory as something which exists prior to and applies onto a set of data. Lewis Binford was a strong critic of the paradigm model of theory; for him, a lot of the problems with contemporary archaeology were due to the way it saw theory as something one *brings* to the data rather than something one *built* as a way to explain or account for that data. For Binford, questions and problems in archaeology should always come from the archaeological record not from some general body of social theory which was developed with very different kinds of data. It is not that Binford argued against the use of such theory but rather *how* it was used. He made a distinction between an interpretive argument, which tried to show how a theory or interpretation is evidenced by archaeological data, and a referral argument, where a theory or interpretation is used to suggest an avenue of research in light of the data. Binford lamented the fact that archaeology too often adopted the former approach.

Binford was no naïve empiricist although he did tend to uphold a general separation of theory and data, and even if he wanted archaeological problems to derive from the archaeological record, there is still a sense that archaeological theory is what made sense of this data. That if data provided the questions, then theory – specifically archaeological as opposed to borrowed theory – provided the answers. But it is precisely such an equation that recent discussions of strong and weak theory have tried to unsettle (see Box 1.4). Strong theory is a theory which exemplifies this quality in a very clear way; it is the view of theory that is seen to provide order and structure on our data to render it meaningful. In contrast, weak theory is argued to be less imposing, to be more open and help facilitate meaning and relevance to emerge from the data rather than dominate it. While I find the distinction between strong and weak theory useful, it also has some limitations, the chief one being that it is hard to define what weak theory is in more positive terms beyond being the opposite of strong theory. The whole distinction between strong and weak theory is largely based on a very concrete characterization of strong theory as a set of structuring principles and concepts which are applied to ones' data. Weak theory thus becomes hard to define except in terms of negatives which is why some see it as sailing dangerously close to naïve empiricism. So even if the "rudderless" nature of weak theory is quite different from naïve empiricism, at the same time, how it actually works remains somewhat enigmatic. The danger here is that perhaps weak theory might still be linked to a notion of theory and data as separate things but with relations between theory and data inverted, whereas in fact weak theory is arguably about the dissolution of the very couplet of theory-data.

Borrowing and Moving

With these points in mind, for the rest of this chapter I want to discuss these issues not in terms of strong or weak theory but how ideas move or circulate. The only time archaeologists usually think in these terms is when they decry theory for its status as a borrower; either the complaint is "why should archaeologists be citing some French philosopher who has never picked up a trowel?" or "why can't archaeology develop its own theory instead of borrowing from other disciplines?" To some extent, these laments are ill-founded as many archaeologists would argue that other scholars are increasingly borrowing from archaeology – and maybe always have. Indeed, borrowing is something we have done and continue to do all the time. Archaeologists borrowed the trowel from the mason and bricklayer; we borrowed the principles of stratigraphy from geology; we borrow the typology we use on our bead assemblage from another archaeologist; we borrow an excavation methodology from a field manual. If I am stretching the meaning of "borrowing" here, it is to make a point: borrowing, when viewed as part of a wider practice of how we do research, is essential. But it is also perhaps better thought of as re-using or re-purposing rather than borrowing as what we do is hardly ever that passive.

The aim here is to see theory as part of a more general practice of doing archaeology; that what we do always involves re-locating a set of ideas or methods from one context to another which consequently also change in the process, and it is this broader phenomenon that matters, not making theory out to be something particularly different or special. Every time you start a new excavation or field survey, you are in effect operating a mobile laboratory as we discussed in Chapter 2. The tools, recording forms, methods of excavation and often personnel which you used on one site are being moved and "applied" to work on another. Every time you analyse an assemblage of finds, you are "copying and pasting" a set of techniques, tools and typologies from previous contexts onto new ones. Normally, we might see this in terms of embedded disciplinary knowledge, codified in field manuals and experience which is simply drawn upon and "reproduced" on each site or assemblage. But this is to emphasize the cyclical over the serial. Rather such "reproduction" is both cyclical and serial, and because each new excavation or assemblage is always different, there is change as well as repetition. By characterizing this process as one of mobility, we are reminded of this ever-present tension between mere repetition and reform or modification. Any piece of original research will always be an amalgam of novelty and mimicry.

What applies to field methods and find analysis, applies no less to more "theoretical" research. The only difference is that this "copy and paste" approach is much less codified and regulated, there is much more freedom in how we go about it and so, more scope for originality. Ultimately, what matters here is the extent to which the source and target situations are similar. The more similar the two are, the more likely your research will be imitative; the less similar, the more scope there is for innovation. With one, the risks of failure are low, with the other, success is rarer. With these preliminary remarks, let us now dive deeper into this and show how it can be used to characterize the nature of research questions and solutions in archaeology.

As I mentioned in the last paragraph, the key to understanding how "theory" works in the research process is not by thinking in terms of applicability and case studies, but as what emerges through the juxtaposition of your material with other material. You always start with something at hand; it may be in an excavation trench or with an assemblage of animal bones, it may be with an interest in gender or time; it doesn't matter if this initial matter-at-hand is an abstract idea or a bunch of bones. Wherever we start, we never just remain with that matter-at-hand. You can stare at the pile of bones all you want, but it only starts to work once you put it to work. Once you start to intervene and connect that pile of bones to measuring tools, a computer, an identification guide, a journal paper on feasting, a report on another "pile of bones" from a different site, a deposit description, a volume on capitalism ... then that pile comes to life. Through such juxtapositions, you start to draw out a web of relationalities between that pile of bones and other things. Similarly, you can reflect on gender all you want, but until you connect it your lived experiences, to how space is structured, to a feminist study on the body, to an archaeological report on a cemetery or to iconography, it won't budge. There are few guidelines here about how to make these connections, but there is no limit on them either. They are as infinite as your imagination. But equally there is no recipe for success; whether you can connect that feminist study on the body to a cemetery report or a zooarchaeological database to feasting is where the real skill and work is needed. And a little luck never hurts.

Thinking about research in these terms then is not about applying theory to data, but about making connections between concrete things – a philosophical text, an artefact assemblage, an ethnographic monograph, a site report, a scientific method. The trouble is, we tend to want to parse these different elements into two groups: theory and data. But in reality, all we are doing is measuring, reading, digging, writing or thinking with a range of different things. If it is anything, theory is what happens in the space between the juxtaposition of these different things. It is the connections that are made. Seeing theory this way means our emphasis is on the nature of these connections and relations, and so in order to understand how theory works under this description, we need to attend to the similarities and differences between the various materials or things being put together. Let's look at some examples, and for simplicity, I will focus on the juxtaposition of just two materials or things but with the implicit recognition that actual research is often a triangulation of multiple materials.

In the 1990s, historical archaeologist George Miller came up with a neat way to explore socio-economic status in excavated ceramic assemblages from nineteenth-century sites in North America. He compiled an index using contemporary price lists which assigned a value to any vessel depending on its form and manner of decoration. By totting up the cumulative values of all vessels in an assemblage, you could compare different assemblages to see how much each household had invested in their purchase of pottery (Figure 6.1). He even then tested these summed values with documented information about the household head (specifically their occupation) and found that these seemed to correlate rather well; that is, middle-class merchants tended to own more costly ceramics than poor farmers. This was a very heavily cited study in the 1990s, and though it garnered some criticism, it was also widely emulated; many other historical archaeologists working in the US used his published indices to run similar analyses on their own assemblages, and it provided a way to talk about socio-economic status and consumption in archaeological assemblages from the nineteenth century across North America.

This is an interesting example, and I have chosen it because it illustrates how difficult it can be sometimes to separate method and theory as this has elements of both. But it is also interesting because it illustrates how ideas move and circulate within archaeology, driving the research process. In this particular example, the archaeologists who copied Miller's approach were essentially using it on similar types of data (ceramics from archaeological assemblages) and similar contexts (nineteenth-century North America). In this sense, the original model and its imitators had a very similar form. In some ways, this is a strong property of most archaeological methods; think of an artefact typology for example. It begins when an archaeologist takes an assemblage of objects and creates a classification such as of Viking Age spearheads; this classification then is used on other assemblages

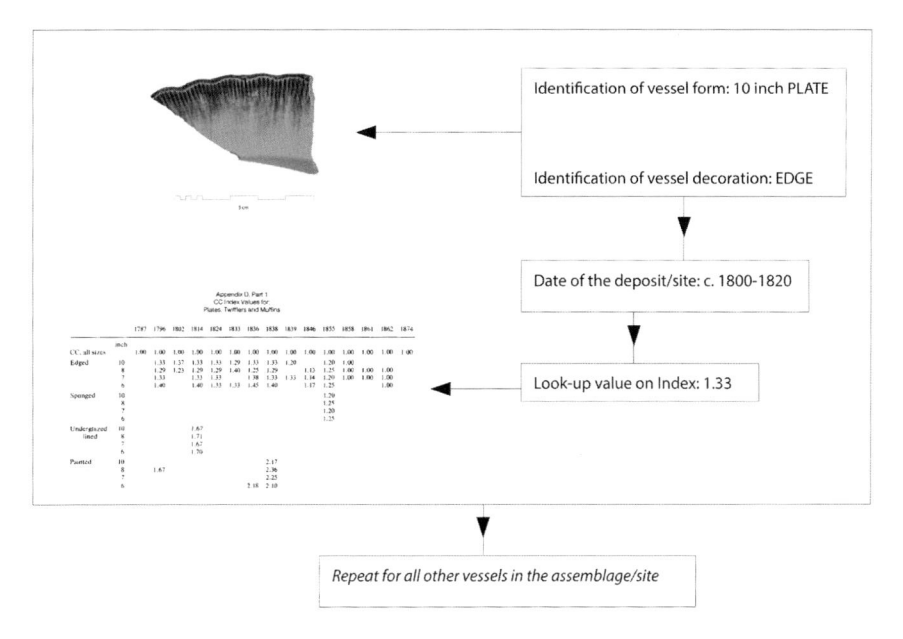

Figure 6.1 Working out the value of a plate using George Miller's CC indices.

or new finds as they are unearthed – but only so long as the new objects and contexts are regarded as sharing the same material and contextual parameters, that is, they look like spearheads and came from Viking Age contexts.

Yet many methods can work more freely of their cultural context; the same excavation techniques, for example, can work as well on a Japanese Neolithic site as an Icelandic medieval farmstead because the same tools and essentially the same materialities (rocks, soil) are involved. Of course, there are always some differences involved, but the point here is that materially speaking, the two cases are similar, even if contextually they are quite different. Let's look at another example to illustrate this. Strontium isotopes have been used in archaeology now for several decades as a way to provenance people and animals. By comparing the levels of strontium isotopes in teeth and bones against background levels in local geologies, archaeologists have been able to suggest whether the individual was born locally or migrated from somewhere else. Some of the earliest studies of this were done by Judy Seeley in South Africa in the 1980s, but others soon emulated her work such as Douglas Price, who adapted the same technique successfully to material in Europe. Once again, what we have here is a case of moving a set of ideas and practices from one context to another, but where the materials – bones, teeth, strontium isotope measurements – remained basically the same. As with excavation techniques, these kinds of scientific analyses translate successfully because even if the contexts of the bones and teeth are quite different, the materials themselves are regarded as identical for analytical purposes.

Box 6.3 The Unrepeatable Experiment?

Philip Barker once famously described excavation as the unrepeatable experiment. But is this true? For Barker it was meant to underline the fact that once you dig a site, it is destroyed and you can't go back and do it again. This is not entirely true of course; there are plenty of examples where archaeologists have gone back to re-excavate a site and of course, ended up re-interpreting it. But Barker still had a point: information is nonetheless lost and destroyed. But in another sense his analogy somewhat missed the mark. No scientific experiments work on the same materials; once you dissect a frog you don't un-dissect it and start again; no, you take a new specimen. When you re-run a chemical test, you use new chemicals. No two experiments are ever alike. One might object and argue that *this* misses the point Barker was trying to make; when you take a new frog or new batch of chemicals, you are assuming for experimental purposes that they are the same; since the kind of information you seek are common to all individuals. For Barker, you cannot treat archaeological sites like frogs; each is unique and has its own unique story to tell. But then this is surely to beg the question: how unique is this site?

This is an issue that Chris Evans has raised in the context of development-led archaeology in Britain. In an inversion of Barker's argument, Evans suggests that what archaeology needs is not flagship excavations – those big, famous sites that become the textbook exemplars or headline grabbers but rather excavations viewed more like experiments. Rather than see each site as unique, we see each for what it reveals about broader patterns. Although this is an important argument, I think there is a more general lesson here about regarding *any* excavation as an experiment. For Barker, repeatability of the experiment seemed to rest solely on the recognition that sites can somehow be treated as equivalent, like our experimental frogs. It is from this presumption of equivalence that similarities and differences start to become meaningful. But this is a one-sided representation of the experimental set-up. Equivalence is not just a presumption made about the object of study, it is something the experimental apparatus itself helps to create. Scientists don't just experiment on *any* frogs – or mice or fruit flies as is more common. They experiment on laboratory-bred organisms, ones that have been highly modified through breeding to conform to the experimental set-up. Now in archaeology, we don't of course control our sites in quite the same way biologists control their specimens. But the way we excavate does affect the way a site appears; we control our excavation methods, so that as much as possible, the same techniques are used in order to make our results comparable. There is a reason so many site plans look like they could be the same site:

> because they are produced under conditions which are meant to generate some degree of equivalence.
>
> Thus what is repeatable about an excavation is not the act itself, nor the results, but the implementation of a set of techniques, methods or protocols. This standardized implementation is what makes an excavation like an experiment. It is a mode of interacting with (and constituting) the archaeological record that is iterable and mobile, facilitated by field manuals which help to establish this iterability and mobility by canonizing these techniques and methods. It establishes a set of reproducible practices through which both fieldwork and the fieldworker are themselves reproduced. Like any experiment, there will always be a tension or trade-off between standardization and imagination, "dogma and design", but these are not so much opposites as complimentary aspects that fuel the process. Excavation is an experiment we repeat every time we go on site.

What these two examples demonstrate is that for ideas to travel from one case to another, there needs to be some degree of similarity between the two cases. Another way to think about such travelling is as forms of analogical thinking. For archaeologists, the concept of analogy most likely conjures up associations of ethnographic analogies, that is, using contemporary or recent non-Western societies as parallels for past communities as an aid to interpretation (see Box 6.4). But analogy as a form of reasoning is much broader and simply refers to any form of reasoning where inferences are made from one particular to another based on some form of similarity, as in metaphor. If I say that psychoanalysis is like archaeology, I am making a one-to-one correspondence and implying some degree of resemblance in these two practices. Importantly, the value of analogy lies in drawing out what these resemblances are and more specifically, discovering something new about the subject or target of an analogy that one hadn't realized. Another way to think of analogy is how does the mere act of juxtaposing two things normally not seen side by side change the way we look at one or both of them? What train of thought is initiated if I put a bag of finds next to a bag of candy? Inevitably not all analogies lead anywhere interesting but sometimes they do. In this sense, analogy stands in sharp contrast to the more common types of reasoning discussed in the last chapter, such as induction, which works by relating a particular to a general, such as the inference that the composition of a pottery assemblage will reflect the socio-economic status of the household based on a sample of cases. Analogy has sometimes been characterized as a type of induction, but it is quite different in this respect and shares much closer affinities with the kinds of reasoning discussed at the end of the last chapter, especially abduction and transduction.

Box 6.4 Analogy in Archaeology

A lot was written about the role of analogy in archaeology between the 1950s and 1980s, but today it is definitely *not* a hot topic. Much of this older discussion focused on how to increase the strength of analogies, and while there was a period in North American archaeology where they were viewed as a means to construct more a generalized, law-like body of knowledge that came to be known as middle range theory, on the whole the value of analogy rested on its degree of similarity with the archaeological case material. Typically, two kinds of analogy were distinguished: formal and relational. Formal analogies were based on similar appearances; in a classic example used by Alison Wylie, a class of perforated, polished stones (called "gorgets") found in North America have been the subject of much speculation over the years. One such theory suggested they looked very much like potter's tools and so the inference was, that is what they were (Figure 6.2). But such formal similarities can be very misleading as it is really the relations such objects have to other things in a material cultural system that is more important, as this tells you how they were used or what meanings they carried. As it turned out, gorgets are found on sites where no pottery was made, so although as a formal analogy it caried some conviction, as a relational analogy it completely broke down.

So how do you go about establishing grounds for strengthening a relational analogy? Clearly it wasn't enough for two objects, for example, to look alike; they had to share other, contextual properties in common make this similarity more robust. Commonly, this meant either a close historical-cultural context or similar generic features like environmental conditions or subsistence strategies. In other words, nineteenth-century ethnographies of native communities from the same region as archaeological sites were better analogues than ones from further away in time or space; analogies for sub-glacial palaeolithic sites were better sought from contemporary hunter-gatherers in the artic that nomadic pastoralists in east Africa. At the same time, these are still quite broad parameters, and it was ultimately realized that however similarity was defined, it could never provide any foolproof guarantees and so attempts to strengthen analogies in this way have been largely abandoned.

Although analogies remain in use by archaeologists today, there is rarely any attempt to qualify their use; rather, their value lies simply in their juxtaposition as fruitful means to engage and think through archaeological material. Their significance lies not in establishing a prior degree of similarity but precisely in the similarity that emerges from their juxtaposition and what that generates. That is, the use of analogy is less about how say an ethnographic case can be used to interpret a prehistoric site

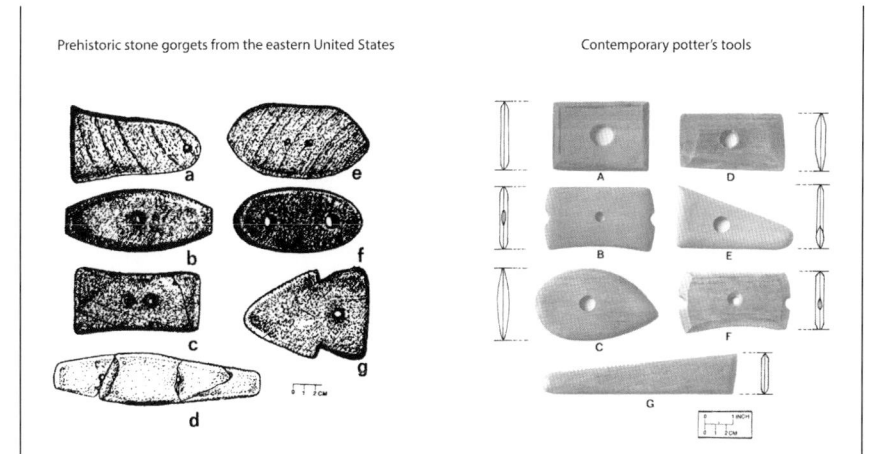

Figure 6.2 Formal analogy between prehistoric stone gorgets and contemporary potter's tools (adapted from Curren 1977).

but rather that the ethnographic example acts as a foil to think through and alongside the archaeological data. That what matters is not how close the analogue fits your prehistoric case but that the juxtaposition of the two together was generative of new ideas that are present in neither on their own. In many ways, this is a bit like the Peircean notion of abduction as the drawing of novel inferences or possibilities from two known state of affairs.

If we can then regard analogy as a way of generating lines of thought through concrete juxtaposition, the same can also be argued for even more abstract, theoretical juxtapositions. As a final example, let me use the case of structuralism. We met structuralism briefly in Chapter 3 where you will recall it is a very abstract body of theory which emerged in the 1960s across the humanities as a way to investigate cultural phenomena. Originally a theory of language, it was transposed onto other kinds of materials and situations such as myths, kinship systems, spatial organization, architecture and artefact design and distribution. While we often talk about structuralism as a classic case of an abstract theory which gets applied to archaeological data, this deeply misrepresents how it actually operates. There are a set of concepts or terms, which though originally constructed to work with spoken language, are migrated and made to work on other materials, just like Miller's ceramic indices, strontium isotope analysis, ethnographic analogies. As they migrate, they subtly change; how Roland Barthes analysed French fashion or food was different to how Claude Levi-Strauss analysed Amazonian communities, and this was different again to how Ian Hodder analysed Neolithic pottery. There is a connection, a shared genealogy, but this is better regarded as a serial process of moving ideas from one context to another than as about reproducing a stock body of theory. If structuralism – and almost any theory in archaeology – has been viewed as something abstract which one applies, this is simply a product of our thinking of theory in paradigmatic terms. Such a view has been perpetuated and reinforced in the humanities and social sciences since the middle of the twentieth century by textbooks and introductions to either particular brands of theory or the array of theory present within any given discipline. It is precisely this view of theory that this textbook tries to subvert.

Surprise and Improvisation

Based on the discussion in the last section, one can suggest that the research process is not about some constant dialectic between theory and data but rather the movement of ideas and things from one context to another. However, in framing it like this we face a new problem. Let me put it like this: when an archaeologist draws on Miller's work with their own material or data set, or uses established methods like isotope analysis or classifications of Viking Age spearheads, how is new knowledge generated? To some extent, one could say one is simply imitating or copying a method or idea, but when you do that, can anything new really emerge? This is certainly one of the common criticisms of theory; that in drawing on, for example, an ethnography of Melanesia to help understand Neolithic England, all one has really done is made Neolithic England look like Melanesia in a colder climate. At the same time, the very similarity is what guarantees the ability to migrate an idea; it is important precisely to copy the protocols of isotope analysis or the criteria of a classification to ensure a valid result. So how can we both imitate and innovate at the same time?

The problem here, as anthropologist Tim Ingold has pointed out, partly relates to the way we set up imitation and innovation as opposites, where copying is characterized as lacking in creativity, while innovation is all about being creative. In practice though, it is easy to see how this simplistic dichotomy is misleading. When you use an existing or established typology to classify your spearheads, there may well be examples that don't quite fit, which may result in a revision to the system. This has happened many times in archaeology; for example, consider the various types of Roman Samian pottery (*terra sigillata*), which are based on an original typology laid out by Hans Dragendorff in 1895 but was subsequently expanded by Déchelette, Knorr and Walters among others over the next decades. But even when using a typology without amending it, innovation is possible; if you identify a type not previously seen in a region or a period, new data are generated. And when scholars use Miller's indices or isotope analysis without making any alterations to the method or protocols as they work with it on their own material, new information is still generated. All archaeology thus involves a complex mix of imitation and innovation.

When borrowing or copying an idea or method developed in one context or moving or translating it into another, sometimes this translation is easy, as with

Miller's ceramic indices; but sometimes it is very hard work, as with structuralism. To some extent, the more work required, the more scope there is for creativity and originality, or, to put it in the terms I used in the last section, the less similar the donor and recipient are, the greater the risk, but also the greater the rewards. Perhaps rather than think in terms of imitation and innovation, it may be better to think of research and learning as a process of improvisation as Ingold has suggested. Sometimes, we need to improvise more, sometimes less, but the more improvisation there is, the greater chance there is of producing something new. I think it is also fruitful to connect the idea of improvisation with speculation, abduction and transduction that we discussed at the end of the last chapter, which were also important sources of novelty. But the advantage of improvisation over speculation is that it encompasses a wider sense of practice and engagement with a situation, whereas speculation has a narrower and more detached connotation.

Most academic research tends to set greater value on originality; funding bodies, awards, even thesis requirements stress it to varying degrees, although ironically, they never define what it is. Indeed, originality is not an unproblematic term as it is entangled with specific politics of knowledge production which values originality over imitation. Yet as feminist scholar Berenice Carroll pointed out many years ago, the academic valuation of originality is often gendered (e.g. "Pitt Rivers is the father of British fieldwork") but also ultimately functions as a reward system in a culture where work attributable to identifiable individuals is paramount (e.g. citation systems). Collective or anonymous authorship is often difficult or impossible.

What is originality then? It is interesting to reflect on how the term embraces two subtly different qualities. On the one hand, we think of an original as something which is the first of its kind, not a copy or derivative; on the other, an original is something without precedent, something that occurs *ex nihilo* or from nothing. In other words, one dimension to originality focuses on the presence of a future, the fact that an original has imitators; while the other dimension focuses on the absence of a past, the fact is that an original has no predecessor. This immediately sets up originality as something outside the normal flow of science, which is mostly then derivative or imitative, which plays into Kuhn's concept of scientific revolutions and **normal science**. Yet it is quite obvious that no work is like this – every work, no matter how "original", has precedents, and by the same token, most acts of imitation involve a degree of innovation. How something is ultimately classed as original or derivative can be a fine line but maybe it should not even matter; the privileging of originality is more a reflection of a desire for a "class system of the intellect" and as a concept for assessing the value of a work, ultimately sterile and reductionist. As suggested earlier, a greater store ought to be put on the process of improvisation and although part of this is circumscribed by the degree of structure around the movement of an idea, part of it is also defined by the degree to which things confound or surprise us, such as when an artefact doesn't fit into a typology or the results of using Miller's indices invert our expectations. Let us now pursue this discussion further through some archaeological examples and focus more specifically on the idea of novelty rather than originality.

158 *Doing Research*

Every archaeological excavation unearths new finds, new features, but does this constitute new knowledge? This all depends on how you see it in the context of existing knowledge of course. What to an undergraduate archaeologist appears new, may not to a senior academic who has seen fashions come and go and even re-appear. When a student on an excavation finds a decorated pottery sherd and feels a wave of excitement because it is nothing like any of the other sherds they have dug up, it elicits no such response from the director because they have seen many like it on other sites. Novelty is certainly relative; but because knowledge is a collective or social endeavour, it is the disciplinary context of knowledge that can be taken to define novelty, not that of any given individual. On the other hand, even at a disciplinary level there may be no consensus on novelty – simply because disciplinary knowledge itself is not a neat, coherent system but a patchwork of different perspectives, problems whose relevance may vary wildly between those in the discipline.

Let me tell you a story which hopefully will illustrate what I see as a key feature of novelty. In the early 1970s, probably the first major urban excavation in Reykjavik took place, led by the Swedish archaeologist Else Nordahl. Apart from remains of an eighteenth-century textile factory, the other major find and one that made most headlines was the excavation of a Viking farm dating to the first decades of settlement. Immediately speculation circulated about whether this was the home of the historical figure recorded as the first settler of Reykjavík, Ingólfur Arnason. The archaeologists generally remained agnostic about this, preferring to focus on the site as evidence of early settlers' lifeways, and on the whole, the discovery of the site matched general expectations of the settlement patterns of Iceland being that of individual farmsteads. Viking Reykjavík was no bustling emporia as seen in the foundation of many other urban excavations happening in Scandinavia at the same time.

Then in 2001, new archaeological excavations began at a plot adjacent to that from the 1970s, and a second Viking hall was discovered. Once again, media speculation flared up – could *this* be the home of Íngólfur Arnarson? How many houses does one guy need? Once again, the archaeologists steered away from such issues, focusing on the implications for settlement patterns; certainly there were other cases of farms with two halls in Iceland, so though unusual, it was not exceptional. But then in 2007, a third hall was found – and yes, you guessed it, old Ingólfur crops up again. But more seriously, the discovery of this site, along with other remains found earlier, such as a wooden trackway, forge and other structures from the same period, have started to throw a big question mark around what we think we know about the nature and density of settlement process during the first centuries of *landnám* in Reykjavík.

So what can we learn from this story? From one perspective, each site on its own did not produce anything new; all the buildings had a similar form and construction as seen on other Viking farmsteads previously excavated in Iceland and the same goes for the finds. Certainly each was unique in its own way and new in a sense, but none of them offered new *kinds* of buildings and artefacts. Collectively, however, it is a different matter altogether; as a group, they are redefining the type of settlement forms we are used to seeing in Iceland from the earliest centuries, and in that sense, new knowledge is surely emerging.

One of the key features of this story was that the empirical evidence seemed to stack up as a series of anomalies; this aspect might be used to tell a story of how conceptual novelty emerges from the proliferation of empirical anomalies. This is in fact the classic view of how theory as paradigms change. But there is more than anomaly going on here; the second and then third farms were not just anomalous with respect to existing knowledge, they were also unexpected. They were a surprise. How did this come about? In the case of the discovery of the second farm, given its location next to that excavated in the 1970s, there was at least some expectation of further Viking remains – outhouses or other contemporary features. But no one expected to find another Viking hall. In the case of the third hall, there was not even any expectation of Viking remains at all, except in the vaguest terms. How do we understand such surprises? Do we just relegate them to random chance, luck, the serendipity accompanying any act of excavation or can we use this as way of reflecting more broadly on novelty?

This is where the wider context of these excavations matter; none of these were research excavations but rather work done ahead of urban development; these sites were dug because someone wanted to build hotels on these plots. Now this non-archaeological reason for digging at a site can sometimes be frustrating, but at the same time, in injecting an element of chance into the archaeological process, it also creates the conditions for new knowledge. In other words, novelty emerges not simply through confoundment but also surprise. And as the example of the Reykjavík Viking halls shows, development-led archaeology is very good at throwing up surprises. I am certainly not suggesting that surprise is absent from research-led excavations. One of the thrills with any excavation is that no matter how much background research and preparation you have done, you can never be quite sure what the earth will reveal as you put your spade or trowel into the ground. Every excavation contains that seed of excitement and anticipation of the unexpected. But what I do want to suggest is that when the conditions for choosing a site are *non*-archaeological, they increase the likelihood of surprise and consequently, confoundment simply because they are not being framed by the research tradition with all its prior assumptions and expectations. There is an element of truth to that old saying, you will only find what you are looking for.

If we can extrapolate from this, one can suggest that novelty emerges in contexts where external forces have a significant impact on archaeological research. In development-led or preventative archaeology, this is unavoidable and often decried, yet it has resulted in some stunning discoveries and changes to the way we understand the past. In the neater and tidier world of academia with its carefully scripted research designs and competitive funding, one usually tries to keep such external forces to a minimum. But even here, the "external element" can prove to be beneficial and ultimately should be something we cultivate. Collaboration with indigenous communities, for example, is not just ethically and politically the right thing to do, it also has epistemic advantages (see Box 6.5). Reading what anthropologists have to say about personhood or philosophers about time is not just for those with an interest in "theory" but has epistemic advantages. At the end of the day, what keeps archaeology alive, dynamic and moving forward is not new data or new theories, but cultivating an openness to the unexpected, the unplanned which means embracing the permeability and fluidity of our disciplinary borders. Archaeology doesn't begin or end as we leave the site to the builders, it doesn't begin or end with your professional colleagues, and it doesn't begin end with archaeological journals or conferences. Its links to other people, other practices and other things are there and it is because of them, that novelty is possible.

Box 6.5   Creativity and Collaborative Archaeology

Saying yes to this collaboration forced me to put aside my own agenda and commit myself to the tribe. By dedicating myself to research serving the needs of others, I had opened the door to worlds of knowledge that I never would have known existed – and forced myself to learn things that I never would have dared to learn on my own.

(Liebmann 2018)

Matthew Liebmann is an archaeologist based in the US who has worked a lot on postcolonial issues in archaeology, and in one particular instance, his collaboration with an indigenous Native American tribe in the southwest proved unexpectedly creative. The Jemez Pueblo approached Liebmann with the idea of getting help on understanding the ancestral use of a culturally important locale, the Valles Caldera National Preserve in New Mexico. It sounded great – only there was one problem: archaeologically, the area was almost a void, with the exception of some lithic scatters. There were no ruins of abandoned villages, no middens bursting with pottery, which were the kinds of things he was used to working with. Moreover, the tribe preferred a non-intrusive field strategy in case any burials should be disturbed. How on earth could he bring anything to the table? But as it turned out, it was quite emancipating.

Working with members of the tribe, Liebmann surveyed 30 sites in the area and retrieved substantial surface collections of obsidian lithics; these they then submitted to XRF analysis with a portable XRF gun to provenance them, comparing them to the five known obsidian sources in the area. The results revealed the predominance of one source of obsidian over four others – a predominance which had no relation to quality or proximity to source but rather spoke of the special, cultural meanings which must have attached to this source. More generally, it demonstrated ancestral occupation of the region for over four centuries. It may not sound like a

Figure 6.3 Jemez tribal member Aaron Tosa collecting obsidian and ceramic samples at the ancestral Jemez pueblo of Kwastiyukwa (photo: Matt Liebmann).

great discovery, but for the tribe, it was of major significance because not only did it agree with their own cultural knowledge, it provided scientific data admissible in a court over a land claim. For Liebmann on the other hand, it was revelatory about knowledge production. In a scientific culture which values project designs guided by strong, academic research agendas, ceding control of the parameters of a project like this can feel inherently uncomfortable. Yet what Liebmann found was the exact opposite: it opened up new perspectives and benefits that a traditional approach would never have given.

So where does all this leave our master's student researching early medieval spearheads? The advice of his supervisor is fairly typical of how many research projects are set up at universities around the world, but in many ways it is deeply flawed. On the one hand, it certainly encourages an awareness of the importance of theory to research. On the other, it paints an image of theory as something separate from data, something which requires application. Theory becomes something like a commodity you shop for or take off the shelf and its role in the research process is all about finding the right theory that suits you. Regarded in this way, theory will all too often exhibit the qualities that we criticize it for: being derivative or imitative, or even worse, as ill-fitting and contrived. Maybe our student needs to get themselves a new supervisor.

Exercises

1. Devise your own list of 25 (or less) "grand challenges" for archaeology; should they be local or global? How do they compare with the list by Kintigh et al. (2014)?
2. Ask your teacher why they do what they do!
3. Take a journal article and see if you can identify what broad "theory" informs its approach; how explicit is the author about this?
4. Using Google Ngram viewer (https://books.google.com/ngrams), type in some key words (like "archaeology and religion") to see how popular different topics are over time.
5. Take a journal article and see what role models or exemplars it imitates; how important do you think originality is to the value of this paper?

Further Reading

Questions and Answers

The "25 Grand Challenges" discussed in Box 6.1 come from Kintigh et al. (2014); for a general discussion of research frameworks, see Darvill (2007), and for the example of the UK, see Belford (2020). On World Heritage and cosmopolitanism in archaeology, see Meskell (2009, 2018) and De Cesari (2010). Mark Leone's personal approach to archaeology can be found in various publications, especially Leone (2003, 2010) while more broadly, a discussion of how issues of standpoint affect one's archaeological approach have been discussed from a feminist (e.g. Wylie 2007) and indigenous perspective (e.g. Nicholas 2016). For a range of papers showcasing archaeologies of the heart, see Supernant et al. (2020), and for Supernant's Grand Challenge No. 1, see Supernant (2020). Whitney Battle-Baptiste's archaeology can be found in her book (2011). For the current reigning "theories" and theoretical fashions in archaeology, pick up any recent textbook (e.g. Harris & Cipolla 2017; Hodder 2012; Johnson 2019). On paradigms in archaeology, see Lucas (2017). Binford offers his own inimitable take on where archaeological questions come from in Binford (2001), while discussions of strong and weak theory in archaeology can be found in Pétursdóttir and Olsen (2018) and Lucas and Witmore (2022).

Borrowing and Moving

On archaeological "borrowing", see Lucas (2015, 2019 esp. ch. 5). The examples of price indexes used in historical archaeology referred to can be found in Miller

(1980, 1991), while the citations to strontium isotope work can be found in Price et al. (2002). For excavation as the unrepeatable experiment, see Barker (1982), Bradley (2015) and Evans (2012). The nature of ethnographic analogy in archaeology is covered in a classic paper by Wylie (1985).

Surprise and Improvisation

On the false dichotomy of imitation and innovation and the idea of learning as improvisation, see Ingold (2013). On the politics of originality, see Carroll (1990), while for discussions of novelty in archaeology, see Ribeiro (2016) and Sørensen (2019). The case study discussed by Matthew Liebmann can be found in Liebmann (2018).

References

Barker, P. 1982. *Techniques of Archeological Excavation* (2nd edition). London: Batsford.

Battle-Baptiste, W. 2011. *Black Feminist Archaeology*. Walnut Creek: Left Coast Press.

Belford, P. 2020. Borderlands: Rethinking Archaeological Research Frameworks. *The Historic Environment: Policy & Practice* 11(2–3): 359–81.

Binford, L. 2001. Where Do Research Problems Come from? *American Antiquity* 66(4): 669–78.

Bradley, R. 2015. Repeating the Unrepeatable experiment. In R. Chapman & A. Wylie (eds.), *Material Evidence. Learning From Archaeological Practice*. London: Routledge, pp. 23–41.

Carroll, B. 1990. The Politics of "Originality": Women and the Class System of the Intellect. *Journal of Women's History* 2(2): 136–63.

Curren, C.B. 1977. Potential Interpretations of "Stone Gorget" Function. *American Antiquity* 42: 97–101.

Darvill, T. 2007. Research Frameworks for World Heritage Sites and the Conceptualization of Archaeological Knowledge. *World Archaeology* 39(3): 436–57.

De Cesari, C. 2010. World Heritage and Mosaic Universalism. A View from Palestine. *Journal of Social Archaeology* 10(3): 299–324.

Evans, C. 2012. Archaeology and the Repeatable Experiment: A Comparative Agenda. In A. Jones, J. Pollard, M. Allen & J. Gardiner (eds.), *Image, Memory and Monumentality. Archaeological Engagements with the Material World*. Oxford: Oxbow Books, pp. 295–306.

Harris, O. & C. Cipolla. 2017. *Archaeological Theory in the New Millennium*. London: Routledge.

Hodder, I. (ed.). 2012. *Archaeological Theory Today*. Cambridge: Polity Press.

Ingold, T. 2013. Making, Growing, Learning: Two Lectures Presented at UFMG, Belo Horizonte, October 2011. *Educaçao em Revista, Belo Horizonte* 29(3): 297–325.

Johnson, M. 2019. *Archaeological Theory. An Introduction*. Chichester: Wiley-Blackwell.

Kintigh, K.W., J. Altschul, M. Beaudry, R. Drennan, A. Kinzig, T. Kohler, W. Limp, H. Maschner, W. Michener, T. Pauketat, P. Peregrine, J. Sabloff, T. Wilkison, H. Wright & M. Zeder. 2014. Grand Challenges for Archaeology. *American Antiquity* 79(1): 5–24.

Leone, M. 2003. The Origins of Questions in Historical Archaeology. In T. VanPool & C. VanPool (eds.), *Essential Tensions in Archaeological Method and Theory*. Salt Lake City: University of Utah Press, pp. 17–22.

Leone, M. 2010. Walter Taylor and the Production of Anger in American Archaeology. In A. Maca, J. Reyman & W. Folan (eds.), *Prophet, Pariah, and Pioneer: Walter W. Taylor and Dissension in American Archaeology*. Boulder: University of Colorado Press, pp. 315–30.

Liebmann, M. 2018. Losing Control in the American Southwest: Collaborative Archaeology in the Service of Descendant Communities. In S. Silliman (ed.), *Engaging Archaeology. 25 Case Studies in Research Practice*. Oxford: Wiley Blackwell, pp. 23–30.

Lucas, G. 2015. The Mobility of Theory. *Current Swedish Archaeology* 23: 13–82.

Lucas, G. 2017. The Paradigm Concept in Archaeology. *World Archaeology* 49(2): 260–70.

Lucas, G. 2019. *Writing the Past. Knowledge and Literary Production in Archaeology*. London: Routledge.

Lucas, G. & C. Witmore. 2022. Paradigm Lost: What Is a Commitment to Theory in Contemporary Archaeology? *Norwegian Archaeological Review*. https://doi.org/10.1080/00293652.2021.1986127.

Meskell, L. (ed.). 2009. *Cosmopolitan Archaeologies*. Durham: Duke University Press.

Meskell, L. 2018. *A Future in Ruins. UNESCO, World Heritage and the Dream of Peace*. Oxford: Oxford University Press.

Miller, G. 1980. Classification and Scaling of 19th Century Ceramics. *Historical Archaeology* 14: 1–40.

Miller, G. 1991. A Revised Set of CC Index Values for Classification and Economic Scaling of English Ceramics 1787–1880. *Historical Archaeology* 25(1): 1–25.

Nicholas, G. (ed.). 2016. *Being, and Becoming an Indigenous Archaeologists*. London: Routledge.

Pétursdóttir, Þ. & B. Olsen. 2018. Theory Adrift: The Matter of Archaeological Thinking. *Journal of Social Archaeology* 18(1): 97–117.

Price, T.D., J.H. Burton & R.A. Bentley. 2002. The Characterization of Biologically Available Strontium Isotope Ratios for the Study of Prehistoric Migration. *Archaeometry* 44(1): 117–35.

Ribeiro, A. 2016. Archaeology Will Be Just Fine. *Archaeological Dialogues* 23(2): 146–51.

Sørensen, T.F. 2019. The Triviality of the New: Innovation and Impact in Archaeology and Beyond. *Current Swedish Archaeology* 26: 93–117.

Supernant, K. 2020. Grand Challenge No.1: Truth and Reconciliation. Archaeological Pedagogy, Indigenous Histories, and Reconciliation in Canada. *Journal of Archaeology and Education* 4: 1–22.

Supernant, K., J. Baxter, N. Lyons & S. Atalay (eds.). 2020. *Archaeologies of the Heart*. New York: Springer.

Wylie, A. 1985. The Reaction Against Analogy. *Advances in Archaeological Method and Theory* 8: 63–111.

Wylie, A. 2007. Doing Archaeology as a Feminist: Introduction. *Journal of Archaeological Method and Theory* 14: 209–16.

7 Defining the Discipline

> **Situation 7: At a Conference**
>
> *It is her first time presenting at a major conference; her research, which revolves around the archaeology of swimming pools, is being presented in a session on "Alternate Landscapes". The abstract for the session sounded like this would be the best fit as it was inviting contributions which would expand the conception of archaeological place and spaces – but having listened to the two previous speakers, she is now feeling a bit nervous. But when her turn comes, she gets up and delivers her 15-minute presentation immaculately and then waits for questions. An old guy sitting in the front raises his hand and starts to speak . . . . "This is more of an observation than a question . . ." whence follows several minutes of personal experiences with pools which seems to bear no relation to her talk. But then, he ends with a bombshell: "Having said all that though, your research sounds to me more like a piece of sociology or ethnography . . . I mean as far as I can see you haven't excavated any pools, or even surveyed them; you have offered no typology. What makes this archaeology?" Some of the audience gasp at this. Most are silent, curious to see how she would reply. She pauses for a moment and is unsure how to respond . . . Later, she found out this "old guy" was none other than a famous Oxford professor, an archaeologist whose works she had read and admired. Now she wonders . . . .*

What Is Archaeology?

"What is Archaeology?" might seem like a straightforward question; I am sure you have your own sense of what it is and if pushed, you could probably offer some kind of definition. For the purposes of this discussion, I am going to use the definition offered by Colin Renfew and Paul Bahn in their famous textbook: ". . . archaeologists study past societies primarily through their material remains". It sounds reasonable – and as a general description, I think it is one that most of us would agree with. Yet if we dig a little deeper, we will quickly realize that this definition leaves a lot still open, and indeed, all its key ingredients – humanity, material culture and the past – have been subject to critical scrutiny by archaeologists over the last few decades. In this section, I want to explore some of the issues and questions raised and in doing so, make you rethink what archaeology is – or can be.

The Past

One of the most defining features of archaeology is that it is concerned with the past. But what is, or when was, the past? Even at cursory glance, it is obvious the past, strictly speaking, can refer to the previous moment, a mere second ago. Is that then, within the scope of archaeology? Traditionally, archaeology has been focused on the distant past and certainly in terms of our disciplinary history, this has generally meant anything medieval or earlier. Archaeological research on post-medieval or modern remains is a field that has only really grown in the last 50–60 years and even then, it varies between countries. At the time of writing, Norway, for example, only legally and automatically protects archaeological remains older than 1537, that is the date of the Reformation, although protection and definition are two different things. Indeed there are many Norwegian archaeologists working on more recent material and the various sub-fields of post-medieval, modern and contemporary archaeology has been one of the boom areas in the last few decades. So even if there are not many archaeologies dealing with the last few seconds, there is a growing scholarship on the archaeology of the last decades and century. Indeed, even back in the 1980s, some archaeologists argued that archaeology is the study of material culture, irrespective of time (or place). Nonetheless, prehistory and to a lesser extent medieval archaeology still remain the dominant areas of research within our discipline which reflects an invisible line or divide in our perception of the past – one based around the division between history before and after writing.

We are all familiar with the role the Christian calendar plays in structuring our timelines; the use of BC and AD, or more commonly today, BCE and CE, reflect a dividing line in human history between time before the birth of Christ and after. Many of us probably don't really give it much thought today, and we use this division as an arbitrary device; in historical sciences, the *anno domini* system is purely secular, a convention with no religious meaning. Despite that, it probably still silently influences the way we think about the past; somehow, BC or BCE is much more distant from our present than AD or CE. Although it doesn't map onto the BC/AD distinction, there is an even more influential division, and that is between prehistory and history. The past where there is writing and where there is none. Where this line is varies between different parts of the world of course, and even where you have written texts, they vary massively. There is a world of difference between the first cuneiform tablets of late fourth millennium BCE Mesopotamia and the massive paper archives of seventeenth-century England.

The line between prehistory and history therefore is not sharp, not even in one place. Yet maintaining the distinction is to uphold the importance of writing, and in a global context, this has a very strong political dimension as it is linked to colonialism as it divides the world into people with and those "without history". Especially in places like North America, the prehistory/history divide creates a false sense of rupture and elides narratives of indigenous persistence and resistance.

Moreover, the presence of writing has played a major role in defining what we consider to be within the purview of archaeology and has influenced the shape of our discipline. Archaeologists studying prehistory often inhabited – and still do inhabit – a very different discipline to classical or medieval archaeologists who work alongside texts. It is not just that working with texts alters the way you work with objects, but historically, prehistory always had a much closer affinity to geology and the earth sciences while classical and medieval archaeologies shared closer links with the humanities. Today, these historical differences are much less distinct and the way prehistorians and historical archaeologists work is not as different as it once was; at the same time, we cannot ignore the way past perceptions of the past have affected the constitution of what archaeology is, the way it is organized and structured. It explains why prehistory remains taught as a separate field to historical archaeology or even how the past is divided up into segments

Figure 7.1 A pavement on Mill Road, Cambridge, England; like an archaeological site, it is mix of multiple past events whose material presence persists in the present (photo: Laurent Olivier).

based on much older schemes – whether it is the Three Age System or the divisions between antiquity, the Middle Ages, and Modernity. These divisions don't just structure disciplinary knowledge, they also embody a particular politics of the past.

So far, I have discussed the past as if it was a line, laid out from the present and stretching back to some origin point – typically, the emergence of hominins and *Homo* species. But it is one thing to decide how much of this line archaeology should cover or how we should cut or divide up the line, quite another to question the line itself. Why do we see the past like this at all? And if we regard the past differently, how might that change the way we regard archaeology? Think about it this way; when you are on an excavation or visiting a heritage site, where is the past in relation to the present? Those flints or potsherds you dig up and that medieval stone church in front of you, are they five hundred or a thousand years away from where you are right now? Or are they, in fact, also right here, right now? The past – the material past – is all around us, it exists only in the present, as French archaeologist Laurent Olivier reminds us (Figure 7.1). The past we imagine as a point or period on a line – 500 AD or 3400 BC – is just that: a product of our imagination. It doesn't exist. Whatever does exist of it – remnants of a building, scattered artefacts, pollen or seeds – exists only here and now, in the present. If archaeology is the study of the past, then surely is it always the study of the past as it exists in the present. To argue that history is a fiction is hard for many to accept, and even if we can acknowledge that the past only exists in the present, it is much harder for most of us to abandon the idea of historical time. These debates remain lively and are by no means over.

Box 7.1   When Did the Neolithic End?

You probably know that the Neolithic is a term used by prehistoric archaeologists in Europe to refer to the span of time that comes after the Mesolithic and before the Bronze Age – all of which are what we call "periods". Although a complex package with various attributes, the most common feature of this period is that it is linked with the emergence of farming and the transition from a hunter-gatherer lifestyle. When it began and when it ended is obviously variable, depending upon what part of Europe or the Old World you are dealing with; but archaeologists generally assume it has ended, and ended a long time ago. But did it? Archaeologists Alfredo Gonzáles-Ruibal and Chris Witmore have both suggested that in fact it was only in the twentieth century that the Neolithic finally ended; what did they mean?

If the Neolithic is defined by a lifestyle based on farming, then most of the world's population have remained "Neolithic" until the last few centuries. Go back a few generations and probably most of your ancestors made their livelihood from the land. In fact over the course of the twentieth century, the proportion of people making their living off farming dropped from c. 50% to 2% in Europe and North America, suggesting that this is the century that really witnessed the end of the Neolithic. Now an obvious response to this is to argue that the Neolithic is more than about farming – it is about monuments, about ideologies, and even about a particular type of farming – horticultural and pastoral. It is about handmade pottery and polished stone tools. It is about a historically specific configuration of materialities that no longer exist except as archaeological remains. All of this is true of course, but it also presupposes a particular way of looking at time and history – as neatly bundled into segments (i.e. periods). An alternative is to focus on specific continuities and ruptures – like the global shift of humanity where only a small percentage are actually engaged in agriculture.

In signalling the twentieth century as the end of the Neolithic, Gonzáles-Ruibal and Witmore are not really engaging with debates about how to define a period like the Neolithic, but rather questioning the very idea of periodization and how we conceptualize time and history. In Gonzáles-Ruibal's paper, the issue comes out with the way we separate modern from traditional material culture in the context of ethnoarchaeology. In his case, the Ethiopian Gumuz among whom he stayed had modern assault rifles alongside calabashes, hoes and handmade pottery. The Neolithic sits side by side with the twentieth century which is not a conceptual problem for the Gumuz, but for archaeologists, they upset our expectations of neat periodization. In Witmore's study of Texan cattle cities, he also connects up the massive changes in societal organization ushered in by the twentieth century with our current environmental crisis. Indeed, the dependence on beef and dairy products in the global north/West and the contribution such large cattle herds are making to greenhouse gas emissions are historical consequences of the early domestication of wild cattle twenty-five centuries ago. Such deep time continuities unsettle our neat periodizations and question our taken-for-granted assumptions about the past.

Humans

In the last section, we saw that even if we define archaeology by a concern with the past, this is by no means straightforward. In this section, we will find the same difficulties with the second ingredient, humans. That archaeology is concerned with the human past seems, again, undeniable. Despite the often, mistaken impression of some, archaeologists do not study dinosaurs, they study people – or rather more usually, contexts where people have once been and the objects they once made or used. This is what separates archaeology from geology or palaeontology. At the same time, apart from skeletal, mummified or otherwise preserved bodies, most archaeology actually deals with things other than people. Is this a paradox? Not really, but it does depend on how you see the relationship between these things and people. Traditionally, archaeologists would say they are trying to get to past humans *through* these things; that things are the immediate or proximate object of study, but people are the ultimate object of our investigations. During much of the twentieth century, there was a lot of debate about what kind of information you could get about people from these things; for some, they gave better insight into practical activities and engagements with the environment, but to learn about people's religious beliefs or cosmologies was considered much harder to access. British archaeologist Christopher Hawkes called this the ladder of inference in the 1950s. In the 1980s and 1990s, many archaeologists claimed to have scaled this ladder, and papers and books on ritual, religion and ideology were very popular.

But whatever position you took on this, there was a general consensus that the things archaeologists studied were essentially proxies or indirect evidence of something else, whether that was social organization or subsistence practices, ideology or trade systems. This is what North American archaeologist Kent Flannery once called, "the system behind the Indian behind the artefact". But then, towards the end of last millennium, archaeologists started to think about these things differently; instead of viewing stone tools and pots as merely *reflecting* these human social and cultural institutions, they started to be seen as active co-creators of them. If one were being honest, this is probably something archaeologists have always been aware of, but what did change was the role given to such things. Up until then, humans were considered to be the prime, indeed sole agents when it came to understanding the human past. It was people who made, shaped and used things, not the other way around. Yet with the recognition of the active nature of material culture in the 1980s and 1990s, it quickly became apparent that things also shaped and made people; this new emphasis on the agency of things became even stronger at the turn of the millennium. Whereas in the 1980s and 1990s, it had largely focused on the way things affect people's mental make-up and perception of reality, in the 2000s and 2010s, things were now structuring people's lives in more tangible ways.

This new perception of the relation between humans and things is most familiarly linked to French philosopher and sociologist Bruno Latour who argued that what humans are cannot be thought without things. Things are no longer secondary or supplemental to humans but integral to them. Latour was tapping into an older genealogy of technology studies, especially in France which goes back to archaeologist André Leroi-Gourhan who in the 1950s was arguing for the closely intertwined relation between people and things over a long-term, historical perspective. These shifts also tie closely to what is known as **posthumanism** – a term which can be defined quite differently but includes the implication that the "human" is an unstable and fluid category, one that cannot be conceived independently of other, non-human things. However, there are other dimensions to this concept, so this must stand as only a partial definition at this point. What this means for archaeology though is that the stuff we study – artefacts, building

Defining the Discipline 171

foundations, animal bones or landscape features – are not a *means* to an end, but both means and the end itself. In studying these things, we are not studying humans at one remove, but studying them directly. Of course, the evidence is still partial and fragmentary, but it is not indirect. Potsherds and flints, walls and ditches, these are as essentially human as speech, feelings, minds and fingers. There is no plausible way to separate these elements and say this stuff is "human" and that stuff is just "human-made".

This shift in how archaeologists have conceptualized the relation between humans and things has had an important impact on the discipline, but it has also opened the door to a very different approach to archaeology. Just as in the last section, when we think of the past in different terms, a different view of what archaeology can be emerges, so when we rethink the human–thing relation, the same happens. If humans and things are bundled closely together so that they are co-constitutive, then the human – as in the traditional notion of a person, bounded by their skin – is only one subject among many. An artefact or a building can also be a subject in its own right, where it is equally defined by its relations to other things as to humans. In other words, we can also explore thing–thing relations as well as human–thing relations. What if we study a building not as something made or occupied by people, or even as something expressive of human ideology, but as an autonomous object? This is not about denying or ignoring the human involvement in the building but rather about re-centring the object of study. Whereas in traditional archaeology, everything comes back to the human as the centre, once you accept that humans and things are co-creations, then what is the justification for keeping humans at the centre? Surely archaeology can also focus on other non-human subjects?

Box 7.2 Archaeological Drift

Drift matters – the stuff that washes up on beaches and coastlines like seaweed and toothbrushes, dead birds and toy cars. Is it cultural or natural? Heritage or rubbish? Its location on the shoreline, between land and sea, metaphorically accentuates its hybrid status of part culture, part nature. A piece of wood, once part of a living organism, sawn into a plank, later washed ashore with barnacles clinging to it. Is this a human thing or a natural thing? The very question makes no sense, unless we force it apart – this part human, that part nature. Its very mixing seems to defy easy categorization and although we might talk about them as an environmental eyesore, as the product of irresponsible human and social behaviour, can we think about them more productively? This is not about denying their ecological impact but about seeing how the way in which we conceptualize drift has in part contributed to the environmental problem.

Drift objects are what archaeologist Þóra Pétursdóttir calls "unruly things" in her study of drift matter in Iceland and northern Norway. Although we might think of drift as "waste", historically it was regarded as a resource in these places; the sea provided things you could use, like driftwood or beached whales. Nowadays, attitudes as well as the composition of drift has changed yet along the coastlines of Iceland and Norway, people still collect and stack drift for anticipated and possible uses. You never know when something might come in handy. Such beachcombing contrasts sharply with more organized forms of beach clean-up, where the point is to remove and get rid of the drift matter. The difference really comes down to this: in one case, this stuff is seen as having a future, it has some potential not yet exhausted, whereas in the other, it is dead, it has no afterlife and it does not belong in our future.

But what has all this got to do with archaeology? We tend to think of archaeology, as heritage, as something from the past. But the fact is, heritage is really all about stuff from the past that we want to maintain into the future; that is why we build museums, spend time and money retrieving and conserving it all. In a sense, archaeologists are no different from beachcombers. Moreover given the hybrid nature of drift – part culture, part nature – can we also not break down the divide between heritage and the environment and talk about ecological heritage? Seeing drift matter as ecological heritage rather than waste means recognizing that these objects, many of them human-made, have afterlives which don't require us to place humans at the centre of their story. In seeing them as waste, we see them as

Figure 7.2 Drift matter in Eidsbukta on the Sværholt peninsula, Finnmark, Norway (photo: Þóra Pétursdóttir).

> purely human-made things, and so when we abandon or discard them, they no longer have a story. This is our hubris, the very thing that is encouraging the environmental problems we now face.
>
> Approaches to the concept of heritage and archaeology as exemplified in Pétursdóttir's study of drift raise all kinds of questions that many in the discipline might find uncomfortable. What kind of discipline studies human-made things in such a way that de-centres or even marginalizes the human? What kind of discipline suggests that what matters is not so much the past lives of these things but their future? These questions go to the heart of the ontological structure which defines archaeology and if we find some of the suggested answers to them uncomfortable, then maybe we need to reflect harder on what we are doing and why.

This is essentially what the critique of **anthropocentrism** argues; that archaeologists can study things like garbage or ruins as autonomous things, not simply as evidence of human habitation or consumption practices. That once we stop privileging the human in the human–thing bundle, once we reject human exceptionalism, then we can start to think of things in the human–thing bundle differently. A lot of contemporary archaeology revolves precisely around this kind of work. The same approach also underlies much of the work conducted under **multi-species archaeology**, which centres or foregrounds non-human organisms. For example, instead of seeing non-human animals as resources of human exploitation or symbolic manipulation, we see the archaeology of such animals from an animal-oriented perspective (Figure 7.3). At an even larger scale, we can think, not just of other, non-human subjects for archaeology, but also about the archaeological record itself as one, giant hyper-object: the **archaeosphere**. This has been proposed by archaeologist Matt Edgeworth who, in relation to recent discussion about the Anthropocene, has indicated that the whole surface of the earth is better regarded as a hybrid human-deposit stratum, and that when we look at it on this scale, again, archaeology becomes something quite different to what we normally think of it. How far you want to go however with this line of de-centring will vary between scholars, and Rachel Crellin has suggested distinguishing between non-anthropocentric and post-anthropocentric positions. The former often has the connotation of totally erasing the human as the subject of archaeology, while the latter preserves humanity as an ingredient.

Material Culture

The third and final ingredient of our definition of archaeology is material culture. In the previous two sections, we have tried to show how recent debates in archaeology have unsettled what we think the past is and what we think the human is. In both cases, openings were made in the wake of these discussions for an archaeology which looks very different from the traditional model. What about material

Figure 7.3 A tree growing around a sign in a park in north London, 2014; for whom does this sign matter? (photo: author).

culture? Is this also more complicated than we might have thought? Material culture is in many ways a somewhat archaic term and one many archaeologists are increasingly uncomfortable with. Why? Well, for one, it implies a distinction between material and immaterial culture; the fact is, we usually don't use the term "immaterial culture", because it is the presumed default setting for culture. Look up any definition of culture and it will probably talk about beliefs, customs, religion, language, etc.; rarely will it mention material things. The concept of culture is, historically, implicitly an immaterial phenomenon related to the mental or spiritual life of a society. The "material" in material culture is by implication a necessary qualification; that aspect of culture which has a material dimension: clothing, tools, houses, etc. The same distinction informs the more recent division between tangible and intangible heritage, only here the situation is reversed. Heritage, as a field that grew out of material culture and archaeology, was by definition material, but when scholars wanted to talk about preserving indigenous languages, music or skills, they used the term intangible to refer to this. This was actually a political move, because traditional heritage with its emphasis on material remains tended to also privilege cultures with a larger, material footprint – think of ancient civilizations with their monuments and cities, compared to small hunter-gatherer communities. Yet despite the good intentions behind this, the distinction of tangible and intangible heritage has perpetuated a very old understanding of what culture and materiality is.

Indeed, the problem here is not just that it perpetuates a normative sense of culture as primarily immaterial, it also sets up tacit understandings around what materiality is. Anthropologist Daniel Miller – who started his career as an archaeologist – has underlined how the notion of materiality has been aligned with negative connotations in Western thinking. In religious discourse, think of the elevation of the soul over the body, of spiritual values versus carnal pursuits; in secular discourse, think of the elevation of immaterial pursuits (knowledge, friendship, love) over the superficiality of materialist consumption (shopping, money, accumulation). Miller has been a vocal force in academia for challenging these dichotomies through his work in material culture studies, showing, for example, how love and shopping are closely entwined. Indeed, since the 1980s, most work on material culture – inside and outside of archaeology – has demonstrated not only the paucity of thinking of material culture as the poor cousin of culture but challenging the very dichotomy of material and (immaterial) culture. Indeed, even if we are told that we live in an increasingly virtual world of cyberspace, its materiality is always present from the devices you use to access this virtual world to the quite substantial servers, cables and energy producers that keep it operational.

So if the divide between material and "immaterial" culture is redundant and with it, the phrase "material culture", how do we refer to the stuff which is the traditional object of archaeology? The potsherds, building foundations, pits and so on? We could just call it all "culture", but the word **culture** is almost as problematic, especially after what we discussed in the last section; "culture" tends to have overly anthropocentric connotations. Alternatively, we could simply talk about **materiality**, and certainly this is the term the discipline has tended towards, at least in some circles; indeed what is interesting is that discussion about materiality has also tended to revolve around either the past or the human–thing relation. In the first, it is about materiality in connection to "remaining" and the temporal properties of materials; after all, what is distinct about archaeological stuff as opposed to the things anthropologists might normally study is that it is residual or remnant from a former "present". It has endured or physically survived. In the second, it is about materiality in connection to human senses and feelings; indeed, it is hard to conceptualize materiality except in relation to sensory affects and properties especially to touch (hardness, roughness, etc.) and sight (colours, shapes, etc.). Thus by considering materiality as a broad, sensory quality, we should also include other senses like taste, smell or sound, as well as emotional and other felt properties such as atmosphere and affect.

Having now reviewed the three major ingredients of archaeology – the past, humans and material culture – and shown some of the ways in which these concepts are not as straightforward as they might seem, what is your view of archaeology now? How much does the traditional view of it still seem viable? This is for you to decide and for many archaeologists, it is business as usual. The point has not been to suggest that the traditional approach of archaeology is wrong; only that there are other ways to conceptualize it. That by examining these core elements and showing how, by thinking about them differently, one can also imagine a different kind of archaeology. That maybe one way of defining archaeology is precisely in terms of how it draws these three dimensions together and because of the flexibility in how this can be done, different archaeologists will have different perceptions of their discipline. Such reflections raise questions about how much diversity there is and can be within the same discipline. To what extent should archaeology have a common set of concerns, objects or methods? And if we are opening up this box, then to what extent is it important to separate it from geology or ethnography, from history or biology? How does the definition of archaeology fit into the wider structure and organization of disciplines?

What Kind of Science Is Archaeology?

What kind of **science** is archaeology? Do you think of archaeology as a science, and if so, in what way? I must admit that very question would have bothered me when I was a student in the late 1980s and early 1990s; the idea that archaeology was a science at all, I would have said was debatable. At this time, the processual-postprocessual wars were in full swing in Britain and calling archaeology a science would have put you in the processual camp straightaway. But things change and so has the status of science in relation to archaeology. The tension can be traced back to older currents in society such as the notion of "two cultures" first coined by C.P. Snow in the 1950s to refer to people trained either in the Arts or Sciences (see Box 7.3). In turn, these "two cultures" phenomenon relates to an even older historical divide between the natural sciences and arts/humanities from the twentieth century. German scholarship made a distinction between what they called *Geistewissenschaften* (humanities) and *Naturwissenschaften* (natural sciences), each of which was considered to have its own methods and data; where the natural sciences were concerned with explanations of observable phenomena in the physical world, the humanities deal with the understanding of meaning as represented though language and other forms of human expression. It was the classic division between nature and culture, two worlds, each requiring their own kinds of science. It is a division that created tensions in many disciplines, especially new ones that emerged at the end of the nineteenth century like sociology and archaeology, which didn't easily fit this division. The result though was that scholars often tried hard to mould their new field to fit into one of these two models. Modern archaeology inherited this split through its two ancestral roots: an old one linked to antiquarianism, art history and the humanist tradition, and a newer one linked to geology and biological evolution which, although it can no longer be mapped onto the separation of prehistoric from historical archaeology, was originally closely linked to it. Part of the debate between processualism and postprocessualism in Anglo-American archaeology of the 1980s was bound up in this divide; processualists saw themselves as scientists, promoting the use of statistics and mathematical modelling, while postprocessualists focused on the articulation of the archaeological record as a meaningful "text" to be read, drawing on the intellectual tradition of the humanities.

Box 7.3 Archaeology and the Two (or Three?) Cultures

Archaeologists have long debated whether their discipline is closer to the sciences or humanities (also see Chapter 4). Andrew Sherratt and Kristian Kristiansen have suggested that it belongs to both, but that it has oscillated over its history, sometimes being closer to one, sometimes closer to the other. Every half a century or so, archaeology swings between a more scientific outlook ("rationalism" or "positivism") and a more humanistic one ("romanticism" or "relativism"). So, for example, between c. 1900 and 1950 when culture historical archaeology dominated, the discipline was aligned with the humanities, while from the 1950s to 1980s under processualism, science was in the ascendant, only to swing back to the humanities under postprocessualism. Today, we are moving back into what Kristiansen calls a Third Science Revolution (Figure 7.4).

Although an interesting perspective that tries to situate archaeology as a discipline in between the sciences and humanities, such a narrative also perpetuates a simple, paradigm-model view of disciplinary change. Michael Smith has argued that rather than see archaeology in relation to Snow's two cultures, which is now woefully out-dated, we acknowledge the existence of *three* cultures: the humanities, natural sciences and social sciences. To be fair, even Snow had anticipated the idea of a third culture in later work, but this was always seen as a kind of "middleman" position, mediating between the sciences and arts which is very different to Smith's attribution of the third culture as the social sciences. Archaeology, according to Smith, clearly belongs – or should belong – to this third culture. At the same time, Smith acknowledges there are other ways to cut the cake; what about the historical sciences which might include archaeology but also geology and even, arguably, cosmology?

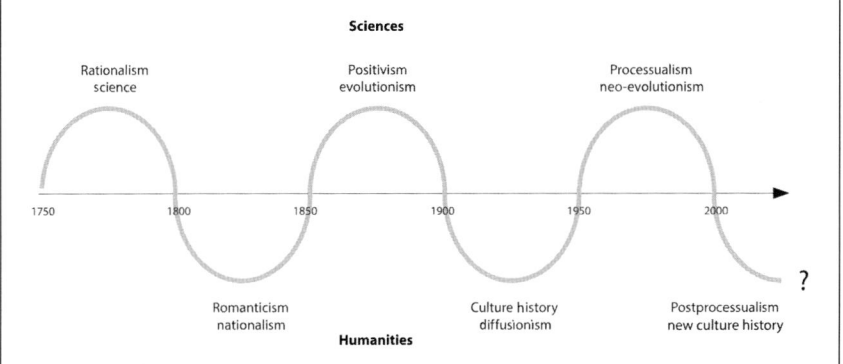

Figure 7.4 The swinging pendulum of archaeology between the sciences and humanities (redrawn from Kristiansen 2014).

> But does adding a third culture really help matters? Tim Flohr-Sørensen has argued that the problem runs deeper for the oscillation or vacillation that characterizes the position of archaeology in the science/humanities divide is less of a gentle swing between poles and more of a destructive wrecking ball. It acts to polarize and create confrontation and rejection which ultimately does no good for the discipline. Flohr-Sørensen argues for plurality rather than polarity, that what matters is not defining where archaeology is or should sit on this divide but embracing the heterogeneity of our discipline.

Nowadays, I am less easily roused by such labels and am quite happy to think of archaeology as a science, especially if we understand this in a broad sense. But still, some qualifications are in order. A common position today is to draw a distinction between archaeological science and scientific archaeology. The former refers to the various scientific methods and techniques that archaeologists use in their research, like radiocarbon, aDNA or isotope analysis; everyone accepts this is a standard part of archaeology, and in fact even in the 1960s, those archaeologists who staunchly defended archaeology as a branch of the humanities recognized this. The second term, however, scientific archaeology is often considered more suspect as it portrays archaeology as a science, like particle physics or molecular biology, that is, using the same general approach of creating hypotheses, testing them and drawing out generalizations. Usually when archaeologists make the distinction between these two ideas of archaeology as a science, it is to affirm the first and distance themselves from the latter.

The problem here though is that in both cases, the term "science" has the same root origin: it is something that is associated with what are known as the hard or natural sciences; in the one case, "science" is confined to method and technique and in the other, expanded to encompass a whole operational philosophy. But in both cases, "science" evokes disciplines such as physics, chemistry or biology. Isotope analysis is a scientific method, a phenomenology of landscape isn't. In other words, it perpetuates the divide between hard and soft sciences or sciences and the humanities and asks archaeology to situate itself on one side of this divide. Indeed, the very distinction is the echo of those debates from the 1980s and 1990s. To move beyond this, we need to stop thinking of science in these terms altogether and regard it more broadly as *scientia* or knowledge. The problem here is one of language; in German, the term *wissenschaft* captures this sense much better and is used as a suffix for all disciplines from physics to literature; in Icelandic, the same sense is denoted by *vísindi*. It is in this broad sense that I use the term here. So, with this in mind, let us ask the question: what kind of science is archaeology?

In this chapter so far, I have discussed archaeology in terms of its object or subject matter and defined three ingredients: the past, humanity and materiality. The trouble with this definition is that it focuses solely on the object or subject matter of archaeology. But archaeology is also a process, a relation which means we must also consider its definition in relation to archaeological practice and to the people and other things which are its practitioners. For some, archaeology is less defined by its object – typically, "old buried stuff" – and more by a set of practices, a sensibility, an imagination, an attitude towards whatever object it happens to engage with. The archaeological is a mode of engagement or interaction, not a thing. In this way, archaeologies of swimming pools, space junk, sea drift, Silicon Valley are all archaeologies because of how these objects have been approached and attended to. So what is this archaeological attention? Archaeologists will define this differently. Some will think of it in very narrow terms like excavation and typology like our Oxford professor in the opening vignette. But a broader definition, one for example that has been proposed by Michael Shanks, is one that prioritizes the physical or material engagement with its subject. It's not simply that our object is material – "stuff in the ground" or wherever, but that we attend to this stuff in physically intimate ways. We get our hands dirty – often quite literally.

Now of course archaeology does not have a monopoly on this; although many historians and anthropologists who deal with material culture may do so "at a distance", many others do handle objects. But the point here is that for most other disciplines, this is just one aspect (and often a marginal or at least optional one) of their main practices, whereas for archaeology it is central. It is the centrality of this material engagement which also makes the archaeological, closely related to other (non-academic) practices like art, design and engineering or building. This physical dimension to archaeology is why Shanks, writing with Randy McGuire, once defined archaeology as a craft. At the same time, archaeology is different to art and engineering, and what makes it different is precisely the object of its attention. As Shanks has underlined innumerable times, archaeologists work on what remains of the past.

So where does this leave us? In some ways, we are back where we started, defining archaeology by its subject matter. However, it's not quite the same, because we have also recognized that the practice of a science like archaeology has to be understood in fairly broad terms. Another way of exploring this question is to see how archaeology "fits" or connects to other sciences or academic disciplines. Traditionally, this question has been addressed in relation to larger disciplinary classifications, as we have already mentioned, in both this chapter and earlier ones: the divisions between the sciences and arts/humanities or between humanities and social sciences. Different countries and even different institutions in the same country will place archaeology differently; in the US, archaeology is typically situated within the four fields of anthropology (archaeology, ethnography, linguistics and physical anthropology). Where, for example, is your archaeology department? Is it aligned with classics? With anthropology? With geography? Is it within the humanities or social sciences? These divisions can be seen everywhere, not just at universities but also with publishers and grant bodies. Academic disciplines are classified and these classifications reflect how a discipline is viewed in relation to other disciplines.

Although many scholars recognize the somewhat arbitrary nature of these placements, they nonetheless have a powerful influence on what gets studied, what questions get asked and how research is done, funded and disseminated. And even though interdisciplinary research is encouraged, the existing infrastructure often makes this quite hard. Archaeology in particular has often been described as a subject which is inherently interdisciplinary: environmental and soil sciences, history, biology, ethnography, chemistry . . . it is not hard to see how archaeology works at the intersection of all these fields because of the fact that it excavates deposits, draws on written sources, studies organic remains, deals with human cultural diversity, analyses the composition of materials. Its' very multifarious nature however may also be partly responsible for its marginal status. It belongs everywhere and so nowhere; its very strength is also, ironically its weakness. Some archaeologists have suggested that our discipline has a low esteem within the broader academic community while others have suggested any inferiority complex is of our own imagining. On the whole, I tend to agree with the latter, yet it is hard to argue with the fact that far more students enrol and graduate in programmes like history than they do in archaeology or anthropology. The reasons for this almost certainly relate to the organization of subjects at secondary school where history is a core subject, while archaeology or anthropology, if taught at all, are marginal at best. Ultimately, the organization of knowledge at secondary school perpetuates the larger divides of the science and humanities, which means archaeology will inevitably get perceived either as one or the other and given the recent resurgence of archaeological science, the trend of the last few decades has been for "archaeology as a science" to be an increasingly popular choice for students and the universities have marketed their programmes accordingly.

And yet maybe this weakness is also its strength. One of the advantages about being a discipline with such clear and obvious trans-disciplinary connections is that it encourages constant movement and critical reflection. As well as having a core disciplinary set of traditions, methods and practices around which it orients itself, archaeology also is constantly re-calibrating itself against developments in other sciences. One way to think about this is in terms of major and minor sciences, after philosopher Rosi Braidotti, who draws on a similar distinction made by Deleuze and Guattari called royal and nomadic science. Major or royal science refers to sciences with strong disciplinary protocols and a clear research subject and is correspondingly well supported institutionally and financially. Think major study programmes and departments. Minor or nomadic sciences in contrast have more open methods and flexibly defined matters of concern and tend to be less well supported institutionally and financially. Think queer studies or material culture studies. They are easily identified by the way they weave across disciplines. Now most academic disciplines are major sciences to some extent, including archaeology, and even some minor sciences often end up becoming major sciences, like cultural studies. Archaeology, on the other hand, is a major science which has the potential to turn the other way – to become a minor or nomadic science. Is this a good thing? Maybe, but perhaps it is more important that we cultivate the minor or nomadic potential of archaeology, because most major sciences probably embody a tension between sticking to a fixed track and exploring connections with others. Where archaeology has an edge is that its potential for nomadism is much greater than many other disciplines.

Box 7.4 Disciplinary Crossings

Archaeology has always looked beyond its own disciplinary borders – whether for ideas, tools, techniques or collaboration. The first scholars to study animal bones from archaeological sites were biologists and radiocarbon dating was first proposed by a physical chemist who had worked on the Manhattan project. The edges of our discipline – indeed any discipline – are like "trading zones" where knowledge and skills move back and forth. Sometimes you might hear an archaeologist claim that we are more borrowers and receivers than givers (see Chapter 6), but that is really a moot point; more relevant is the issue of cross-disciplinarity itself and what forms it takes. You might hear all kinds of phrases bandied about like multi-disciplinary, inter-disciplinary or post-disciplinary – but what do these all mean?

Liv Nilsson Stutz has addressed the diversity of these terms and following other scholars has tried to clarify some of their differences by suggesting we see such collaboration as part of a continuum (Figure 7.5). At one end is multi-disciplinary work, where two or more subjects tackle a common issue. Say the issue is environmental change in a region; you might have archaeologists studying settlement patterns, geologists studying land erosion and soil accumulation rates and historians studying references to climate and weather in the written sources. All three disciplines work together on a common topic, but they maintain their disciplinary identity through the use of their own methods and theories. With interdisciplinary projects, the collaboration is more integrated, and as a result, there is more interaction in the methodologies and theories used; thus in the previous example, geological research on erosion might lead to archaeologists adapting their work on settlement patterns to consider how this affects issues such as building repair rates. Here, the working methods of each discipline are subtly influencing each other. Finally at the other end of the scale are trans-disciplinary collaborations where disciplinary boundaries are the most blurred; sticking with our same example, we might start to question the very separation of environmental and human spheres and adopt a theoretical position which blurs some of the key assumptions underlying the definitions of geology, archaeology and history. Post-disciplinary is another term which has been used, which can be similar in meaning to trans-disciplinary – or its radical conclusion: the dissolution of all traditional academic disciplinary divisions. Which of these kinds of collaboration do you think most characterizes cross-disciplinary work in archaeology?

182 *Defining the Discipline*

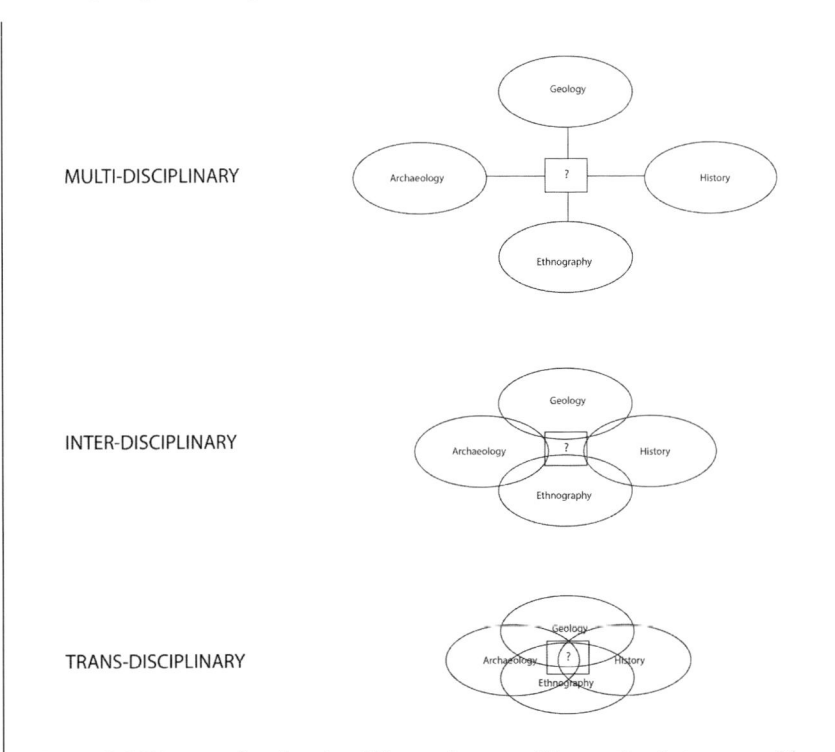

Figure 7.5 Diagram showing the different degrees of integration between multi-, inter- and trans-disciplinary research.

Nilsson Stutz's discussion of these differences is framed within larger contemporary concerns, especially the role of archaeology and the Third Science Revolution on the one hand, and issues of multivocality and the interaction between archaeology and the wider, non-academic community on the other. In many ways, her argument for a trans-disciplinary archaeology acts as real response to portraying archaeology as oscillating between the poles of the humanities and science (see Box 7.3).

Part of the issue here relates to what aspect of archaeology we want to foreground. Let's go back to our three ingredients of archaeology: the past, humanity and material culture. Which of these we foreground will also affect how we see its relation to other disciplines (Figure 7.6). If we foreground the past, then archaeology is aligned with other historical sciences, including geology and cosmology as well as history; it is a historical science as opposed to an experimental or actualistic science the latter of which would include sociology, ethnography and particle physics. What is nice about this division is that it disrupts and cuts across the usual science/humanities divide. What's problematic about it is that it is premised on a

History, cosmology, geology   *Art, design, museums*

```
        Past              Material
                          culture
              ARCHAEOLOGY

               Humans
```

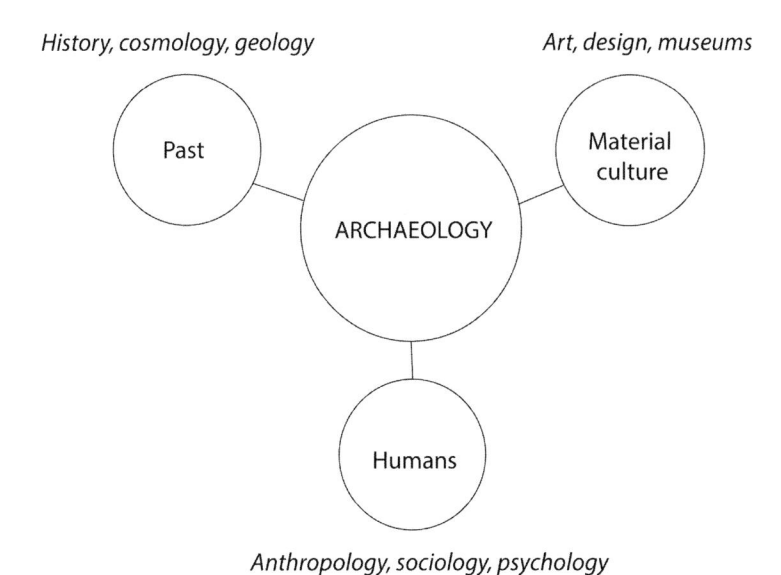

Anthropology, sociology, psychology

Figure 7.6 Different ways to align archaeology depending on which aspect is privileged.

very particular view of the past and time, which as we saw in our earlier discussion is not the only way to conceptualize archaeology. Indeed, if the past is seen as not distinct from the present but part of it, this whole division of historical versus actualistic science is suspect.

If we choose to foreground humanity as the main ingredient – which is, in fact, the most common and usual assumption – then archaeology becomes one of several sciences focusing on humans, including ethnography, sociology, history, psychology and so on. This is how Renfrew and Bahn pitch it in their textbook, as part of a broad discipline of anthropology, whose specialism is *past* humans through their *material remains*. This of course underlines the more prevalent split between the humanities and social sciences on the one hand and the natural sciences on the other and runs the risk of perpetuating a divide between nature and culture. Yet given recent work under the label of posthumanism and the proliferation of various kinds of humanities such as digital or environmental humanities, to what extent can we assume that the "human" in this three-part recipe is a stable or coherent ingredient anyway?

If we privilege material culture, the relations are shuffled yet again insofar as we align archaeology with disciplines like art history, design studies and museum studies, although note that the "culture" in material culture carries within it a presumption of materiality associated exclusively with humanity. Yet as we saw in our earlier discussion of material culture (and humanity), the boundaries here can be very blurred and in fact this is where inter- or even trans-disciplinary aspects of archaeology become very relevant. So relevant in fact, they even de-stabilize

184 *Defining the Discipline*

any unity to what archaeology is or might be. Is it still possible to save a sense of archaeology as a coherent enterprise?

In many ways, the problem here lies in seeing these three ingredients – the past, humanity and materiality – as separate. Depending on what we focus on, we can align archaeology differently. But the thing is, archaeology deals with all three *together*, not separately; the archaeological object is an inherently composite entity. A flint axe lying in the backfill of a pit is both human, material and temporal all at once. If we really want to get to grips with what archaeology is about, we cannot treat these as separate properties but rather consider them as a package. So let's start again and this time, ask the question: what is the archaeological?

What Is the Archaeological?

The best way to begin is to look at how archaeologists think about their object in its immediacy and especially the words they use to describe it: the archaeological record, archaeological remains, archaeological sources, archaeological evidence.... I am sure you could add to this list. But what stands out are two things: first, a sense of material persistence, something that has carried over from the past into the present. And second, a sense of these things as testimony to that past. Regarding the archaeological as a record or source is in fact indicative of a much older and broader metaphorical view of nature as a book to be read. Indeed archaeologists were not alone in using literary and textual metaphors for physical traces of the past, it was a motif adopted equally by geologists in the nineteenth century. In the German and Central European tradition, archaeologists typically treat archaeological remains as "sources" and even adapt historical methods of source criticism towards them while in Anglo-American archaeology, the archaeological "record" is normally appraised through sampling theory and formation theory.

There are problems with this conception however, not least in how it establishes a division from the start between present physical remains and past events or processes. Just as a document which inscribes an eyewitness testimony of an event is not the same as the event itself, so the scattered remains of buildings and rubbish are testimonials of some past activities and not part of those activities. Yet it doesn't take much reflection to realize how problematic this is; because actually those building remains and rubbish *are* an intimate part of those past activities in a much more direct way than any *post hoc* written testimony. In describing them as a "record", surely we are laying down some preconceptions from the very start which we should be more wary of. This is an argument that John Barrett has made repeatedly, arguing that archaeological remains are better viewed as the material conditions of past human life, not as a record of past events.

At the same time, one of the key points made in earlier chapters is that these remains don't really have any meaningful status except in the context of our interventions; whether it is walking along an earthwork or excavating the foundations of a Roman villa, these physical traces are, in part, constituted by our engagements with them and these engagements are, in turn, equally constituted by the

Defining the Discipline 185

records we make. To be more precise, doing fieldwork, making records and the physical remains themselves are – all three – bundled together into a complex, co-constitutive relation. Given that, thinking about the physical remains as a record or archive is perhaps not so problematic after all. Viewed as an archive, the notions of the past, materiality and humanity are still held together with the archaeological; moreover, the etymology of both words are revealing as they share a similar root in the ancient Greek word *arkhē* which has at least two different meanings: one is ancient or pertaining to the beginning, the other is sovereignty or authority. Archives play more on the latter (through *archeion*, a public building belonging to city officials) while archaeology on the former (through *archaia*, old things), yet the entwined etymologies are perhaps more revealing than either on their own.

Yet the archaeological is not synonymous with the archive, especially if we understand the archive in its literal sense as inscribed records or documents preserved as evidence. The metaphorical affinities are undoubtedly valuable and informative but the nature and processes behind the formation of manuscripts in a state repository and artefacts buried in the soil are quite different. There is a whole branch of study in archaeology devoted to this, known by various names including sampling and formation theory and other books will cover this in detail. Here, I want to focus on the broader theoretical implications of this work, especially in how it impacts our understanding of the archaeological. The first thing to notice is how these studies articulate a tension between loss and transformation (Figure 7.7). We shouldn't see these two ideas as an either/or as they stimulate our work in different ways, especially our sense of time. Where loss tends to underscore the notion of a past irrevocably out of reach, cut off from the present, transformation reminds us of the connection between past and present, of the past which exists in the present. In other words, the tension speaks to the tension within time itself which we also discussed earlier in this chapter. So let us now

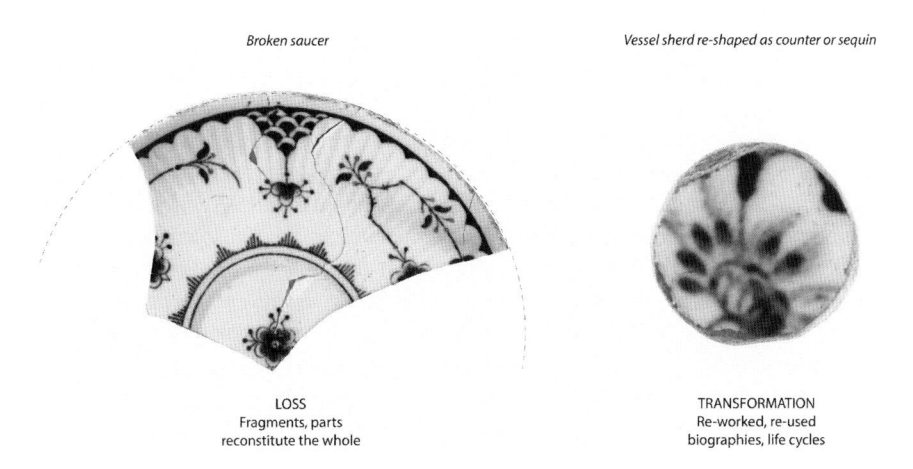

Broken saucer   *Vessel sherd re-shaped as counter or sequin*

LOSS   TRANSFORMATION
Fragments, parts   Re-worked, re-used
reconstitute the whole   biographies, life cycles

Figure 7.7 The artefact as metaphor for two ways of looking at the archaeological record: as loss or as transformation (objects not to the same scale).

examine in more detail how archaeology has approached these two aspects in coming to terms with the "archaeological".

We all know that a lot of stuff never survives in the archaeological record: organic material like textiles, leather, wood or body tissue especially are usually very poorly preserved except in unusual circumstances. You only have to look around you and ask yourself what items in your room or on your body would survive. This of course has often prompted remarks about how cautious we should be interpreting the past from what does survive. Even though all archaeologists acknowledge this, it is also something we frequently and conveniently forget. So yes, there are large gaps in our "archive" because of physical processes of decay, but also, of course, intentional destruction or removal; if a burial lacks grave goods, it could be through robbing as much as preservation, though luckily, we can often tell the difference. Some archaeologists have portrayed this loss as a fundamental way to define the archaeological record, as a cumulatively depleted source from the moment things enter the ground until they end up in an archaeological publication. It is meant to illustrate how little has survived, how fragmentary and scrappy out record really is and so how cautious we should be in making any inferences from it. Despite this, what is important here is the way the "archaeological" maintains a connection between time, materiality and humanity but in a very special way. That over time, materiality and humanity are denuded, stripped away and further back we go, the fainter they are, the harder to discern so only the most hardy elements survived. In other words, just as only the most durable material survived, so only some of the more durable aspects of human society have survived – those which had the closest connection to "nature". Technology and subsistence strategies we can deal with; religion and ideology – forget it!

Yet in tension with this view of the archaeological as one marred by loss is another which stresses its transformation. Under this view, the archaeological record is not a reduced version of what once was, but a transformed version of it. Bones or organic finds don't simply vanish or disappear; they decay, break down into finer elements and become minerals in the soil or food for worms; these transformations leave traces like phosphates we can measure in the soil. Of course, a phosphate reading is not the same as having the bones, but in focusing on transformation, we keep open the possibility of still recovering something. The focus is on what remains, not what has been lost. But transformational views of the archaeological record also highlight another dimension, one which is perhaps more important; it's not simply that objects themselves are transformed, but their associations are too. Even if objects survive in the soil, they can move around through various processes such as burrowing animals, freeze-thaw action, ploughing . . . the archaeologist Michael Schiffer wrote a famous book about these processes, which he called n- and c-transforms, or natural and cultural formation processes.

But Schiffer didn't just discuss the transformations that happen to things in the ground; he saw transformation as something that happened all the time, even while things were still circulating in ancient societies and being discarded or abandoned. Transformation was a constant feature of the material world, from the manufacture, use, discard and burial of stuff that archaeologists ended up studying. Clay is transformed into a pottery vessel, a pottery vessel is transformed as it is used for cooking, is transformed into sherds when it breaks and in all these stages, its associations – spatial, contextual – also change. Schiffer's work underlined the importance of understanding how use life, discard rates, depositional and post-depositional processes among many others are all necessary to understand the archaeological record.

But as revolutionary as Schiffer's work was, it shared with the simpler, reductionist view of the archaeological record, a notion of an "original context". With the reductionist model, the archaeological record was seen as a severely fragmented and partial version of what once was; with the transformational model, the archaeological record is seen as a distorted or warped version of what once was. That even if transformation was a constant feature of the material world, the aim was still always to re-wind the tape and stop at a point – whichever point you want – and try to reconstruct how the past was at that moment. The job of the archaeologist was, like the conservator of a corroded lump of iron, to clean off the corroded mass and get back to the original inside, or at least whatever was left of that original that was recoverable. This notion of an original can be linked back to our earlier discussion of the archaeological record as a literary metaphor and the archive; just as in philology, scholars have tried to reconstruct an original document from surviving multiple, later copies which may have distorted the original, so do archaeologists often view their task. But what if there is no original? What if the "corruptions", like iron corrosion, are just part of the thing itself?

Some archaeologists have taken this question to heart and have argued that this is really what archaeologists should be thinking about. If the archaeological fundamentally has this nature, should we really be trying to roll back time at all? Should the aim rather not be to embrace the deep, transformational temporality of the human past in its wholeness? At least two very different responses to this question have emerged in archaeology which have focused on two very different aspects of the archaeological record. One emerged from a theory called **time perspectivism** pioneered by the British archaeologist Geoff Bailey, who argued that the archaeological record is temporally "corrupted" in the sense that it hardly ever – except in rare instances – presents us with access to a moment in the past. Time in the archaeological record is compressed so the past is always a composite overlay of multiple events which cannot be dissected, which is why it is thought of as a palimpsest. It is a chimera to think we can recreate the past at time scales experienced by humans as our cousins in anthropology or history can; rather than see these "corruptions" as something we must try and undo, we should rather embrace them to see what larger scale, long-term patterns and processes are visible in human history – and ones that are invisible to disciplines working at human scales of time like history or ethnography. The archaeologist Charles Perrault has defined this as macro-archaeology, to contrast it with what he sees as the conventional and misguided approach that most archaeologists cling to: to conduct archaeology as a study of micro-scale processes that operate over days, years or decades.

188 *Defining the Discipline*

A very different approach can be seen in the French school of **archaeogeography** and the related work of French archaeologist Laurent Olivier who we met earlier in the chapter. They too see the archaeological record as a composite overlay of multiple events, a palimpsest; but instead of seeing this as a form of time compression, they see it as a form of time sedimentation. It's about how the past persists into the present, but in variable and partial ways to create bundles of contemporaneous materials from different times. It sees the archaeological record as a heterochronic or polychronic ensemble, much like our own present where a medieval church stands next to a twentieth century shopping mall and both follow the line of an old Roman road. For Olivier, such perspectives don't mean abandoning the humanistic approaches that time perspectivism eschews, but it does mean abandoning the notion of conventional, linear histories.

So what is the archaeological? Although we are no closer to a resolution of this question, we have seen from the previous discussion how complex the issue is, and moreover, how you define it will have implications for what you think archaeology is – and can do. What we can say though is that archaeology is a practice that is defined both by its object and its mode of engagement with that object. Moreover, how we define that object, whether through some of its prime ingredients like the past, humanity, materiality or through a composite of them, the archaeological record or archive, and how we define its mode of engagement – as a science, a craft, or an attitude both have a fairly wide latitude and plasticity. Ultimately, defining archaeology is not something we can do in a textbook, it is not something we can lay out in advance because what archaeology is changes over time. It changes because of the way our object and practices vary, both between practitioners, institutions, places and countries and as these objects and practices transform in the course of our disciplinary history. Defining the discipline is like defining the archaeological as we discussed in Chapter 2, in effect, something we do every day.

After the session, our slightly shaken speaker was able to sit down and reflect on what she should have said to that comment from the Oxford professor. It's always this way: at the time, you stand there like an idiot and only later do you find the right words to answer. Part of her wants to search the professor out and tell him what she should have said. But she realizes this won't make her feel any better and in fact may just give his comments too much importance. No, the moment has passed; what matters is that she does have an answer, even if she could not articulate it at the time. What is archaeology? She knows what it is, because that is what she does.

Exercises

1. Come up with your own definition of archaeology (either individually or in groups) and discuss in class.
2. Come up with an alternative organization of academic departments, faculties or schools and where archaeology would sit in this new structure (either individually or in groups). Discuss in class.
3. Can anything be archaeological?

Further Reading

What Is Archaeology?

Renfrew and Bahn's definition of archaeology can be found in Renfrew and Bahn (2016). Issues of how archaeology is affected by its views of the way the past has divided the politics of periodization are discussed by various authors; for the prehistory/history divide see Orser (2013) and Panich and Schneider (2019); for the Three Age System, see Maynes and Watner (2012). More radical discussions of the nature of time and the past can be found in Olivier (2011) and Witmore (2013); Gonzáles-Ruibal and Witmore's discussions of the "end of the Neolithic" can be found in Gonzáles-Ruibal (2006) and Witmore (2018). On humanity as the subject of archaeology, traditional views can be found in J. Hawkes (1968), C. Hawkes (1954) and Flannery (1967). For a recent discussion of posthumanism and archaeology, see Crellin and Harris (2021); much of this work draws from the feminist scholar Rosa Braidotti (2019a, 2019b). For Þóra Pétursdóttir's study on drift, see Pétursdóttir (2020). For multi-species archaeology, see Pilaar Birch (2018), while Edgeworth's concept of the archaeosphere can be found in Edgeworth (2018). For critiques of the "material culture" concept, see Thomas (2007), while Miller's approach to materiality can be found in Miller (2010). On the new materialisms, see Witmore (2014), while for sensory archaeologies, see Hamilakis (2013).

What Kind of Science Is Archaeology?

The position of archaeology in relation to the sciences and humanities is widely debated, but see Sherratt (1996), Kristiansen (2008, 2014), Smith (2017) and Sørensen (2017). On the distinction between archaeological science and scientific archaeology, see Ion (2017) and Martinón-Torres and Killick (2015). On archaeology viewed primarily as practice and craft, see Shanks (2012) and Shanks and McGuire (1996). On major and minor science, see Braidotti (2019b) On cross-disciplinarity, see Ion (2017) and Nilsson Stutz (2018).

What Is the Archaeological?

On the nature of the archaeological record, see Lucas (2012), while a more general discussion of the archaeological can be found in Nativ and Lucas (2020) and Olsen et al. (2012). For time perspectivism and macro-archaeology, see Holdaway and Wandsnider (2008) and Perrault (2019), respectively. On archaeogeography, see Watteaux (2017).

References

Braidotti, R. 2019a. A Theoretical Framework for the Critical Posthumanities. *Theory, Culture and Society* 36(6): 31–61.

Braidotti, R. 2019b. *Posthuman Knowledge*. Cambridge: Polity Press.

Crellin, R. & O. Harris. 2021. What Difference Does Posthumanism Make? *Cambridge Archaeological Journal* 31(3): 1–7.
Edgeworth, M. 2018. More Than Just a Record: Active Ecological Effects of Archaeological Strata. In M. de Souza & D. Costa (eds.), *Historical Archaeology and Environment*. New York: Springer, pp. 19–40.
Flannery, K. 1967. Culture History v. Culture Process: A Debate in American Archaeology. *Scientific American* 217: 119–22.
Gonzáles-Ruibal, A. 2006. The Past Is Tomorrow. Towards an Archaeology of the Vanishing Present. *Norwegian Archaeological Review* 39(2): 110–25.
Hamilakis, Y. 2013. *Archaeology and the Senses. Human Experience, Memory, and Affect.* Cambridge: Cambridge University Press.
Hawkes, C. 1954. Archaeological Theory and Method: Some Suggestions From the Old World. *American Anthropologist* 56(2): 155–68.
Hawkes, J. 1968. The Proper Study of Mankind. *Antiquity* 42: 255–62.
Holdaway, S. & L. Wandsnider (eds.). 2008. *Time in Archaeology. Time Perspectivism Revisited.* Salt Lake City: University of Utah Press.
Ion, A. 2017. How Interdisciplinary Is Interdisciplinarity? Revisiting the Impact of aDNA Research for the Archaeology of Human Remains. *Current Swedish Archaeology* 25: 177–98.
Kristiansen, K. 2008. Do We Need the 'Archaeology of Europe'? *Archaeological Dialogues* 15(1): 5–25.
Kristiansen, K. 2014. Towards a New Paradigm? The Third Science Revolution and Its Possible Consequences in Archaeology. *Current Swedish Archaeology* 22: 11–34.
Liv Nilsson Stutz. 2018. A Future for Archaeology: In Defense of an Intellectually Engaged, Collaborative and Confident Archaeology. *Norwegian Archaeological Review* 51: 1–2, 48–56.
Lucas, G. 2012. *Understanding the Archaeological Record.* Cambridge: Cambridge University Press.
Martinón-Torres, M. & D. Killick. 2015. Archaeological Theories and Archaeological Sciences. In A. Gardner, S. Lake & U. Sommer (eds.), *Oxford Handbook of Archaeological Theory*. Oxford: Oxford University Press.
Maynes, M.J. & A. Watner. 2012. Temporalities and Periodization in Deep History: Technology, Gender, and Benchmarks of "Human Development". *Social Science History* 36(1): 59–83.
Miller, D. 2010. *Stuff.* Cambridge: Polity Press.
Nativ, A. & G. Lucas. 2020. Archaeology Without Antiquity. *Antiquity* 94(376): 852–63.
Olivier, L. 2011. *The Dark Abyss of Time: Archaeology and Memory.* Lanham: AltaMira Press.
Olsen, B., M. Shanks, T. Webmoor & C. Witmore. 2012. *Archaeology. The Discipline of Things.* Berkeley: University of California Press.
Orser, C. 2013. The Politics of Periodization. In A. González-Ruibal (ed.), *Reclaiming Archaeology: Beyond the Tropes of Modernity*. London: Routledge, pp. 145–54.
Panich, L. & T. Schneider. 2019. Categorical Denial: Evaluating Post-1492 Indigenous Erasure in the Paper Trail of American Archaeology. *American Antiquity* 84(4): 651–68.
Perrault, C. 2019. *The Quality of the Archaeological Record.* Chicago: Chicago University Press.
Pétursdóttir, Þ. 2020. Anticipated Futures? Knowing the Heritage of Drift Matter. *International Journal of Heritage Studies* 26(1): 87–103.
Pilaar Birch, S. (ed.). 2018. *Multispecies Archaeology.* London: Routledge.

Renfrew, C. & P. Bahn. 2016. *Archaeology. Theories, Methods and Practice* (7th edition). London: Thames & Hudson.

Shanks, M. 2012. *The Archaeological Imagination*. Walnut Creek: Left Coast Press.

Shanks, M. & R. McGuire. 1996. The Craft of Archaeology. *American Antiquity* 61: 75–88.

Sherratt, A. 1996. Settlement Patterns or Landscape Studies? Reconciling Reason and Romance. *Archaeological Dialogues* 3(2): 140–59.

Smith, M.E. 2017. Social Science and Archaeological Inquiry. *Antiquity* 91(356): 520–28.

Sørensen, T.F. 2017. The Two Cultures and a World Apart: Archaeology and Science at a New Crossroads. *Norwegian Archaeological Review* 50(2): 101–15.

Thomas, J. 2007. The Trouble with Material Culture. *Journal of Iberian Archaeology* 9(10): 11–23.

Watteaux, M. 2017. What Do the Forms of the Landscapes Tell Us? In J-M. Blaising, J. Driessen, J-P. Legendre & L. Olivier (eds.), *Clashes of Time: The Contemporary Past as a Challenge for Archaeology*. Louvain-la-Neuve: Presses universitaires de Louvain, pp. 195–220.

Witmore, C. 2013. Which Archaeology? A Question of Chronopolitics. In A. González-Ruibal (ed.), *Reclaiming Archaeology: Beyond the Tropes of Modernity*. London: Routledge, pp. 130–44.

Witmore, C. 2014. Archaeology and the New Materialisms. *Journal of Contemporary Archaeology* 1(2): 203–24.

Witmore, C. 2018. The End of the Neolithic? At the Emergence of the Anthropocene. In S.E. Pilaar Birch (ed.), *Multispecies Archaeology*. London: Routledge, pp. 26–46.

Coda
Theorizing Without Theory

In this short, concluding remark, I want to revisit the question posed at the start: what is theory? I don't want to give any final answer to this question but rather trace out some of the issues that have emerged from the chapters of this book that impinge on this question. This will not be a summary of what has been covered but rather an attempt to articulate what we have learnt about theory since it first became an explicit domain within archaeology more than 60 years ago. At the end, I would simply invite you to ask yourself the same question: what is theory to you?

In Chapter 1, I cited several different statements about theory and suggested they fall into two groups. One focused on theory as substance or content: a set of ideas, a framework, that helps us make sense of the stuff we encounter. The other was more about theory as an attitude or style of thinking: critical, imaginative, open-minded. Both seemed to capture something of what theory is, but what do we make of them now, having traversed the topics discussed in this book? Let's start with the first one. One of the problems with defining theory as a set of ideas or framework is that it posits theory as lying over or above our data. It comes to be something we apply, that we have to operationalize and as a result, automatically starts from a position that puts theory as something separate. Recall our student in the opening vignette in Chapter 6 how he was advised to find a theory that he could use on his study of early medieval spearheads. Theory as a set of ideas or framework makes theory both alien to archaeology and at the same time, hegemonic with respect to research; that is, it dictates and determines the course of investigation and interpretation.

Throughout this book, I have tried to portray a view of theory as something that works from the inside, not above our material. In this way, theory is in fact just another component of the research process. But when we do this, we cannot just leave it at that; we have to crack open this monolithic shell that surrounds theory and break it apart. Otherwise, we are just playing games with words: theory is now a set of ideas or framework that works within, not over your data. This won't do; as soon as you topple theory from its perch above data and bring it down to earth to mingle with our stuff, it no longer has the unity or homogeneity that it once had. The same in fact applies to our stuff. Our stuff is not just data, it is drawings, potsherds, databases, flint arrowheads, photographs, just as our theory is now not just a set of ideas or a framework, but a paper by Binford, a moment of confusion on site, Heidegger's *Being and Time*, a conversation in the coffee room.

DOI: 10.4324/9781003098294-9

In fact when you level everything off, what is theory and what is not becomes very hard to parse. This does not mean everything is the same, but it does mean that theory has lost its sharp edges. For me, this is one way to understand the difference between what is called strong and weak theory. But potentially, it also means theory is losing its purchase as valuable concept. Hold that thought for now.

So what about the other way of defining theory? As more of an attitude or way of thinking: critical, imaginative? This at first seems to hold out more promise, but quickly we realize we are back with the problem we ended in the last paragraph. Surely critical and imaginative thinking is something we always strive for, it lies at the basis of academic scholarship. Remember one of the problems Åsa Berggren had when she tried to implement a reflexive methodology on a development-led project? A large part of her staff was incensed because this is what they thought they were doing all the time. Just because you follow protocols in excavation and recording doesn't mean you turn into mindless drones; the excavators are always thinking hard about what they were doing and the same applies to almost any archaeologist working on their material. But if theory is just about being reflexive, critical, open-minded, then how is it really different to the basic model of scientific investigation? Of course, you can always be *more* critical, *more* imaginative and there is no doubt that when following protocols during fieldwork and lab work, you often black box those protocols and take them for granted; so maybe theory is really about this kind of critique? In some ways, that certainly fits with much of the tone of this book where we have explored various archaeological situations and practices and tried to prise open and question what is in these black boxes that constitute archaeological practice. But even then, the line between doing archaeology and theorizing about archaeology is not always very clear, and so once again, can we really differentiate between archaeological theory and archaeology?

The implications of reflecting on these two aspects of theory are that what theory is – as distinct from whatever else we do in archaeology – has started to disappear before our eyes. We think we know what we mean by theory, yet if we take to heart the lessons from what has been happening in archaeological theory over the last couple of decades, then the very concept starts to slip through our hands like sand. Should we be worried? There is certainly a danger in abandoning a concept that the discipline fought so hard to put on the map. I have lived through a large part of this struggle, and so I understand only too well what is at stake. Indeed, given the resurgence of archaeological science in the last decade, arguably the need for theory is more urgent than ever, to stop us from repeating the errors of earlier times when a naïve empiricism seemed to dominate. At its best, theory has been a critical political tool for dissent, for pushing against the status quo and challenging its assumptions, for developing and enriching our discipline in fundamental ways. In many ways, it is what has prevented us from ossifying into what was called a royal or major science in the last chapter. How can we abandon something that has been such a force for good? Yet at the same time, how can we applaud something which seems to lack any obvious substance or coherence? If theory did all this, why do we find it so hard to pin down what theory is?

194 *Coda*

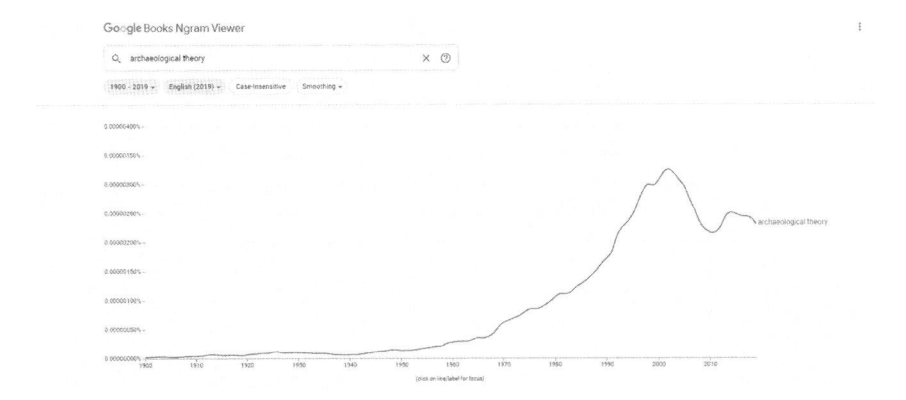

Figure 8.1 A plot from Google Ngram viewer using the search term "archaeological theory". How well does this reflect the status of theory in archaeology and if it does, what does it mean?

Personally, I find this paradox troubling. Maybe it doesn't bother many of my colleagues, but for me, we are reaching a moment in our discipline of great potential in terms of how we think about theory. When I look at developments, for example, among some philosophers of science, the concept of theory was abandoned in the 1990s because of some of the same issues I have raised here, and yet these same philosophers did not stop what we might call "theorizing". Is the same now happening in archaeology? (Figure 8.1). The philosophers abandoned a discourse which elevated this thing called "theory" above what they were interested in: the history and practice of science. Yet even they have not escaped the paradoxes I have alluded to here. One of the most influential ideas to come from this field was ANT which we briefly mentioned in Chapter 3; yet the irony is, ANT is not really a theory and its very designation as such is something of an oxymoron. I suppose what I am straining for here is a suggestion that the best way out of this paradox is somehow to keep the generative and affirmative effects of "theorizing" without invoking a special term to designate this activity. Theorizing without theory. Is this even possible? I don't know, but let me end by alluding to Wittgenstein's ladder, the penultimate words of his famous work *Tractatus Logico-Philosophicus*, where he essentially recants the whole book as a mere means to an end. What he says about his work may be extended to archaeological theory: it got us to where we needed to be, but now it has served its purpose, maybe we can kick it away.

Index

Note: entries in **bold** are suggestions for a do-it-yourself glossary though students are encouraged to create their own lists of alternative or complementary terms.

abduction 124, 134–5, 153, 155, 157
abstraction 10, 25, 54, 85–6
actor network theory 3, 71, 73, 194
agency 8, 16, 29, 35, 71, 73–5, 86, 93, 106, 132, 170
ambiguity 34, 87–9, 101, 131
analogy 117, 131, 152–5
animism 73, 109
ANT *see* actor network theory
Anthropocene 173
anthropocentrism 173, 175
archaeogeography 188
archaeosphere 173
archive 77–8, 91–5, 101; objective 24; *vs.* publication 95; relation to archaeology 185–8
argument: interpretive *vs.* referal 147; logic of 117, 124–7; as mode of writing 105–6, 116
assemblage theory 71, 147

borrowing 148, 156, 162

care 145–6
cartesian dualism 70–1, 136
case study 99, 101–2, 115
certainty 34, 87–8, 131
citation 104, 108–9, 116, 157
citizen science 46
classification 13, 36, 56, 62–3, 66–8, 70–1, 76–8, 117, 135, 150, 156, 179; emic *vs.* etic 67–8
closure 87–8, 92, 95; mechanisms of 87–8
collaborative archaeology 43–6, 160
common sense 1, 5–6, 9, 18
community archaeology 43–5, 47
confirmation bias 119
cultural relativism 75

culture 66–8, 70–1, 135–6, 171–2, 174–6, 183; *see also* material culture; two cultures
culture history 6–7, 146, 177
cyborg 79

Darwinian archaeology 147
data: as ampliative 57; big 8, 19, 60–3; cleaning 88; distinct from evidence 117; distinct from facts 54–5; distinct from theory 8–9, 11–18, 127, 131, 147–8, 150, 156, 192; meta- and para- 63; pyramid (*see* DIKW pyramid); raw 8, 54, 57, 61–2, 95; trail 57
de-colonizing methodology/archaeology 76, 144
description: and interpretation 25–9, 32, 62, 98; as a mode of writing 105–6, 110, 116
detection 131
diagnosis 128, 131
dialectics 135–8
DIKW pyramid 54–5, 57, 135
disciplinarity: inter-, multi- and trans- 181–2
doubt 87–8
dualism 70, 136, 138; *see also* cartesian dualism

empiricism 8, 11–13, 54, 61, 148, 193
epistemology 63–4, 70, 91, 93, 109
evidence 1, 87–8, 105, 117–18, 121–5, 127–8, 131–2, 134, 171, 184–5
evidential reasoning 118, 124–7, 131, 134

fact: big *vs.* small 54; *see also* data
feminism 7, 9, 17, 40, 87–8, 109, 144–6, 149–50, 157

field 23
forensics 131–2
formation theory 184–5
fragmentation: of the archaeological process 89–92, 95; of the archaeological record 87, 89, 171, 186–7

grand challenges 142–3, 145
grand narrative 16

hermeneutics 128–32, 135
humanity 14, 36, 76, 166, 173, 178, 182–6, 188
hypothesis: auxiliary 130; testing 12, 118–22, 124–5, 127, 130, 134

images: *vs.* text 57–8, 85, 90, 95–6, 109–10
improvization 156–7
induction 12, 61, 116, 119, 124, 134–5, 153
inference to the best explanation 118, 121–4, 134
interpretation: and description 25–9, 32, 62, 98
intervention 29, 31, 47, 56, 77, 84–5

ladder of inference 170

macro-archaeology 187
Marxism 5, 7–9, 14, 40, 144
material culture 35, 66, 69, 79, 166, 169–70, 173–5, 179–80, 182–3
material engagement theory 71–3
materiality 8, 66, 175, 178, 183–6, 188
middle range theory 13–14, 154
multi-species archaeology 173
multivocality 45, 94, 182

narrative 102, 105–6, 108, 116, 128; *see also* grand narrative
New Archaeology 7
normal science 157
novelty 134, 149, 157–60

objectivity 25, 33, 35–6, 58, 104
observation 29, 31, 56
ontology 63–4, 69–70, 80; and classification 63, 65–6, 77; indigenous 73–6; relational 70–3
originality 149, 157

palimpsest 187–8
paradigm 7, 9, 146–7, 177; evidentiary 131
past 166–9
performative: fieldwork 28; recording 76–7; text 105; theory 17–18
perspectivism 75
phenomenology 3, 7, 36, 70–1, 73, 178
positivism 11–13, 177
postcolonialism 16, 40, 43, 144, 160
posthumanism 135, 170, 183
post-positivism 11–13
postprocessualism 2, 6–8, 67, 146, 176–7
presencing 106–7, 110
processualism 6–8, 16, 146, 176–7

questions 8–9, 23, 42, 44, 60, 116–17, 130, 141–9, 180

realism 58, 95
representation: crisis of 105; *vs.* presencing 106–7, 110; and recording 29, 36, 53, 77, 86, 110
research agenda 142, 144, 161

scepticism 1, **88**
science: *vs.* humanities 7, 103, 146–7, 167, 176–8, 180, 182–3; major *vs.* minor 180; royal *vs.* nomadic 180
semiotics 133–4
slow archaeology 32
speculation 1, 11–12, 124, 134–5, 157
standardization 35, 56, 153
standpoint 104, 143
structuralism 8, 67–9, 136, 155–7
subjectivity 27, 33–6, 38

theory: death of 8; definitions of 9–11; grand 8, 14; high 9, 13; levels of 10, 13–14, 16, 135; strong *vs.* weak 15–17, 148, 193; *see also* middle range theory
thinking: analogical 153; binary 71, 135–8; critical 10; dialectical 137; nomadic 128, 134–5, 138; tree- *vs.* rhizomes- 135–6
time perspectivism 187–8
transduction 134–5, 153, 157
two cultures 176–7
typology 62, 68, 124, 148, 150, 156–7; *see also* classification

vagueness 88–9